Alan Millard

DISCOVERIES FROM THE TIME OF JESUS

A LION BOOK

Oxford · Batavia · Sydney

For Margaret
with love and gratitude
for twenty-five years
1964–1989

Published by
Lion Publishing plc
Sandy Lane West, Littlemore, Oxford, England
ISBN 0 7459 1207 9
Lion Publishing Corporation
1705 Hubbard Avenue, Batavia, Illinois 60510, USA
ISBN 0 7459 1207 9
Albatross Books Pty Ltd
PO Box 320, Sutherland, NSW 2232, Australia
ISBN 0 7324 0136 4

First edition 1990

Bible quotations are from *The Holy Bible: The New International Version*,
copyright © 1978 by New York International Bible Society
published by Hodder & Stoughton

British Library Cataloguing in Publication Data
Millard, A.R. (Alan Ralph)
  Discoveries from the time of Jesus
  1. Bible. Historicity. Archaeological sources
  I. Title
  220.9'3

  ISBN 0-7459-1207-9

Library of Congress Cataloging-in-Publication Data
Millard, A. R. (Alan Ralph)
  Discoveries from the time of Jesus/Alan Millard — 1st ed.
  p.   cm.
  Includes bibliographical references.
  ISBN 0-7459-1207-9
  1. Bible. N.T.—History of contemporary events. 2. Bible. N.T.—
Antiquities. 3. Palestine—Antiquities. 4. Excavations
(Archaeology)—Palestine. 5. Bible. N.T.—History of Biblical
events. I. Title.
BS2410.M45   1990
225.9'3—dc20

Printed in Spain

CONTENTS

PREFACE

Thousands of people flock to the Holy Land to see the sacred sites each year—to 'walk where Jesus walked'. On Galilee's lake and hills the Gospel stories are easy to imagine, other places are greatly changed. What was it like to live in first-century Palestine?

Discoveries in the past thirty years have given a far richer picture than earlier generations expected. There are the Dead Sea Scrolls and early copies of the Gospels. There are Herod's grand palaces and the houses of Jerusalem. In fact there are so many discoveries from archaeology and historical research, old and new, that I have decided in this book to concentrate on the forty-year period of the Gospel story. Even so, coverage is not complete: in some areas only examples can be given, and literary and theological studies are left aside.

The discoveries presented mostly provide background information. They are stage properties for the Gospel story, which help the reader to view it more clearly. But several discoveries do make the meanings of sayings or events plainer, so improving our understanding of the message of the Gospels.

This book follows the pattern of *Treasures from Bible Times*, but has to include much more history in detail, and so the sources of that history are outlined. I have followed the standard works listed in the list *For Further Reading*. Without the devotion of generations of scribes, the Gospels would not have survived. Evidence for their work, recently re-evaluated, and the continuing recovery of early manuscripts deserve wider recognition than they have so far received.

The experience of living in Jerusalem as a Fellow of the Institute for Advanced Studies at the Hebrew University in 1984, and the kindness of friends in Jerusalem, especially Professor Nahman Avigad, stimulated me to write this book. I am grateful to them and to many others who have advised me or provided photographs, and in particular to Dr Walter Cockle of University College, London, and Dr John Kane of Manchester University, who kindly read and commented on several chapters. My wife's support and patience has enabled me to complete this work, and I thank her most of all.

Alan Millard

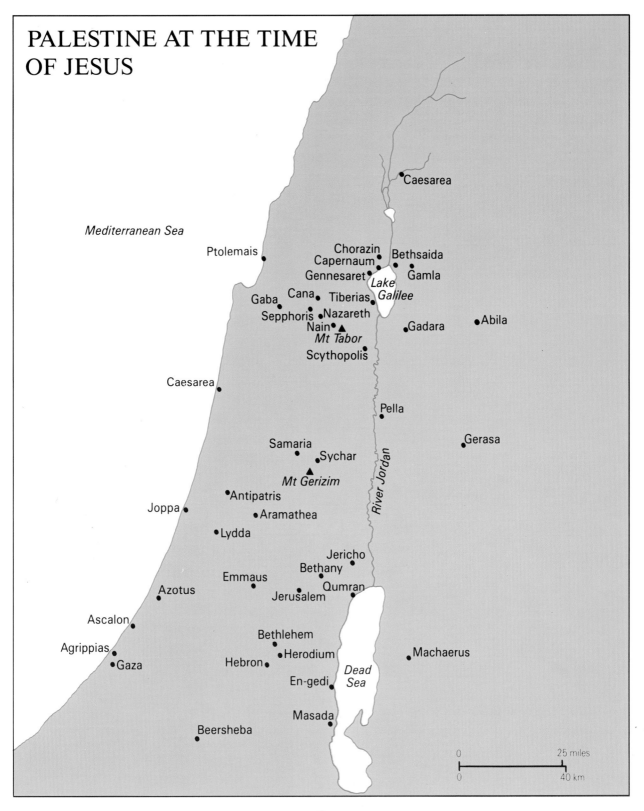

PALESTINE AT THE TIME OF JESUS

Mediterranean Sea

Caesarea

Ptolemais

Chorazin
Capernaum
Bethsaida
Gennesaret
Gamla
Lake Galilee
Gaba
Cana
Tiberias
Sepphoris
Nazareth
Nain
Gadara
Abila
Mt Tabor
Scythopolis

Caesarea

Pella

Samaria
Sychar
Gerasa
Mt Gerizim

River Jordan

Antipatris
Joppa
Aramathea
Lydda

Jericho
Bethany
Emmaus
Qumran
Azotus
Jerusalem

Ascalon

Bethlehem
Agrippias
Herodium
Machaerus
Gaza
Hebron
Dead Sea
En-gedi

Masada

Beersheba

0   25 miles
0   40 km

PART ONE

DAILY LIFE

Jesus spoke to people in their houses, in towns and in the countryside. He told stories about the ordinary activities of home and field, about men and women, family and business. Digging up ruined houses from those days, with their pots and pans still in place, helps to give more realism to those stories and to incidents in the life of Jesus. Discoveries in Jerusalem and other towns allow us to say, 'This is what it was like.'

'Show a light!' Even the faintest light helps in a dark place. The common lamps of Jesus' time could be held in the hand. With oil in the bowl and a wick in the spout, a lamp set on a shelf could light a room. Often one was left alight in a tomb, like this example which still has the ancient soot on its lip. The light was a sign of life.

THE BURNT HOUSE

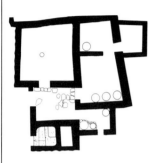

This plan of the Burnt House is based on the original drawings in N. Avigad, Discovering Jerusalem.

Among the finds at the Burnt House were stone weights, one of them scratched with the owner's name: Bar Kathros.

The sounds of swords clashing, the screams of the dying, and crackling of flames echo from deep below a new apartment block in old Jerusalem. Foreign soldiers are attacking the city, killing and looting. The sounds are modern, the story they tell is an old one, vividly re-created in the ruins of the Burnt House. Israeli archaeologists shifted a great depth of rubbish piled up over the centuries and uncovered part of the house where a prosperous Jewish family lived until Roman soldiers burnt it down in AD 70.

When the rubbish was cleared away, in January 1970, the walls of rooms began to appear. They covered an area about 10 metres/32 feet square, being apparently the basement of the building. As the archaeologists dug into them they met great quantities of ash and burnt wood, and everything they found was covered with soot. Here was a vivid demonstration of the work of the Roman army. There was no doubt this was a house burnt in AD 70, for scattered on the floor were coins issued by the Roman governors

of Judea, mixed with others issued by the Jewish rebels in the years 67, 68, 69, and none later. Broken pottery and other objects are also of known first-century styles. Looters had been through the house, throwing what they did not want into heaps on the floors.

Perhaps it was one of the defenders running away who left his short iron spear in one corner of a room. But another did not escape so easily. Against the doorway of one room were the bones of a human arm, the hand spread out to grasp the step. No more of the skeleton remained, but later destruction had carried away everything outside the entrance. The bones belonged to a woman in her early twenties, maybe a servant in the house, who, we may imagine, staggered a few yards to die from her injury.

What did she, and other people, do in those rooms? In the opinion of the excavator, N. Avigad, part of their work may have been to prepare incense for the Temple services. Among the finds pointing to this are many perfume bottles of pottery and glass (see *An Alabaster Jar of Perfume*), some stone mortars and pestles, weights, measuring-cups, and ovens. The heavy soot that clung to everything could have come from oily materials burning. Whether this deduction is right or wrong, two pottery inkpots also found in the ruins indicate that writing was a regular activity in the house.

On one of the stone weights is scratched the owner's name: Bar Kathros. In the Talmud that name is listed among the families of the High

Priests who used their power to line their own pockets. The Bar Kathros family were attacked for misusing their pens, which may mean they spread false rumours or misinformation. Although someone may have carried this weight from another house to the place where it rested for 1900 years (it is only about 8 cm/3 ins in diameter), the Bar Kathros family certainly had a house in Jerusalem, and this one is a good candidate.

The rooms unearthed were workrooms and a kitchen, and a small ritual bath (see *Cleanliness is Next to Godliness?*). Their furnishings were few, apart from ovens, large jars, and stone tables. Before this discovery the furniture of Jerusalem houses in the first century was unknown, for woodwork decays rapidly when buried. Now several stone tables illustrate it. There were tables with rectangular tops about the size of a tea-tray (50 cm/20 ins × 75 cm/30 ins), slabs of stone cut smooth and decorated around the edges, supported on a single central leg of stone, about 75 cm/30 ins high, carved like a pillar. Other tables had round tops, about 50 cm/20 ins across, with three carved wooden legs fitted beneath them. Roman sculptures and paintings show the shapes of the legs. They also indicate that people reclined on couches around the circular tables to eat, the food and drink being served from the others.

Stone was also used for making dishes, cups, jars, and bowls, besides the common pottery. Previously scholars had supposed that stone was kept for special, expensive vessels, but the excavations produced so many— some finely finished, others only roughly cut on the outside yet polished within—that another explanation had to be found. Both Jewish writings and

the New Testament gave the clue: stone vessels avoided some of the problems caused by the laws of ritual purity (see *Cleanliness is Next to Godliness?*).

In the Burnt House is preserved an illuminating glimpse of first-century life, and a horrifying reminder of Jerusalem's fall. Staring at the ruined walls, the ovens, cooking-pots and tableware, the visitor can imagine a house of that time more realistically than any words can describe. If the imagination can run a little further, it is permissible to suggest that people who worked in these rooms may have run to wave branches before Jesus as he rode into Jerusalem, or that those who drank from the cups and goblets may have been among those who cried 'crucify him'.

Until 1970 the remains of this wealthy first-century AD Jewish house in Jerusalem lay buried under rubbish. When this was cleared, among the rooms unearthed was the kitchen, with its ovens, jars and stone tables.

RICH MEN'S HOUSES

'Sell everything you have and give it to the poor.' That was a key step, Jesus told a rich ruler who came asking him how to get eternal life (Luke 18:18–23). The man went away sad because he was very rich.

Recent discoveries in Jerusalem have revealed how the rich lived at the time. A visitor from another part of the Roman Empire would have found houses furnished as well as those in the major centres of Roman culture. In Jerusalem the best example is so splendid that Professor Avigad, who discovered the ruins, called it the Palatial Mansion. It covers an area almost 30 metres/100 feet long. Later buildings damaged some of the walls, so the position of the entrance has been lost. In the middle was a court-yard. A doorway at one side opened into a passage leading to several rooms. Perhaps because it was a busy place, the passage had a mosaic floor.

Two doorways led into a hall. This was a huge room, over 11 metres/36 feet long, its walls covered with panels of white plaster cut to look like fine stone masonry. Pieces of plaster fallen on to the floor seem to have decorated the ceiling. They were moulded with geometric patterns in relief. Our visitor would be familiar with such designs, for they echo the work of interior decorators in houses of the first century BC at Pompeii.

Other rooms were brightly painted. Panels of different colours imitated the marble slabs which only princes could afford. Imaginary windows and columns gave an air of greater space. Able artists painted lifelike fruit and leaves on some walls, and friezes of leaves in regular designs. A lot of this painting was done while the plaster was wet, so that the colours soaked into the wall. (This is fresco painting, the technique Michelangelo used in the Sistine Chapel in Rome.) When a householder grew tired of a design, he could not call a decorator to scrape it off like wallpaper, or cover it with a

Mosaic patterns decorated the living-room floors of a very few houses in first-century Jerusalem. This is the finest example of the simple geometric patterns. A coin of AD 67 was found on this floor.

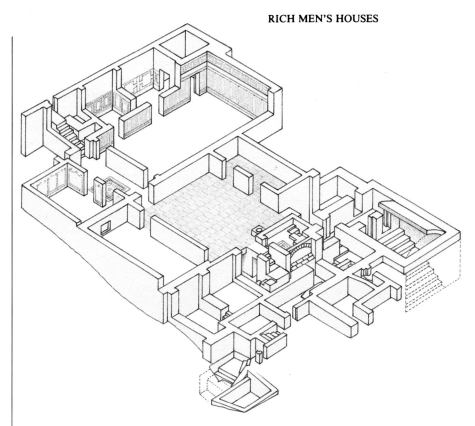

This plan of the Palatial Mansion is based on the original drawing in N. Avigad, Discovering Jerusalem

coat of paint. He had to have a new coat of plaster put on the wall, then painted. Often archaeologists have been able to chip away a damaged layer to uncover an earlier one underneath. Pieces of painted plaster are found in so many places in Jerusalem that it is clear most rich men's houses were decorated in this way.

As in many Roman houses, painters and plasterers worked with a third group of craftsmen, those who laid mosaic floors. They set tiny cubes of stone, black, red and white, into cement to make patterns and pictures. In the Palatial Mansion the passageway and one reception room had mosaic floors. (Other rooms may have had them but if so they have entirely disappeared.) Where there was little heavy furniture to be moved, floors may have been polished plaster, covered with carpets or mats. Fire and damp would quickly have destroyed floor coverings of this kind, assuming that they were not stolen.

Elegant as these painted walls and mosaic floors were, a non-Jewish visitor from Rome would think them very tame. There are none of the people and animals, gods and goddesses that chase around most Roman walls and floors. Gods and goddesses, of course, had no place in Jewish thinking, but there were ancient Jewish heroes and famous stories like

The colours on the plastered wall of one room in the Palatial Mansion stayed bright, despite the fire that covered the ruins with soot in AD 70.

Well-to-do people had high quality glass vessels on their tables. One famous maker was Ennion. A glass jug from his foundry was unearthed in Jerusalem. This cup came from a tomb in Cyprus. Ennion's name is moulded on the side.

that of David and Goliath which would have made good pictures. Yet there were only geometric patterns, rosettes and waves on the floors, with one or two flowers and leaves, and walls panelled in the styles already described.

The reason for this is religious. First-century Jews were strict in following God's command: 'You shall not make for yourself an idol in the form of anything.' Pictures of animals or human beings might lead to idolatry. Most people applied this rule, but no authority had the power to impose it on everyone. At least one householder dared to disregard it, mildly. Plaster fallen to the floor in a room near the Temple was moulded with pictures of animals running through the countryside.

The visitor to the Palatial Mansion would have found more mosaic floors in the bathrooms. Set on a cement base, mosaic pavements were waterproof, so bathers could move freely in and out of the water. In one elaborate suite in another house the bath-tub itself had a mosaic floor. In other houses, there were rooms with under-floor heating (hypocausts) to create fashionable Roman steam baths.

These were baths for normal washing. What would have surprised the Roman visitor was the number of other baths. They are tanks of various sizes cut in the rock, lined with waterproof plaster, and vaulted with stone. Bathers walked down a flight of steps which often took up the whole width of the tank, and were faced with

a blank wall! They were not stepping into a swimming-pool. If the tank was well filled, the bather could easily go down to the lowest step and duck his head under the water to be totally immersed. That was all that was needed. Then he could turn and climb out. If the water-level was lower, or the bath was small, he would need to crouch to go under the water's surface. These were ritual baths, designed to enable religious Jews to fulfil the laws of purity (see *Cleanliness is Next to Godliness?*).

The biggest bath in the Mansion had eight steps running across its 4 metres/13 feet width, and was almost 5 metres/16½ feet long. It had two doorways so that people coming out clean did not brush against those going in unclean. Water for these baths had to be spring or rain-water, so cisterns were essential to collect and store it. Sometimes a cistern fed the bath next to it through a narrow pipe in the wall —so that the pure water which flowed into the bath also purified the water brought into the bath. Baths like these,

and smaller ones, were found in large numbers in buildings near the southern end of the Temple, where its main entrance was (see *Temple Tourists*). Houses in that area may have served as hostels for pilgrims who would want to purify themselves before entering the Temple. The care and expense taken to make these baths inside Jerusalem underlines the central role that ceremonial washing had in the daily life of religious Jews in the first century.

Carefully following religious laws

Archaeologists were astonished at the perfect condition of these objects hidden over 1850 years ago. Jewish rebels fleeing from Roman soldiers had put bronze jugs, iron knives and keys in the basket as they left their homes.

was not a bar to luxury for a rich man. Bits and pieces of stone, metal, pottery and glass hint at the equipment of the houses. Woodwork perished in the destruction, together with leather and fabric. A clue to fine wooden furniture is a cast-bronze foot from the leg of a table, shaped like an animal's paw.

The stone that could be carved into vessels (see *Cleanliness is Next to Godliness?*) also provided slabs for table-tops. Some of these rested on wooden legs, some on a single stone pillar. The latter were side tables for serving dishes. Leaves, flowers, geometrical designs (and in one case a fish) were carved around the edges of the table-tops. A very few tables are inlaid on the top with mosaic patterns. Tables like these could also be seen in Roman houses in Italy.

Jugs, cups, bowls and plates which stood on the tables in Jerusalem also had much in common with those used all round the Mediterranean. Bronze jugs had gracefully curving handles, and beside them were bowls and saucepans and ladles, some in styles known from excavations as far away as Roman London. High-class glass vessels were in use. In the Palatial Mansion were pieces made by the master glass-blower Ennion, who put

his name on them. Other products of his workshop have been found in Cyprus and Italy. Local craftsmen were active in casting and blowing glass (rubbish from a glass factory was tipped into old buildings as hard core for a street laid in Herodian times). Fine red pottery with a shiny surface adorned some tables. This was imported from factories on the coast of the Mediterranean, perhaps from Greece.

Local potters made serviceable cooking-pots and storage jars, kitchenware and delicate, painted tableware. They also made the small pottery lamps that could be set on a ledge to light a room after sunset. The rich did better, having bronze stands from which metal lamps could hang like flowers, or on which they could stand.

The remains found in first-century Jerusalem give some idea of the riches which Jesus' inquirer was told to sell. Such a comfortable, even luxurious lifestyle was hard to part with. Nicodemus, Joseph of Arimathea, and some of the priestly families probably lived at the same level of cosmopolitan fashion, while maintaining their distinctive Jewish behaviour.

AN ALABASTER JAR OF PERFUME

Jewish burials from Gospel times do not give great golden treasures to archaeologists, or even dozens of pots and pans, as do the tombs of earlier ages. Often nothing lies in the coffin or the bone-chest except the dead person's bones and a little bottle. These little bottles are commonly made of pottery, sometimes of glass. People often call them 'tear' bottles, although the idea of mourners gathering their tears in them to leave with the dead is fanciful. (The translation of Psalm 56:8, 'gather my tears into your bottle', seems to give some

support, without referring to burials at all.) These simple flasks were made for the cheaper scented oils in daily use. Costly perfumes deserve expensive containers.

The alabaster jar the woman broke over Jesus' feet at Bethany was probably carved from stone, for the 340 gm/ 12 oz of perfume in it was estimated to be worth over 300 denarii (more than a year's wages) according to the account in Mark's Gospel (14:3–5). Pliny the Elder, writing later in the first century, stated that ointments kept best in alabaster boxes. If the jar

in the story had a long neck, like the examples illustrated, it is easy to see how the excited woman would break it off, not stopping to unseal the top, releasing all the perfume at once, so that 'the house was filled with the fragrance of the perfume' (John's Gospel 12:3).

Cheap perfume and oils were kept in small pottery flasks. These examples made in the first centuries BC and AD come from the Jerusalem area and Petra.

These glass perfume flasks were laid in tombs of the first century on the edge of the Valley of Hinnom.

DAILY LIFE

In 132 Jewish patriots began the Second Revolt against Roman rule. After three years they were crushed, and the Emperor Hadrian rebuilt Jerusalem as a Roman city (named Aelia Capitolina) which no Jew was allowed to enter. Caves in remote valleys by the Dead Sea were the last hiding-places for some of the rebels. Israeli explorers found their bones and many of their personal possessions in the caves. The very dry atmosphere had preserved them in excellent condition. People living in Palestine a hundred years earlier used similar things, as discoveries at Masada show.

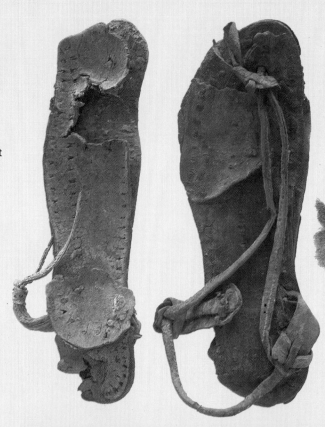

'After me,' said John the Baptist, 'will come one the thongs of whose sandals I am not worthy to stoop down and untie' (Mark 1:7). 'Wear sandals, but not an extra tunic,' Jesus told his disciples when he sent them out to preach in the country (Mark 6:9). The upper sandal was fastened with a sliding knot, others were tied.

The dry heat at the top of Masada stopped pieces of clothing left in the ruins from rotting away. The blue stripe in this scrap suggested to the excavator, Professor Yigael Yadin, that he had found a prayer shawl (tallith) worn by one of the devout Jewish rebels who held Herod's fortress against the Romans until AD 73.

'No one puts new wine into old wineskins' (Mark 2:22). As skin-bottles grew old, the leather became hard and would not expand with the fermenting new wine. This sheepskin water-bottle was carefully sewn up, the front legs tied together as a carrying handle.

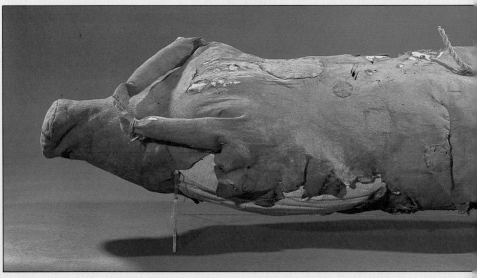

Pottery, bronze and wooden vessels, a wooden spoon and an iron knife with a wooden handle were left in the caves by the rebels. They are good examples of the ordinary kitchenware of a Jewish housewife.

The Jewish refugees took these keys with them to the caves where they hid, hoping to keep their homes and possessions safe against thieves.

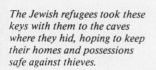

CLEANLINESS IS NEXT TO GODLINESS?

'They don't wash their hands before they eat.'

Many parents may say that about their children today: the Jewish religious leaders said the same thing to Jesus about his disciples. Cleanliness was one of the most important things for religious Jews in New Testament times. It mattered, not simply for health but because anyone who was ritually unclean could not approach God.

The need to avoid uncleanness had led to a great many regulations endeavouring to stop people breaking any of God's commands in the laws of Moses. They had all sorts of results which made life difficult for ordinary men and women who wanted to please God. Eating with un-washed hands made the food unclean, and so the eater became unclean. He would then have to immerse himself in a bath to become clean again. The same thing was required if a man went to the market and touched someone who was not a Jew. On returning home he would have to immerse himself to become clean again.

In recent years archaeology has dis-covered how carefully these rules were obeyed in the first century. Ritual baths have been uncovered in the houses of the rich citizens in Jerusalem as well as in the ruined community

centre at Qumran—and even among the build-ings of the religious nationalists, the Zealots, who occupied King Herod's fortress on the top of Masada in the Judean desert.

Often the baths are quite small, designed so that a person could step down and squat under the water. Some are larger, to display the owner's wealth, or for public use. They may have two doorways with a partition down the steps so that the unclean entered at one side and left, clean, at the other. In every case, care was taken to make sure that rainwater or water from a stream was fed into the pool; water brought entirely in buckets or jars was not satisfactory.

Cleanliness applied to furniture and household utensils, too. They could become unclean in all sorts of ways, developed from the laws in Leviticus, chapter 11. Washing completely in pure water would cleanse them, except in the case of pottery vessels. Most pottery in ancient times was earthenware, so it absorbed a little of any liquid put in it. Therefore it could not be thoroughly cleaned: so, if its contents became unclean, it had to be broken. Metal pots and pans overcame that difficulty, but they were always expensive.

Discoveries in Jerusalem reveal another way of avoiding the need

constantly to replace kitchenware: the production of cups, bowls, jars and trays from the soft limestone of the Judean hills. Stone containers needed washing only if they became un-clean. So many examples have been found in Jerusalem that it is clear there was an industry devoted to making them. The best quality pieces were turned on a lathe, beautifully smoothed inside, cut and polished with simple decoration outside. More roughly cut jugs and measuring-cups were kept for kitchen use.

From these discoveries it is easy to see what lies behind various verses in the Gospels. The six large stone jars in the house at Cana where Jesus went for a wedding feast are described as 'the kind used by the Jews for ceremonial washing' (John's Gospel 2:6), and large quantities of water would be needed in order to follow the regulations at a banquet (see *Stone Water Jars*). Mark, relating the

Pharisees' complaint about Jesus' disciples, had to explain for the sake of his non-Jewish readers:

'The Pharisees and all the Jews do not eat unless they give their hands a ceremonial washing, holding to the tradition of the elders. When they come from the market-place they do not eat unless they wash. And they observe many other traditions, such as the washing of cups, pitchers and kettles.'

Jesus answered the complaint quite harshly because, he said, the religious leaders had become so insistent on people obeying all these regulations that they forgot their real purpose. They even invented ways to avoid their effect. What is vital, Jesus said, is the state of the person himself. 'Nothing that enters a man from the outside can make him "unclean".' Rather, 'what comes out of a man is what makes him "unclean"' (Mark's Gospel, chapter 7).

Stone jugs, bowls and dishes were widely used in Jerusalem. They could be washed and used again if they became ritually unclean, but earthenware pots had to be broken.

Wherever religious Jews lived in first-century Palestine they built baths for ritual washing. Many were found in Jerusalem; this carefully plastered example is at Qumran by the Dead Sea.

STONE WATER JARS

At the wedding in Cana there were 'six stone water jars, the kind used by the Jews for ceremonial washing, each holding from twenty to thirty gallons' (John 2:6). The servants filled them with water, and when they drew some of it, and the host tasted it, it was wine!

Excavators have found several stone jars in the ruined houses of first-century Jerusalem. At least six of them stood in the basement kitchen rooms of the 'Burnt House'. They are 65–80 cm/2–2½ feet tall, each cut from a block of stone that could weigh as much as half a ton. They were shaped and finished on a very big lathe, given a pedestal foot and simple decoration. Such stone jars would hold large quantities of water for washing and kitchen needs—up to 80 litres/17 gallons. Flat discs of stone served as lids. The jars at Cana may have been similar to these.

Large stone jars were used for storing liquids. Many were found crushed in the houses of Jerusalem, and have been reconstructed.

CAPERNAUM

Excavations between the synagogue and the shore of Lake Galilee have uncovered several blocks of small stone houses. They were part of the fishing town which flourished from the first century BC to the sixth century AD. Although they were altered over the years, their basic plan did not change. A door led from the street into a paved courtyard and various rooms opened from that, some leading to other rooms. Stone pillars helped to hold up the flat roofs, and there were stone steps to climb up onto the roofs.

Some of the houses had a row of low arches in place of a solid wall. Perhaps these were to let in light or air, or maybe they were entries to animals' byres or to stores.

In the fifth century an octagonal church was built between the synagogue and the Lake. This had been a special place for Christians for a long time. Excavations reveal that the church stood on one of the houses, preserving a central room. The walls of the room had been plastered and visitors coming to it before the church was put up had scratched prayers naming Jesus on the plaster. This was the house, those early Christians plainly believed, where Peter lived —possibly the room where Jesus cured Peter's mother-in-law, or where he had lived.

Ruins of a fine white stone synagogue were found at Capernaum in 1905. Later the Franciscan owners partly rebuilt them. This synagogue was erected late in the fourth century and was richly decorated with carved stonework. Inside the synagogue the stone step seating can be seen along the walls.

Underneath the white synagogue's walls, archaeologists have found parts of an earlier building of black basalt stone. This was apparently in use in the first century, and so may be the synagogue a centurion gave to the town (Luke 7:4,5). The walls are not well-preserved, so it is not judged worthwhile to remove the later remains in order to uncover them.

THE 'JESUS BOAT'

A picture of a small sailing boat was worked into a mosaic pavement at Magdala, early in the Roman period.

There was a drought in Israel in 1985. With little rain, farmers needed more water for their crops. The Israeli water system draws heavily from Lake Galilee, and so more water than usual was drained from it. At the same time, less water than usual flowed into it. As a result the level of the Lake fell. This was bad for the ecology and, if it should happen often, would put the country's irrigation system at risk. But one benefit came from it: the timbers of an old boat appeared, and it was excavated.

The timbers had survived, sunk in the mud beneath the water for centuries. They were black and water-logged, but still kept their shape. After the boat sank, the movement of the water and the anchors of other boats damaged the upper part, so that only the hull remains in good condition. It is 8.2 metres/26.9 feet long and 2.35 metres/ 7.7 feet wide.

Its planks do not overlap in the familiar clinker-built style of many European fishing and small sailing boats: they butt against each other (a style called carvel building). Roman boats, preserved in places spread across the Empire, show that this was the common method at that time. Mortice and tenon joints hold the planks of cedar and oak together. To make the shape of the boat, a series of ribs were laid across the planks, curving from the upper edges to the centre. They do not continue round from one side to the other, as in modern boats. Study of the boat and preservation of the wood will take several years, and full publication will make more details available. Meanwhile, it is kept at Ginosar on the shore of the Lake, north of Tiberias.

What was this ancient boat?

Its style, and objects found with it—a cooking-pot and a lamp—point to an age of about 2,000 years. The 'carbon 14' test applied to the wood gave the same age. Journalists were quick to name it the 'Jesus boat' or 'Peter's boat'. Certainly the boat belongs to the Gospel period, or very close to it.

One suggestion links the boat to the war against Rome. In AD 67 Roman soldiers overran the town of Magdala and sank their boats in the Lake. This could be one of them, for Magdala was the nearest place to the shore where it was found.

Of course, there is no way to prove any connection between it and the Gospel characters. Only a name painted or carved on the side, 'Zebedee and Sons', could do that! Like so many more discoveries, the boat from Galilee's waters allow us to see what something the Gospels mention was like, and to picture the events they record more vividly.

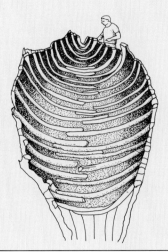

This drawing, made from a photograph, shows the construction and scale of a boat dating from the time of Jesus. The waterlogged vessel was taken with great care from Lake Galilee and each part carefully identified.

A TOWN THE ROMANS CONQUERED

East of Lake Galilee the Golan Heights rise sharply from the shore. In winter and spring, water from rain and melting snow rushes down into the Lake, and over thousands of years the water has cut steep-sided valleys for its course. About 11 km/7 miles to the north-east of the shore is a place where five of these valleys meet at an acute angle. There a promontory stands up, precipitous on one side and sloping heavily on the other. The ridge has a humped outline when seen from the side, joined by a long narrow rock to the Golan plateau at the east. This hill has a good defensive position, and it commands a view directly down the valley to the edge of the Lake, to Bethsaida and Capernaum.

An Israeli explorer went surveying in the hills after they had been seized from Syria during the 1967 war. He found ruins of stone buildings on the sloping side of the promontory. Broken pottery lying among them showed that people had been living there in the first century AD. Round stones the size of a baseball looked like the missiles shot by Roman siege-engines.

What was this place?

Archaeologists often have a problem in identifying the places they discover. In ancient times towns did not usually have convenient signs at the roadside to identify them. Only under the Roman Empire were milestones put along the main roads to help travellers. Anyone arriving at a town would ask where they were. The archaeologist has no one to ask, so he has to search among the records that

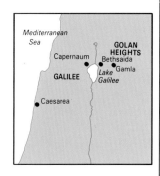

survive to see if they give any help.

In this case the explorer's reading suggested the answer. Apart from the New Testament, the only Jewish history-writing to come down to us from the first century AD is the work of Josephus (see *Josephus the Jew*).

Describing the war against Rome of AD 67–70, Josephus tells of a town called Gamla whose citizens defied the Roman army. He knew the place because he himself had built some of the defences at the start of the revolt. The story of its capture is best read in his own words.

'The houses were built against the steep mountain slopes, astonishingly huddled together, one on top of another, and the town seemed to be hung in mid-air.'

When Vespasian arrived he saw that the town could not be surrounded, so he set his legions to begin the siege from the eastern neck. Soon the Roman equipment was in position and the defenders were hard pressed.

'Their leaders encouraged them and led them to the walls. For a while they kept at bay those who were bringing up the siege machines, but the first of the catapults and stone-throwers drove them back. Then the Romans brought battering-rams against these different points and broke through the city wall. With trumpets sounding, the clash of arms, and battle-cries, they poured through and closed with the defenders. At first those in the city held their ground and checked their advance. But the Romans were too many, so the men of Gamla fled to the higher parts of the town where they could push the Romans down the uneven slopes. The Romans were unable to drive back the enemy above them and they could not force their way back through their own ranks pressing on from behind, so they took refuge on the roofs of the enemy's houses. Crowded with soldiers, and not made for such weights, the roofs soon fell in. As one fell it brought down several others below it, and they in turn, carried away those lower down. In this way a lot of Romans were killed because they had nowhere else to turn and went on leaping on to the roofs, although they saw the houses collapsing. The ruins buried many, some were pinned down while trying to escape, and more died choked by the dust.'

Harassed by the citizens, the Romans withdrew. Such a disaster was bad for Roman morale. Vespasian spoke to his troops to give them fresh courage. Some of them then undermined one of the towers, causing confusion among the people. The Romans pressed in, driving the defenders to the high part of the town. There they threw whatever they could at the Romans, but the wind was against them, deflecting their arrows.

Led by Vespasian in person, 'the Romans mounted the crest and quickly surrounded and killed them. Hemmed in on every side, despairing of their lives, many threw themselves headlong with their wives and children into the ravine which had been dug deep below the citadel.' In fact, more died in that way than at the hands of the Romans. Gamla was left empty; nobody returned to live there again.

The sloping site of the hill northeast of Galilee and its humped shape made it a prime candidate for

identification as ancient Gamla, although there is no definite proof. The name Gamla means 'camel(-town)' and the hill looks like a camel's hump. Excavations began on the hillside in 1976. Running up the slope facing the neck of the peninsula is the hint of a town hall. At one point a gateway leads through it. Within the town are ruins of streets and houses, all built of dark grey basalt stones from the hills, and standing one below another on the slope of the hill, as Josephus described.

The walls against the hillside still stand several feet high; others have tumbled down the slope. Small copper coins found in the ruins show that the town was occupied in the first century BC and the first century AD. The pottery belongs to the same period. Everything points to the place coming to a sudden end. Iron arrowheads lay in the gateway and in other buildings. Some of them have bent points, the result of hitting the hard stone walls. Many of them had evidently been shot into the town by enemies outside the wall.

Arrowheads were not the only missiles that came hurtling in. Scores of stone balls were strewn among the ruins. They were lumps of basalt from baseball size upwards to some half a metre/20 ins diameter, chipped and hammered into shape. These were surely the balls shot by Roman catapults!

Everything agrees with Josephus' description of Gamla and its fate. There can be little doubt, with the evidence of its violent end, that this is the site of that town. It is, naturally, a poignant place for anyone of Jewish descent to visit. It is also of great interest for the study of New Testament times. Here is a town, here are the houses, where people lived who saw and heard Jesus as he moved across the hills of Galilee.

The town of Gamla, devastated by the Romans, was abandoned in the first century AD. This steeply sloping hill north-east of Lake Galilee (which can be seen in the distance) seems the most likely site. Excavation began in 1976.

A SYNAGOGUE OF JESUS' DAY

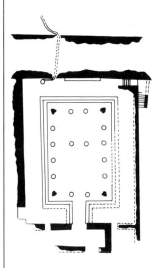

A plan of the synagogue at Gamla, based on the plan from S. Guttman in L.I. Levine, Ancient Synagogues Revealed, *Israel Exploration Society, Jerusalem, 1981.*

One of the first buildings the excavators uncovered in Gamla was an unusual one. It was clearly not a house. A porch led into a pillared hall some 20 metres/65½ feet long. Four rows of stone steps, each about 50 cm/19 ins high, ran from the doorway along either side. At the far end they joined a similar row of four steps. A space almost 2.4 metres/8 feet wide separated the walls from the edge of the top step. Stone pillars placed at intervals round the central area held up the roof. The tops of these pillars were carved with geometric designs, and the pillars at the corners were not round but heart-shaped in cross-section. Along the foot of the rows of steps the floor was paved, but in the centre it was simply bare earth. This building was set along the slope of the hill, so one side stood on a terrace high above the street. Here a flight of steps led up into the back corner of the hall.

The ruins showed that this building had been taken over in the siege by the defenders. They had built fires in it for cooking their meals. The reason for that is clear. The east end buts on to the town wall, and just to the north is a gateway through the wall. It was obviously an important position. Further signs of that were the numbers of stone catapult balls and iron arrowheads lying about, especially at the eastern end, where the attack had come. When the town fell, this building caught fire. Iron nails from the roof beams lay in the burnt debris.

In a Jewish town, what could such a building be? There was one obvious answer: a synagogue. If that is the right answer, the ruins of Gamla have yielded the oldest synagogue so far found in Palestine. The New Testament and the books of Josephus tell us that there were synagogues in the towns of the first century, so it was to be expected that remains of one might eventually be uncovered. Yet how can anyone be sure it is a synagogue? Without an inscription no one can be certain, and it is unlikely, in a Jewish town, that there would be a notice on it. (In Corinth a stone was found cut with Greek letters forming parts of the words 'Synagogue of the Jews'.) However, there are two good reasons for identifying the Gamla ruin as a synagogue.

First, the plan of the building is almost the same as the plans of buildings uncovered at other places around Galilee. These date from the third century AD and later, and they were certainly synagogues. In some of them were Hebrew and Aramaic inscriptions recording the gifts prosperous men made for parts of the structures, or their decoration. Words like 'this holy place', and the prayers included, show beyond doubt that these buildings were synagogues. Indeed, it is hard to think of any other use for such halls in Jewish communities. Some of them have heart-shaped columns in the corners like those at Gamla. Examples can easily be seen in the famous ruins at Capernaum.

The second reason for calling the building in Gamla a synagogue is the discovery of what are likely to be two more synagogues of the first century

The ruined hall beside the town wall of Gamla is probably the only synagogue of Jesus' time yet found near Galilee.

AD. Both lie south of Jerusalem, far from Galilee. They were not purpose-built; the Zealots and other Jewish rebels converted parts of other buildings during the revolt against Rome.

In King Herod's fortress and burial-place at Herodium, 6 km/3½ miles south-east of Bethlehem, the Zealots altered the dining-room, a hall 15 metres/49 feet × 5 metres/34 feet. They took stones from other rooms to construct a platform along three sides, with two steps at the inner edge, making benches. A pillar was set at each corner of the floor to hold up the roof. Just outside the doorway a ritual bath was carefully made in a small room. These features together suggest that this room served as a synagogue, although they cannot prove it.

The second building is in King Herod's amazing fortress on top of the isolated rock of Masada beside the Dead Sea.[1] Herod's architects had designed a double wall to run along the edge of the mountain-top, with guard-chambers and store-rooms built between the walls. One of these rooms in the north-west sector projected inwards from the line of the wall. When Professor Yigael Yadin's

volunteers cleared away the sand and rubble they found a room with four tiers of plastered benches around its sides, and places for pillars in the middle of the room. It was nearly the same size as the hall at Herodium, about 15 metres/50 feet × 12 metres/40 feet. Was this a synagogue? The excavators hardly dared express their hopes. Had they found the place where the last of the Zealots to stand against the Romans had prayed and read the Holy Scriptures?

In one corner a small room had been built, but its purpose is not clear. Careful digging revealed a pit dug through the floor. At the bottom of it was a piece of dry, rolled-up leather. Not far away, patient work traced the edges of another pit. At the bottom of it lay part of another scroll. As soon as the dust was blown off, eager eyes read familiar words from the Book of Ezekiel, chapter 37, the vision of the valley of dry bones! The first piece had to be unrolled in a laboratory. When it was open its words were clear: it contained the last part of the Book of Deuteronomy. Finding two books of the Bible might point to a sacred place, but pieces of others came to light in other parts of the fortress, so they do not by themselves prove that this room was part of a synagogue.

It is all the evidence taken together which points to the conclusion that the bench-lined halls at Masada and Herodium were synagogues. In both cases they were obviously so important to the rebels fighting the Romans that they were prepared to build these clearly non-military structures inside their strongholds. Knowing that the rebels were intensely religious makes the synagogue interpretation all the more plausible.

The likeness of the Gamla building to these halls strengthens the case for identifying this one too as a synagogue. It also makes sense of some of the other features found. Outside the porch was a cistern cut in the rock, carefully plastered, and entered by a few steps, set in a convenient place for the worshippers to wash before going to pray. In the building itself, by the north-west corner, was a recess in the wall. This could be a cupboard for the scrolls of the Scriptures. Across the central floor was a line of paving-stones with a pillar at each end. The excavators think this was the place where a reading-desk stood.

Here then, surely, was a synagogue used by people who were among the crowds listening to Jesus at the lakeside. Gamla's synagogue is the only one of the first century near Galilee. Were others in the area like it? No one can be sure. However, the fact that some of the later synagogues there were similar in many ways suggests that they were. Given that no one can be certain, we may use the Gamla ruins to build a picture of the synagogues Jesus knew.

Luke's Gospel describes him going to the synagogue at Nazareth 'on the Sabbath day, as was his custom'. Citizens of Nazareth had walked along the streets, some pausing to wash at a pool, to the doorway of their prayer hall. Entering, they climbed the steps and walked along to find a place to sit. Men and women may have had separate sections, that is not clear. They sat in rows along the steps, leaving the central area empty. The floor there was probably covered with rugs, giving a splash of colour. Men wore prayer shawls, white, some with long fringes (see Matthew's Gospel 23:5).

When everyone was seated, the leader could begin the service. An important moment was the reading of the Bible lessons. The scrolls of the Law and the Prophets would be brought respectfully from their ark or cupboard, carried through the congregation and laid on the reading-desk in the centre. On that occasion in Nazareth Jesus was reading the second lesson, from Isaiah's prophecy. The Dead Sea Scrolls show us the sort of book he read from (see *The Bible of Jesus' Time*).

The discovery at Gamla helps us to imagine more clearly the setting in which Jesus began his teaching, and the synagogue from which he was expelled.

[1] See *Treasures from Bible Times*, pp. 176ff.

THE BIBLE OF JESUS' TIME

Jesus 'went to Nazareth . . . and on the Sabbath day he went into the synagogue, as was his custom. And he stood up to read. The scroll of the prophet Isaiah was handed to him. Unrolling it, he found the place . . .' (Luke 4:16,17).

What was it like, that scroll from which Jesus read? Scrolls read in synagogues today are big and bulky. Judging by the Dead Sea Scrolls they were rather smaller in the first century. One of the first of those scrolls to come to light happened to be a copy of Isaiah. It is also the only biblical scroll found complete (see *A Treasure from Buried Books*). If the synagogue in Nazareth owned a similar one, it would have been about 7.5 metres/24½ feet long, and 26 cm/10 ins high. Seventeen leather sheets were sewn side by side to make the roll, and on them were fifty-four columns, each with 29 to 32 lines of writing: 1633 lines in all. The reader held the book and unrolled it with his left hand, taking the outer edge in his right and rolling it again as he read, column by column. To reach Isaiah 61, the chapter he read in the synagogue, Jesus would have unrolled most of the scroll and re-rolled it again.

The dozens of copies of Old Testament books found among the Dead Sea Scrolls suggest that it was not hard to obtain a biblical scroll in first-century Palestine. Of course, the Scrolls belonged to a very devout Bible-reading community, and in a country town like Nazareth probably only a very few people had the leisure to read, or owned any Bible scrolls themselves. Even so, books were not expensive. Calculations put the time needed to copy a long work like Isaiah at almost three days, so its price had to cover three days' wages for a scribe, and the cost of materials.

This is in line with the price of one and a half to two and a half denarii for a cheap copy of a papyrus scroll, unlikely to be as long as Isaiah, which the poet Martial quoted in Rome later in the first century. In second-century Egypt, the cost of copying 1,000 lines of Greek was two denarii. A working man determined to buy a copy of Isaiah would expect to pay three or four days' wages for it. To own a complete Old Testament would cost a lot more, and would mean not a single book but a pile of scrolls.

By the time Jesus read from Isaiah's prophecy in the synagogue at Nazareth, this copy of Isaiah was over 100 years old. It had been read over and over again and repaired where it had torn. Where the copyist missed out some words by mistake, they were inserted afterwards, running down the margin where the space on the line was too short. The join between two sheets of leather is visible to the left. The photograph is of Dead Sea Scroll Isaiah A (the original is in the Shrine of the Book, Jerusalem).

THE LANGUAGES THEY SPOKE

Talitha kumi, ephphatha, abba are all words in Aramaic, the language of Jesus reported in the Gospels. In the days of the Old Testament prophets the Jews spoke Hebrew. When they went as exiles to Babylon, in 586 BC, Aramaic was normal there, and they began to speak it themselves. Aramaic is a sister language to Hebrew and was spoken in Syria. Trade and Assyrian deportations spread it across the Near East and it became important as the administrative language of the Persian Empire. Although Greek invaded the same area (see below), Aramaic remained the speech of most ordinary people.

Those words in the Gospels are important relics of first-century Palestinian Aramaic. Scholars wanting to reconstruct the sayings of Jesus as the disciples might have heard them, had hardly anything else from his time. They had to work back from the phraseology of Jewish and Christian books of the third to seventh centuries, which made their studies

Alexander Jannaeus, the Jewish king who ruled 103–76 BC, struck coins with his name in Greek on one side and Hebrew on the other.

less than satisfactory.

With the discovery of the Dead Sea Scrolls the situation has changed. They include books, or fragments of books written in Aramaic in the first century BC and up to AD 67. Their language lies between the language of the Persian Empire and that known from the third century AD onwards. Among the scrolls are paraphrases of Old Testament books, including some like the later Targums, and several apocryphal and visionary compositions. These all have a formal, literary flavour. Scribblings and notes on pottery vessels, and especially the notices scratched on ossuaries, add examples of the languages in daily use.

If Aramaic was the common language, what was the role of Greek? Alexander the Great's

campaigns left Greek generals ruling and Greek soldiers settled all across the region, so Greek replaced Aramaic as the language of government. Coins minted in Syria, Babylonia, Persia and further east carry rulers' names in Greek. The same was true in Judea. When the Hasmonean priest-kings started to issue their small copper coins, they had their names and titles stamped on them in Greek on one side.

Inscriptions in Greek were set up in Jerusalem to commemorate generous gifts to the Temple. There were also notices in Greek intended for foreign visitors (such as the Theodotos inscription and the 'Forbidding Stone', see *Temple Tourists* and *Herod's Great Temple*).

Again, names or descriptions of contents scratched or painted on

pots and pans, and ossuary texts, show that Greek was not limited to the ruling class. Among the Dead Sea Scrolls are pieces of books in Greek, biblical translations and others, demonstrating that some religious Jews read their sacred literature in that language in first-century Palestine. In the course of their daily duties the Roman governors certainly spoke Greek, and Jesus may have answered Pilate's questions at his trial in Greek.

Josephus recorded the display of warning signs in Latin beside the Greek ones in the Temple. Latin was the formal language of Roman rule, and of military command. (Papyri written in Latin were left at Masada by Roman soldiers.) The priestly authorities would be concerned that Roman officials and their staff should be alerted to the rule forbidding entry to the sacred area. Pilate's inscription in Caesarea is engraved in Latin (see *Pilate's Own Monument*).

Pilate wrote the title for Jesus' cross—'Jesus of Nazareth, the King of the

This inscription in Aramaic, from an ossuary, states that these were the bones of 'Simon the builder of the temple'.

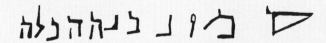

The Greek writing on this ossuary includes the names Joseph and Mary.

Jews'—in three languages: the local language, Aramaic; the official language, Latin; and the common language, Greek.

Aramaic, Greek, Latin . . . was Hebrew spoken, too? For years scholars believed not, or that it was restricted to religious circles, synagogue readings and prayers, and the Temple. Counting in favour of a wider knowledge is the presence of Hebrew inscriptions on the other side of- Hasmonean coins. That might mean no more than Latin legends on coins of recent times—a grand style which the educated could understand.

However, recent discoveries have thrown new light on the question. Books in a style of Hebrew imitating the Old Testament yet distinct from it, and some in Hebrew more like that of the Mishnah (see *Jewish Writings*) make up a large section of the Dead Sea Scrolls. They could be dismissed as the products of a religious sect had not other documents been found with them, and in other caves, which come from secular life.

There are letters and legal deeds, admittedly of slightly later date, connected with the revolt of Bar Kochba (AD 132–35). This false Messiah had letters written in Hebrew, Aramaic and Greek. From first-century houses in Jerusalem, from Herod's castles (Herodium and Masada), and from other places have come pots with Hebrew words or names painted on them. There are ossuaries, too, with labels which are clearly Hebrew.

Within each of these languages there were dialects, hard to trace now, plain to those who heard them. Matthew 26 records the serving girl's recognition of Peter's Galilean accent in the High Priest's house. The language used by peasants and by the uneducated workmen was Aramaic. Hebrew was probably taught in synagogue schools everywhere and spoken in some places near Jerusalem, by religious zealots and by nationalists. Except for those in the remotest villages, craftsmen, businessmen and traders would have learnt enough Greek for commercial purposes at least. A Jewish craftsman's son brought up in Nazareth, a town on a main road, could be expected to talk in Aramaic, to use Greek when necessary, and to have more than a reading knowledge of Hebrew.

SMALL IS BEAUTIFUL

A sharp-eyed bedouin picked up this tiny leather packet in the Qumran area. It is a first-century head phylactery. When it was unstitched, it opened to reveal four tiny parcels tied with hair. Both pictures are actual size.

Each of the parcels in the leather packet is a piece of very thin skin containing verses from Exodus and Deuteronomy in minute writing (actual size).

Most people would not have noticed the tiny blackened object. To the sharp-eyed bedouin, hunting for treasure in the caves by the Dead Sea, it was something that they might be able to sell. They were used to finding pieces of old leather scrolls (see *A Treasure from Buried Books*): this was a tiny leather package. Presently they took it to their agent, and it found its way to the shop of an antiquities dealer in Jerusalem. In January 1968 the dealer sold it to Yigael Yadin, then Professor of Archaeology at the Hebrew University. He knew what he had bought, a fascinating antiquity which he set about studying and described in detail in a book published the next year.

The package is a piece of leather, folded in half and sewn together along three sides. It is tiny, 20 mm/0.79 in. long and 13 mm/0.51 in. wide. When it was unsewn, it opened to reveal four minute parcels, tied with hair, each lying in a hollow in the leather. To unwrap these was a delicate task. They proved to be folded pieces of very thin parchment, with lines of very small writing on one side. The largest piece is 2.7 cm/1.06 ins and 44 mm/1.73 ins wide, and carries twenty-six lines of writing. The letters are about 0.5 mm/ 0.02 in. high.

Although no one was ever expected to read them, a scribe had copied on to these sheets passages from the books of Exodus and Deuteronomy.

Several more tiny sheets were found among the Dead Sea Scrolls. There are also a dozen or so more of the leather packages, but none of them is as well

preserved as the one Yadin bought. All of them are about the same size.

Four times in the 'Law of Moses' a command comes to the Israelites from God: 'Fix these words of mine in your hearts and minds; tie them as symbols on your hands and bind them on your foreheads' (Exodus 13:9,16; Deuteronomy 6:8; 11:18). How should Jews who wanted to obey the Law put this command into effect? Perhaps it was not meant to be taken literally, but many Jews thought it should be.

At least as early as the second century BC devout men had the words of these commands written on slips of parchment to tie on to themselves as reminders of God's Law. By the first century AD this was a custom for religious men. Later, the rabbis laid down rules about them which are still in force today. One package is tied inside the left arm, above the elbow, where it is nearest to the heart. In it is a single piece of parchment with the texts of Exodus 13:1–10, 11–16 and Deuteronomy 6:4–9; 11:13–21. To the forehead is bound a package with four sheets inside, containing the same texts.

Nowadays these are worn for morning prayers, except on the Sabbath and holy days. In the first century it is possible they were worn more often, even all day. Certainly there were some variations in the texts included, although it is not clear if these were definite patterns. The men who wore them would hardly be likely to know exactly which texts were inside, unless they were scribes who made their own. At Qumran we find that a scribe added the Ten Commandments in Deuteronomy 5:1–21 and the following verses 22–33, and several other sections.

The Hebrew name for these packages is *tefillin*, which seems to mean 'prayers'. In the New Testament a Greek word is used for them which has passed into English as 'phylactery'. This word meant a safeguard or an amulet, and it is easy to see how other peoples could think that what the Jews wore were amulets just like theirs. Everywhere in ancient times men and women wore amulets and charms to protect them from accidents and disease, from evil and misfortune, much as they do today. Sacred words engraved on metal or written on parchment supposedly have special value. It is not surprising, therefore, to learn from rabbinic writings that some Jews did treat their phylacteries in the same way. However, their real purpose was clearly to remind their wearers of God's Law.

That is how 'the teachers of the Law and the Pharisees' used them in Jesus' time, undoubtedly. Jesus condemned those religious leaders, not for wearing their phylacteries but for making them wide (Matthew 23:5). Until the example from Qumran came to light, it was hard to envisage what was meant. Now it is clear that some phylacteries were so small that they would hardly be visible on the wearer from a distance. These specimens from Gospel times would surely have won Jesus' approval. Smaller ones can hardly be imagined. By contrast, phylacteries of recent times may be three times as large, with heavy straps to hold them in place. Jesus' teaching is plain: religious duties are to be done without display or fuss. It is not a person's apparent piety which pleases God, but the faithful and humble spirit.

Whereas the first-century phylacteries found near the Dead Sea would have been hardly visible on the wearer's head, modern phylacteries are very obvious.

GEHENNA—'THE EVERLASTING BONFIRE'

Wherever people live they leave rubbish. When they live in towns or cities they have to find a place to dump it. Today you can see piles of refuse outside some towns, whereas at other places it is buried in the ground. Ancient people had the same problem of waste disposal as we do. If a river or the sea ran by the town, it was easy to throw things into the water. If not, heaps of rubbish would build up outside the city wall, or in a convenient ditch. Sensible citizens would make sure they tipped their rubbish where the wind would not carry the smell across their houses.

Archaeologists are often glad to find the rubbish heaps of an ancient town. Ruined houses may have very little left in them, if the owners moved out peacefully. Much more can be discovered about their life-style from the things they threw away. Broken pots, worn-out metalware, pieces of glass, lost coins, waste paper, lie in the soil made by rotting food, decayed clothing, old woodwork and the sweepings of streets and houses. Dead animals might be thrown on a rubbish heap, too, and even, in many places, unwanted children. (The habit of leaving babies exposed to die in this way was accepted in Babylonia, Greece, and Rome. It only ended as the spread of Christianity brought a new appreciation of the value of the individual life. Kind-hearted or childless couples sometimes rescued and adopted exposed babies.) Digging through the layers of a tip can reveal evidence from all types of rubbish, if the earth is carefully analysed for bones, traces of pollen and other organic remains.

The positions of some cities, and their climates, made it unhygienic to leave the refuse rotting in a heap, so it was set on fire. Heat destroyed some of the dangerous by-products of decay (although ancient people did not understand that), and reduced the size of the tip.

The people who lived in houses on the rocky hills of Jerusalem had no river to wash away their rubbish, so they dumped it. At the south of the city, running to the west, is a steep-sided valley which was probably the site of their refuse tip. There they could dump what they did not want, possibly throwing it over the edge of the valley, and set it on fire. Even if flames were not always shooting out, the piles of rubbish would always be smoking and smouldering. Much of what was not burnt, or would not burn, gradually decomposed, as worms and insects gnawed and burrowed, or corrosion and rust ate into it.

That valley was named the Valley of the Sons of Hinnom, or just the

The Valley of Hinnom was Jerusalem's ancient refuse tip.

Valley of Hinnom, in Old Testament times. There Jews who turned to foreign religions performed horrible ceremonies, burning their children in honour of pagan gods (see Jeremiah 7:30,31). In the first century it was the fires of burning refuse that lit the valley. By that time its name had been put into Aramaic as Gehenna, and had become a common Jewish word for hell.

Knowing this, some of Jesus' words strike the modern reader with greater force, as they would have hit their first hearers. He told his followers, 'Anyone who says, "You fool!" will be in danger of the fire of [gehenna]' (Matthew 5:22). And he warned them, 'If your eye causes you to sin, pluck it out. It is better for you to enter the kingdom of God with one eye than to have two eyes and be thrown into

[gehenna], where "their worm does not die, and the fire is not quenched"' (Mark 9:47,48, quoting Isaiah 66:24). Take care, he was saying, that you don't end up on God's rubbish tip!

That was the danger for some of the Pharisees, with their self-righteous stress on the particular details of the laws they had multiplied, contrary to God's intention (see Matthew 23:15,33). It is the danger anyone faces, Jesus taught, who rejects God's way and lives for his own self-satisfaction. The parable of the rich man and Lazarus, recorded in Luke 16, illustrates his point. The rich man has ignored the needs of the poor all his life, and after death it is too late. Tortured by the searing flames he begs in vain for a sip of cooling water.

PART TWO

RULERS OF THE LAND

The country of Palestine, where Jesus and his friends lived, presents a peculiar political picture. There were Jewish kings, then a Roman governor in Jerusalem. The Roman Emperor demanded taxes, and foreign soldiers enforced the law. Learning about the political background makes parts of the Gospel story easier to understand. Archaeological discoveries illuminate the history told by Josephus and other ancient writers.

This head of Augustus in glass is 4.9 cm/1.9 ins high. It is an idealized portrait of the emperor at the beginning of his rule, although it was probably made soon after his death in AD 14.

PEACE AT LAST·

Peace, peace at last! For thirty years the people of Palestine had been free from foreign invasion and murderous civil war. A whole generation had grown up without the fear of hundreds of soldiers suddenly seizing their goods and burning and killing, or of flight to the hills and caves while their homes were ruined. Peace meant better food, more time for family life, easier travel, meeting for religious festivals, prosperity and contentment.

That was the picture when Jesus was born in Bethlehem about 6 BC. His grandfather, or his elderly uncle, the priest Zechariah (John the Baptist's father), could have told him of the hardships they had lived through: the brothers raising forces to fight each other for the High Priest's crown; Pompey's invasion; Jerusalem besieged and taken again and again, and squads of soliders enforcing the payment of Roman taxes (see *Caesar's Image*).

In 40 BC armies had come from the east, from Parthia (Iraq and Iran). Bribed by a would-be High Priest-King they marched on Jerusalem and captured it, looting everywhere. Roman power drove the Parthians out of Syria and Roman support in the end helped prince Herod conquer Palestine. He, too, laid siege to Jerusalem, gaining control in 37 BC only after many weeks of battering and fighting.

Since then, peace had reigned, but at a price, for peace is never free! The price was the rule of King Herod, nearly over when Jesus was born.

What had been happening in Palestine? How did the Romans gain control? Who was Herod? And how did he become king of the Jews?

Fighting for the crown

'I want it!' 'You can't have it; it's mine!' The two brothers fought and squabbled. When they were children their mother had intervened. Now she was dead, and they were fighting over their inheritance. The mother in question was Salome Alexandra. When her husband, the Jewish King Alexander Jannaeus, died in 76 BC she took over the rule of Judea. She could be queen, but she could not follow her husband as High Priest, so she had her elder son Hyrcanus put in that position. By right he should have become king, too, when Salome died in 67 BC, but his jealous brother, Aristobulus, was challenging him. With Mother gone, who could stop the quarrel? Outside help was needed.

Aristobulus built up an army and beat Hyrcanus. He gave up his crown and his High Priesthood in return for a quiet life. It did not last long. His father had put a man named Antipater in charge of Idumaea in the south, and Antipater saw his chance of power in siding with Hyrcanus. He took him to Transjordan and won the support of Aretas, king of the Nabataeans.

With a Nabataean army, Antipater and Hyrcanus marched back to Jerusalem and shut Aristobulus in the temple. Before they could overpower him, an order came to break off the siege. The command came from a power neither Antipater nor the Nabataeans could ignore. It came from Rome.

Since Rome had made a treaty with Judea in 161 BC, to help her fight the Syrians, there had been little contact. Now Syria was securely under Roman rule, so the turmoil next door was unwelcome. If Rome could stop it, she would add to her power. The great general, Pompey, who had settled affairs in Turkey and north Syria, sent his assistant, Scaurus, to Jerusalem. There he sent the Nabataean troops home, and made Antipater and Hyrcanus leave Aristobulus in possession of the city.

In 63 BC Pompey came to Damascus. The two brothers went to put their cases to him. Aristobulus sweetened him with the gift of a golden vine, but his actions were too independent to suit the Roman. Pompey followed Aristobulus to Jerusalem, where he gave himself up. Even so, his followers barricaded themselves in the Temple, where they held out for three months.

October 63 BC saw the Roman soldiers enter the Temple. Judea was now under Roman control; Hyrcanus was set up as High Priest again, without the title king. Pompey paraded Aristobulus in triumph in Rome, executed his supporters, and made the land pay tribute to Rome. All the towns on the Mediterranean coast, others in Transjordan, and Samaria, were added to the province of Syria. Aristobulus' ambition left him in chains, his country impoverished, under Roman control and open to Roman interference in its life.

Julius Caesar—the Jews' friend

All was quiet for a while after Pompey left, then Alexander, a son of Aristobulus, raised an army and occupied three forts in the Jordan Valley. The Romans drove him out in 57 BC. The next year Aristobulus and another son escaped from Rome, tried again to pounce on Palestine, and were quickly beaten back. Aristobulus returned to Rome in chains once more. Alexander was still at large, and his soldiers started to kill any Romans they could find. That brought Gabinius, the governor of Syria, to the attack, and Alexander's force was crushed near Mount Tabor.

One of Gabinius' main activities as governor was to line his own pockets. In 54 BC he was called back to Rome and found guilty of extortion. The man who succeeded him was Crassus. He joined with Pompey and Julius Caesar to rule the territories won by Rome. Crassus' aim was military victory over the Parthians pressing in from the east, and he needed money for his war. What Pompey had not done, Crassus did: he took the 2,000 talents of gold from the Temple in Jerusalem, with a great hoard of other treasure kept there. It was all wasted. Crassus' army failed and retreated: the Parthians killed him (53 BC).

The next years saw the growth of civil war in Rome, as different generals jockeyed for power. Each of them used every means he could to gain support and money from the provinces and from client kings. In the turmoil Aristobulus and his son Alexander were killed. After Pompey's murder, Hyrcanus and Antipater joined Julius Caesar, bringing supplies and men to help him out of a tight corner in Egypt, where the Egyptians had shut him up in the palace at Alexandria.

Caesar made his thanks plain. He strengthened Hyrcanus and Antipater as all but independent rulers, making Antipater a Roman citizen and freeing him from paying taxes. The walls of Jerusalem were rebuilt and Jews were allowed to judge Jewish matters. Caesar also gave Joppa and other places by the coast back to Judea, which meant the country had a sea-port again, bringing great benefits in trade and revenue. One other privilege was that Roman legions should not spend the winter in the country or levy recruits there. This was a valuable relief to the people, because the soldiers were usually billeted on them to be fed and housed without making payment.

Caesar had already built up an

enormous fortune through his conquests in France and Germany, so he could afford to be generous. He also understood the benefits to Rome of a peaceful and contented province. Outside Judea he decreed respect for the Jewish faith and liberty for Jewish communities to function in their own way. That meant, among other things, the freedom to send the annual half-shekel tax to the Temple in Jerusalem (see *At the Moneychangers' Tables*). Caesar's decrees stayed long in the memory of the Jews.

After Caesar's murder in 44 BC one of the assassins, Cassius, took command in Syria. He needed money and when some towns in Judea did not pay he sold the inhabitants as slaves. Antipater made sure of Cassius' protection by paying him a large sum himself. Unhappily for Judea, troubles were multiplying rapidly. Antipater was poisoned. His enemy Malichus took command in Jerusalem, ousting Antipater's elder son Phasael. In Galilee, Phasael's energetic younger brother Herod was in charge, and he persuaded Cassius to approve the execution of Malichus (43 BC). The next year Cassius joined Brutus to fight Mark Antony and Octavian, Caesar's heirs, at Philippi in Greece. Defeated, he committed suicide.

After centuries of war, by the time Jesus was born the land knew peace. This picture, looking towards Bethlehem, captures the tranquil scene.

HEROD—KING OF THE JEWS

HEROD'S KINGDOM

Tyre

GALILEE

Tiberias

Sebaste/Samaria DECAPOLIS

SAMARIA

Jerusalem ——— PEREA

JUDEA

IDUMEA

NABATAEANS

Herod was born about 73 BC. He was the son of Antipater, ruler of the Idumean people who lived in the south of Palestine. When the Jewish king John Hyrcanus (134–104 BC) was ruling, he had conquered the country and forced the people to become Jews. Later, King Alexander Jannaeus (103–76 BC) set up Antipater's father, an Idumean nobleman, as his governor in Idumea. Antipater seems to have succeeded him. His family was rich from sheep-farming and from its shares in the trade which went across their land from Arabia and Petra to the ports at Gaza and Ascalon. This was the route for the caravans of perfumes and incense going to Rome.

Antipater was shrewd and well-informed. As we have already mentioned, he was quick to use the unambitious Hyrcanus, the legitimate Jewish priest-king, to increase his power. He also foresaw the rule of Rome: his own security lay in becoming Rome's faithful ally. New generals held power in Rome every few years, and Antipater became adept at changing sides to win the favour of the man of the moment, although he did not always succeed.

Antipater strengthened his political position by marrying Cyprus, a noble lady of Petra, capital of the Nabataean Arabs. They named their first son Phasael, their second Herod. They had two other sons, Joseph and Pheroras, and a daughter, Salome.

Many Jews disliked Antipater. Although he was said to be pious and just, he was not thoroughly Jewish. Unlike Alexander Jannaeus before him, and Herod after, Antipater was certainly not responsible for large-scale executions and massacres. Some Jews preferred to support Hyrcanus' brother Aristobulus and his sons. Others wanted a return to rule by true descendants of their first High Priest, Aaron. All the time groups of men tried to overthrow the rulers, some for religious or patriotic reasons, others simply for their own gain.

When Herod was twenty-five years old (in 47 BC), his father put him in charge of Galilee, with Phasael governing the Jerusalem region. Herod took up his task energetically. Bandits were terrorizing the area, so he rounded them up and put them to death, including the leader, Hezekiah. Naturally, the local people were very pleased to be rid of this burden, and so was the Roman governor of Syria. In Jerusalem there was another view. Herod had acted high-handedly. Only the Sanhedrin, the court in Jerusalem, could pass the death sentence. Jealous for their rights, the priests and nobles called Herod to appear before the court. Antipater advised him to comply.

Herod went to Jerusalem with a strong guard, but the Sanhedrin moved to condemn him. Before they could do so, Herod escaped. The Roman governor of Syria had sent a letter to Hyrcanus, who presided over the Sanhedrin, ordering an acquittal. So Hyrcanus interrupted the trial and secretly warned Herod.

The sequel reveals something of Herod's character. He was furious at this treatment. He got control over

Lebanon and Samaria from the Roman governor, collected an army and advanced to attack Jerusalem and dethrone Hyrcanus. Antipater and Phasael rushed to meet him, eventually persuading him that any such action would be counter-productive—Rome would be bound to interfere again. But Herod had made his mark. For the moment he went back to Galilee, yet within ten years he would be king in Jerusalem.

Still hovering in the background, hoping for power in Palestine, was Antigonus, the younger son of Aristobulus. The vacuum left by Cassius seemed to open the way for him to take his uncle Hyrcanus' place. He had some support, but Herod stopped him. However, the tyrant of Tyre took over some towns in Galilee.

After the battle of Philippi, Asia fell into Mark Antony's hands. Herod immediately went in person to affirm his loyalty, and to make him a generous present. At the same time, a large number of Jewish nobles went to complain against Phasael and Herod, and the way their father had behaved, but Antony ignored them. He gave the two brothers the title 'tetrarch', which meant ruler of part of a province, and he made Tyre give back the towns in Galilee.

This happy situation quickly passed; a fresh storm broke as the Parthians burst out, overrunning Syria. Antigonus saw another chance, bribed the Parthians, and at last climbed on to the throne in Jerusalem. Herod managed to escape. Phasael was caught and died a prisoner of the Parthians. Hyrcanus was taken captive and Antigonus had his ears cropped. This physical maiming disqualified him from being High Priest. Parthian soldiers looted all they could. Although Antony's general soon drove the Parthians out of Syria, Antigonus ruled until 37 BC.

Herod, the Romans' friend

Herod escaped from the Parthians to the safety of Idumea. Then, on hearing that Phasael was dead, he set out for Rome to ask Mark Antony's help. He travelled by way of Alexandria, where he brushed aside an offer of military command from Cleopatra, was almost shipwrecked, and had to stay for some months in Rhodes. At Rome, Antony introduced Herod to his colleague Octavian.

Octavian admired Herod's energies and skills, and Herod reminded him of

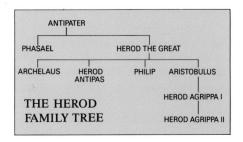

THE HEROD FAMILY TREE

ANTIPATER
PHASAEL — HEROD THE GREAT
ARCHELAUS — HEROD ANTIPAS — PHILIP — ARISTOBULUS
HEROD AGRIPPA I
HEROD AGRIPPA II

the good relations that had existed between Herod and Antipater and Julius Caesar. Caesar had named Octavian, his grand-nephew, as his heir. When Octavian and Herod met, the Roman was about twenty-three years old, Herod ten years his senior.

Antony and Octavian did more for Herod than he had hoped. Antony saw him as a tool to help defeat the Parthians in Syria and Palestine, and proposed that the Senate make him king of Judea. Whatever his future subjects might think, from now on to challenge Herod would be to challenge the might of Rome.

Early the next year (37 BC) Herod landed in Palestine. He went first to Masada where he had left his wife, his mother, and his mother-in-law safe in the castle guarded by his brother Joseph. Antigonus, the Parthian-appointed king, had tried to capture the fortress, and failed. Herod moved on to Jerusalem but a Roman official's interference obstructed him.

After clearing more bandits out of Galilee, and going to help Mark Antony in Turkey, Herod returned to Jerusalem in the spring of 37 BC. Supported by eleven Roman legions, he laid siege to the city, broke through the walls and fought yard by yard until all was under his control. The Roman soldiers killed the defenders without mercy and only by giving each soldier a handsome present did Herod save the city and the Temple from total destruction.

King Antigonus was captured and sent to Mark Antony, who had him executed in Antioch. It was the first time, people said, that the Romans had executed a king. The king they created, Herod, sat on his throne in Jerusalem.

Although Herod always enjoyed Antony's favour, things became awkward when Antony fell under the spell of Cleopatra. The queen of Egypt wanted to be as great as her ancestors, and their kingdom had stretched through Palestine into Lebanon. Herod was in the way: he should be removed. That was too much to ask, even of the infatuated Antony. How could he dethrone the king the Senate had so recently created, when he had been a loyal ally? There would be constant rebellion among the Jews, too.

To mollify the queen, Antony gave her a choice piece of Herod's kingdom, the date-palm orchards and gardens of balsam[1] around Jericho. Herod had to agree, even though the Jericho crops were a major source of income for him. He made a neat arrangement by which he continued to farm the region, paying a heavy rent to

[1] Balsam was the sap of a bush. It had antiseptic qualities and a pleasant smell, and was widely used for dressing wounds.

Cleopatra. That meant her officials had no reason to be busy in his kingdom. When Cleopatra made more trouble for Herod, by taking sides with his mother-in-law against him and making charges against him to Antony (see *Herod, the Great Murderer*), Antony still refused to act against a faithful helper.

Cleopatra's hatred prevented Herod joining the army she and Antony gathered to fight Octavian. Instead, they sent him to bring the Nabataeans to heel. When Octavian won the battle of Actium in 31 BC, Herod knew he had to change sides. He went to Octavian and told him he would be as loyal to him as he had been to Mark

Antony, Octavian, who wanted to settle affairs, assured him that his position would not change. Soon afterwards, in 30 BC, with Antony and Cleopatra dead, Octavian gave Herod back the Jericho estates and added other towns to his kingdom, among them Gaza and Samaria.

Herod was quick to make his thanks to Octavian public. In 27 BC the ruler of Rome took the title Augustus. In 25 BC Herod founded a new city where ancient Israel's capital, Samaria, had been. Here 6,000 men from his army of foreign soldiers were given plots of land. Herod named the place Sebaste, the Greek for 'Augustus' town'. High above the roofs of the

The Citadel at Jerusalem stands on the site of a stronghold built by Herod at the north end of his palace. The largest tower remains from Herod's time, the typical large stone blocks having finely smoothed margins.

Herod's castle at Herodium towered over the countryside, a sign of his rule visible to all. Excavations revealed traces of the elaborate arrangements inside Herodium—baths, a dining-room, an enclosed garden, and the great tower.

houses reared a temple. It was dedicated to Rome and Augustus. In 21 BC Herod began another city, a great new port which took twelve years to build. This he called Caesarea.

Augustus gave more lands to Herod —in 23 BC and again when they met in Syria in 20 BC. They met in Italy a couple of years later, and again in 12 BC, when Herod took two of his sons to Rome for the emperor to settle a charge of conspiracy. There is doubt about a third visit by Herod to Augustus in Rome.

Herod sent the emperor many messages on all sorts of matters. When they were not about imperial policy and the intrigues of his neighbours, they were about his family. Herod's problems with his sons were endless, to Augustus they became a nuisance. 'I would rather be Herod's swine than Herod's son,' he said. He was playing on the Greek words for 'pig' and 'son' which are similar (*hys* and *hyios*), and on the Jewish objection to pigs.

Augustus aimed to rule a peaceful empire. By putting down brigands and ne'er-do-wells, Herod extended the peace. In fact, Augustus gave him lands in south Syria, because they were controlled by robber bands under robber barons who threatened the peace. Herod was able to subdue them. Doing that, he went farther than he should have done. His army went into the Nabataean kingdom to catch some of them and the Nabataeans complained to Rome.

Augustus was angry; Herod had broken the peace. The emperor wrote a harsh letter ending their friendship. There was not much hope for Herod without that, so after about a year he sent a favourite courtier to put matters right. The courtier's speech, and events that took place, changed Augustus' mind. He wrote again to Herod, warmly. For the rest of his rule, Herod had the good will of the Roman emperor.

THERE'S NO GOD THERE!

Pushing past protesting priests, the Roman general strode through the heavy curtain and into the Holy of Holies. He stopped, astonished, turned, and marched out. His officers gaped in surprise. 'There's nothing there!'

In Athens the great statue of the goddess Athene stood in her temple, the Parthenon. At Ephesus the famous temple of Diana guarded her ancient stone which had fallen from heaven. Egyptian temples, too, had sacred statues in shrines where only priests could see them. No one knew what was hidden in the heart of the Temple in Jerusalem. There was great treasure there, so surely there would be an impressive holy object. The Roman general Pompey went to see—and found just an empty room!

Pompey won the praise of Cicero in Rome and, later, of Josephus because he took nothing out of the Temple. He did not touch the golden table and golden lampstand, golden dishes and bowls that stood in the main hall, nor did he seize any of the funds in the stores (2,000 talents of gold—over 52,000 kg/50 tons).

Even so, the fact that he went into the holy place was sacrilege. Not even the most devout Jew could go in there! No religious Jew could overlook this conduct. When the Egyptians with whom Pompey sought refuge killed him in 48 BC, many Jews said it was divine punishment.

The shrine in the temple of Bel at Palmyra, dedicated in AD 32, would have held a fine statue of the god, with valuable ornaments. Like other great statues of ancient gods and goddesses, it was destroyed long ago. Today the shrine stands empty—as Pompey found the holy place in the Temple at Jerusalem.

RULERS

EMPERORS OF ROME

Augustus	31 BC–AD 14
Tiberius	AD 14–37
Caligula	AD 37–41
Claudius	AD 41–54
Nero	AD 54–63
Galba	AD 68–69
Otho	AD 69
Vitellius	AD 69
Vespasian	AD 69–79
Titus	AD 79–81

JEWISH KINGS OR RULERS

Herod	37–4 BC
Archelaus	4 BC–AD 6 (Judea)
Antipas	4 BC–AD 39 (Galilee, Perea)
Philip	4 BC–AD 34 (Gaulan, Bashan)
Agrippa I	AD 37–41 (Gaulan, Bashan, Abilene)
	AD 41–44 (Gaulan, Bashan, Abilene, plus Judea and Samaria)
Herod	AD 41–48 (Chalcis in Lebanon)
Agrippa II	AD 50–53 (Chalcis)
	AD 53 (Gaulan, Bashan, etc.)
	AD 54–93? (Gaulan and Galilean towns)

CAESAR AUGUSTUS

Portrait of Augustus on a silver coin (tetradrachm) from the province of Asia, 19 BC.

The entrance to the temple of Rome and Augustus at Ankara. On the walls is engraved the account of Augustus' rule in his own words, in Latin, with a Greek translation. The building survived being converted into a church and later being partly used as a mosque.

Coins were a very good way to spread information. They were easy to make in large numbers, and could reach all the population. The Romans used coins as a means of propaganda, like every other state: Rome ruled and everyone should know it. Soon the emperor's head was recognized everywhere (as Jesus' question about the tribute money proves—see *Caesar's Image*).

Statues of the emperor standing in temples and public places helped to remind people that he was in control. Smaller figures stood in shrines or private houses. In Rome, during his lifetime, Augustus did not allow people to worship him as a god. Rather he was the father or creator and upholder of the state. In the provinces of the

east he was treated as a god, which made his portrait or image even more offensive to Jews.

Over 230 statues or busts of Augustus are known to have survived —everything from miniatures to life-sized sculptures. No doubt originally there were more, some placed in the temples Herod built in Caesarea, Samaria, Paneas and other towns of Palestine which were not Jewish centres.

In his lifetime Augustus could make his actions known through his agents. He also took care that they should be remembered after his death. At his tomb in Rome a great notice engraved on bronze sheets set out his own account of his greatness. Copies were made for temples in other towns. The bronze plates are lost, as are most of the copies, but one that is almost complete can still be read on the walls of a temple in Ankara, Turkey. The proud proclamation makes the emperor's position clear: Rome ruled the world.

At home Augustus improved the state of the country and its people. Abroad his armies fought battles to win peace through victory. Kings beyond the frontier of the empire made pacts with him. Ambassadors and princes came from far away with valuable presents: from Persia and India, from Britain and Rumania. The senate and people of Rome honoured him for his 'courage, mercy, justice and piety'. His enemies in Rome did not live to tell a different story.

Augustus was enormously rich. Besides his family estates, he took

over the properties of the enemies he overcame before his reign began, including the treasure of Egypt which belonged to Cleopatra. Important Romans left money and estates to him in their wills. With his wealth, he paid for grain to feed the poor in Rome on more than one occasion. He improved the regular grain supply system and also constructed new aqueducts to give the city a better public water supply.

Using his wealth for show was essential to keep his name popular. He transformed his capital city with temples, theatres, bridges and government offices. 'I found it brick and left it marble,' he boasted. That meant good employment for craftsmen and labourers. For the people's amusement he staged gladiator shows with as many as 10,000 men, and mock sea-battles. About 3,500 wild beasts fell as prey in the mock 'hunts' he held, 260 lions and thirty-six crocodiles being killed on one occasion.

The emperor must live in the greatest splendour, although Augustus avoided the excesses of gluttony and ostentation that began to appear in Rome. In later years, gold and silver plate and jewellery from the imperial palaces were melted down or looted. Only a few examples survive from the first century AD to suggest the magnificence of the imperial household.

HEROD—THE GREAT MURDERER

Herod then with fear was filled,
'A prince,' he said, 'in Jewry!'
All the little boys he killed
In Bethlehem in his fury.

Bethlehem's babies, the Holy Innocents, were far from being Herod's only victims. He was suspicious of anyone whom he thought could try to take the throne away from him. One-time friends, servants, countless enemies, priests, nobles and all who happened to cross him in some way were killed. In such a crowd, a few baby boys would hardly be noticed. In fact, we would not know about them if the baby Herod wanted to kill had not escaped (Matthew 2:13–18).

The list of Herod's individual victims is horrifying and damns his memory. He had one of his ten wives (the favourite one) executed. And he ordered the deaths of three of his own sons, a High Priest, a former High Priest and ex-king, and two of his sister's husbands. What threat were they to him?

The first to fall victim to Herod's jealousy was an innocent teenager, Aristobulus. He was the son of Alexander and grandson of the Aristobulus who claimed Hyrcanus' crown (see *Peace at Last*). His mother was Alexandra, Hyrcanus' daughter, and his sister Mariamme was Herod's second wife. Aristobulus, as the last eligible male in the Hasmonean family, was the rightful heir to the high priesthood. Herod had appointed someone else in order to limit the power of the Hasmoneans to rival him.

Aristobulus' mother made Cleopatra put pressure on Herod, so he deposed his appointee, making his young brother-in-law High Priest. All the time Herod watched Alexandra, and stopped her when she tried to leave Judea, smuggled out in a coffin with her son in another. When Aristobulus caught the people's attention in the Temple, for he was a good-looking sixteen-year-old, Herod acted. A party was held in the winter palace at Jericho, the guests played in the garden pools—and Aristobulus drowned (36 BC). Herod ordered a fine funeral; Alexandra worked for revenge.

The second victim was Herod's uncle, Joseph, who had married Herod's sister Salome. Salome and Mariamme, Herod's wife, were enemies. While Herod was away with Mark Antony, answering Cleopatra's charge that he had murdered Aristobulus, Joseph had the care of Mariamme. On Herod's return, Salome told him that her husband Joseph was Mariamme's lover. Mariamme convinced Herod that this was a lie, but she also told him that Joseph had disclosed Herod's order that she was to be killed if he failed to return from the meeting with Antony. The order was a secret one, and Joseph could have let it out only if he had been very close to Mariamme. Salome saw her husband Joseph executed and her enemy Mariamme forgiven (34 BC).

The cruellest of Herod's murders was the killing of Hyrcanus. Although he had been king and High Priest, Hyrcanus was now over eighty years old, quite happy to live at peace in his own home, no threat to anybody. Yet Herod feared Hyrcanus might be the focus of a rebellion, while he himself went abroad to make friends with Octavian. Hyrcanus and the Nabataean king had been writing friendly letters to each other. Herod found treason in that, and so had the old man condemned.

In addition to killing his wife's grandfather, Hyrcanus, before he went away Herod shut his mother-in-law and Mariamme in one of his forts, leaving his sons by Mariamme with his mother, and his sister Salome in Masada. They were all safe, but the plotting continued. Mariamme did not welcome the king on his return, and Salome fed him more false tales about her. At length Herod came to believe that his wife had been unfaithful to him. Despite his love for her, he had her put on trial, condemned and executed in 29 BC. So strong was his passion for Mariamme that Herod made himself ill with remorse. It took another plot to cure him.

Herod's illness was the opening Alexandra, Mariamme's mother, wanted. Alexandra thought she could take over the kingdom. Loyal officers of Herod reported her secret moves to him. At his command, his mother-in-law's life was ended, too.

One more execution brought in a calmer period for Herod's family. After the death of Joseph, Salome was married to Costobar, governor of Idumaea. Now she accused him of conspiring against her brother, Herod. Since he had been forgiven previously for co-operating with Cleopatra, when proof of conspiracy was found he was killed (about 27 BC).

Herod and Mariamme had two sons, Alexander and Aristobulus, who were the king's favourites. His eldest son, Antipater, born by the wife Doris whom he divorced when he married Mariamme, was banished from Jerusalem except for special occasions. The brothers were sent to Rome for education in the emperor's entourage.

Herod brought them back in 17 BC, arranging good marriages for them. Their popularity in the country, coupled with their royal descent through their mother, led them to rash behaviour and outspoken statements. They alone had rights to the throne; their mother's murder should be avenged.

Herod's sister Salome hated them as she had hated Mariamme. She started spreading rumours again, with her brother Pheroras to help her: Alexander and Aristobulus were leading a plot to overthrow Herod. He was hard to convince, but to counter them he called Antipater back to court. Antipater saw that he could build up his own cause. Even from Rome, where Herod sent him to meet Augustus, he wrote in concern about his father's safety and his half-brothers' behaviour. In 12 BC, Herod appeared before the emperor with his two sons, charging them with intent to murder him. Augustus saw through the situation, ruled the charge untrue, and reconciled father and sons. However, Herod changed his will: Antipater was to be king, with Alexander and Aristobulus ruling under him.

No one was content, except Herod. The rivalry and intrigue grew worse. Salome, Pheroras, Antipater, Alexander and Aristobulus, Alexander's powerful father-in-law (king of Cappadocia in Turkey), and other characters hatched schemes to hoodwink Herod into thinking this son or that was, or was not, about to assassinate him. Alexander and

Excavations in the area of Herod's palace at Jericho have uncovered the remains of two pools. The archaeologists suggest it was in one of these that Herod had the young High Priest Aristobulus, drowned.

Aristobulus were the objects of many accusations. All proved ill-founded. Yet in 7 BC, Herod, suspicious as ever, supported by a letter from Augustus allowing him to act as he saw fit, had the brothers pronounced guilty and strangled. Salome, at least, had some satisfaction.

Antipater could not wait for his father to die. He started to build up support, forging a link with his uncle Pheroras. That disturbed Herod, so Antipater went to Rome to escape attention. Then Pheroras died and some of his servants suspected he had been poisoned. An inquiry found that there was poison, obtained by Antipater for Pheroras to feed to Herod! Antipater was recalled by Herod, who did not reveal to him what had been discovered until he reached

the palace. There he was arrested, tried, and found guilty. Herod reported to Augustus and received his permission to execute Antipater. By now mortally ill, Herod rewrote his will. There were other sons still alive. Three were to share the rule: Archelaus was to be king, his brother Antipas tetrarch of Galilee and an area in Transjordan, and Philip, son of a different wife, tetrarch of the former brigand country in the Golan and further east. He gave three cities to his loyal sister Salome.

Herod died in March 4 BC, aged about seventy. The historian Josephus, who preserved so much information about him, commented, 'Fortune made Herod pay a terrible price in his own household for his public successes.'

HEROD—
THE GREAT CASTLE BUILDER

★ Herod's fortresses
● Towns built or rebuilt by Herod

Keeping safe and keeping his crown were Herod's goals. Executing imagined rivals was one way to make sure he remained king. But suppose there were a war or a large-scale rebellion? Against this possibility Herod built castles where he could live securely. Each held stores of weapons, and a strong garrison. His engineers gave them good water supplies. All over his kingdom he built castles. Where there were old ones, he made them stronger, and on strategic sites he erected new ones. Their ruins were identified long ago. With the rise of archaeology in Israel, excavators have uncovered some of the defences and the splendid apartments Herod had designed for himself.

The old fort in Jerusalem was at the north end of the Temple. Herod rebuilt it at the start of his reign and named it Antonia, for Mark Antony. But it has disappeared in the convulsions of the city's history. In the west Herod created his new palace. He could not rest easy in Jerusalem without defences, so he ran a wall with towers around the palace, setting three extra-large towers at the north end.

Josephus said, 'The king made the splendour of these works a means of expressing his own emotions, naming the towers after the three persons he cared for most, his brother (Phasael), friend (Hippicus), and wife (Mariamme).'

Today the lower part of one tower still stands in the 'Citadel', a striking reminder of royal power. The palace itself has vanished, except for traces of the platform on which it stood and some cuttings in the bedrock. Josephus reports that it was magnificent beyond description, luxuriously decorated and furnished with gold and silver. Its colonnades led past green lawns and trees, round two great pavilions. The palace passed from Herod's son Archelaus to become the residence of the Roman governor, the Praetorium where the Gospels record that Pilate washed his hands at the trial of Jesus.

The richness of Herod's palaces is best revealed in the amazing rock fortress of Masada.[1] Equally rich and well-protected was Herodium—the castle Herod named after himself. On a hill south-east of Bethlehem his workmen erected an extraordinary round fort. Two concentric walls crowned the hill, with semi-circular towers protruding on the north, south and west sides, and a round one on the east. Towers and walls still stand 10–15 metres/33–50 feet above the inside ground level; their foundations are 5 metres/16 feet or more below. Architects calculate two storeys have fallen, so that the whole rose 25 metres/80 feet above the floor, and the eastern tower certainly soared even higher.

Those who visited Herod here climbed 200 steps to the doorway. They saw the fort not as a massive stone drum but as a great hill crowned by the wall and towers. Hiding the outside, as high as the now existing walls, was a great tip of earth and stones, giving the appearance of a conical hill. Herod's labourers carried away the top of the next hill to heap up this one. From the top of the stairs, the visitor stepped

Herod's eye for a well-defended site is shown by the location of Machaerus on a steep hill. It was here, according to Josephus, that Herod Antipas held John the Baptist prisoner and then executed him.

Keeping watch over Herod's winter palace at Jericho (foreground) was the fortress of Cypros. Its ruins lie on the peak in the distance, guarding the road from Jerusalem to Jericho.

through a room in the double walls into a cloister. The pillared walks surrounded a space, 33 metres/36 feet long, which was probably planted as a garden. On the side were the main entertaining rooms of the palace.

There was a large dining-room, which the Zealots apparently turned into a synagogue during the revolt of AD 67–70, and a well-built bath-house. This was the latest Roman amenity, which Herod introduced. Heated air circulated under the floor and up the walls of the hot room, floors were paved with mosaic, and walls painted. The domed roof of the warm room is still complete. Bedrooms were most likely in an upper storey here. Courtiers might lead privileged visitors up to the top of the great tower, where the king enjoyed the breezes and the panoramic views over the country he ruled, right across the Dead Sea to his castle at Machaerus in the mountains of Moab.

Anyone building a palace on top of a hill must solve the problem of water-supply. At Herodium three very large cisterns were hewn from the hill below the palace, near the staircase. They collected rainwater, or could be fed from an aqueduct Herod made to carry water from a spring 6 km/3½ miles away (at Artas, south of Bethlehem). A shaft in the palace area gave access to another cistern from which water could be drawn by bucket. That cistern seems to have been filled by hand from the lower ones.

The castle on the hill was only part of Herod's grandiose design. On the ground, at the foot of the hill, spread other opulent structures. A major feature was a great pool, 70 metres/230 feet long, 46 metres/150 feet wide, and about 3 metres/10 feet deep. A round, pillared pavilion stood in the middle. Gardens and a pillared walk surrounded this big pool, making an oasis in the dry summer landscape. There were long halls, and a bath-house bigger than the one in the castle, as well as storage and service rooms. An unexplained narrow terrace runs

for almost 350 metres/380 yards to the west of this area, overlooked by the ruins of another palatial building. Parts of more elaborate structures await examination.

Herodium was both a fort and a palace. It was to be more, for this was Herod's tomb. But precisely where his body was buried is a mystery explorers still hope to solve.

Between Herodium and the Dead Sea was a small fort, Hyrcania. Herod used it as a prison. Cisterns and a few walls survive, taken over by monks who had a monastery there.

Across the Dead Sea, and visible from Herodium, was Machaerus in the mountains of Moab. High on a rocky ridge Herod set up a wall with defensive towers to enclose another palace. Again, a series of cisterns ensured enough water in time of siege. Limited excavations have uncovered parts of the building.

Two strongholds watched over the lower Jordan Valley. Cyprus, named after Herod's mother, was near Jericho. On the hill guarding the south side of the ancient road from Jericho up to Jerusalem remains of cisterns, baths and other buildings show that this fortress was as well-served as Herodium and Masada, even though it was smaller.

Some 30 km/18 miles up the Jordan Valley, atop another commanding hill, lay Alexandrium. As soon as he entered Palestine, Herod took this fort and rebuilt it, equipping it no doubt as well and as strongly as the others.

Through smaller forts, watch-towers, and the garrisons of the cities he ruled, Herod was able to keep a tight grip on the whole of his kingdom.

[1] See *Masada—the Last Stronghold* in *Treasures from Bible Times.*

HEROD—THE GREAT CITY BUILDER

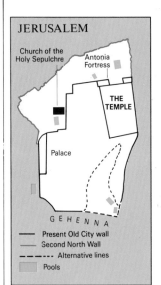

JERUSALEM

Church of the Holy Sepulchre

Antonia Fortress

THE TEMPLE

Palace

G E H E N N A

— Present Old City wall
— Second North Wall
- - - - Alternative lines
Pools

Castles could impress and control the people; cities provided them with streets and buildings where they could enjoy themselves or carry out their business. Herod, like many other kings, founded a number of cities. His name would live on, he hoped, as a generous benefactor in all the major towns of his kingdom, and a large number of places beyond.

On the way to Rome to meet Mark Antony, Herod had to stop at Rhodes to find a new ship. To that city he gave funds for repairs and he rebuilt the temple of Apollo which had burnt down. When Augustus built his new city of Nikopolis in honour of his victory over Mark Antony at Actium, Herod gave liberally to the work, in part, at least, out of duty. Other cities in Greece benefited from his generosity. Perhaps the least expected gesture was Herod's revival of the Olympic Games. He acted as president for one celebration (12 BC) and gave enough money to make sure they would continue.

In Syria Herod was free with his giving. Citizens of Antioch on the Orontes, once the capital of Syria, walked along a muddy main street. Herod supplied a wide stone-paved road with colonnades on either side, 4 km/2½ miles long. Byblos, Beirut, Tyre and Sidon, Tripoli, Damascus, and other cities too, received walls, halls, theatres and gymnasia.

In Palestine Herod did even more. Towns he rebuilt were named after Herod's family and friends and his patron: Antipatris for his father, Phasaelis for his brother, Agrippias for

his friend who was Augustus' right-hand man, Sebaste for the emperor himself. Overshadowing all was Caesarea, also honouring Augustus.

Building began in 22 BC and the city was dedicated twelve years later. Caesarea rivals Jerusalem as Herod's most ambitious project. Although he never saw the Temple fully finished, Caesarea's monumental harbour was ready for the opening. Josephus praised the harbour as one of the biggest in the Mediterranean. Whereas ports usually grow around a creek or bay, here only a small harbour had existed. Herod's engineers had to erect huge artificial breakwaters to provide shelter for the biggest Roman ships.

The new city was to become the major shipping point for trade between Asia and Europe. After Herod's time, Caesarea was the centre of Roman administration and for a long time the major port, despite earthquake damage in AD 130. Neglect and shrinking trade resulted in the gradual collapse of the harbour works, so that today there is nothing to be seen, and some have doubted Josephus' account.

Proof of his accuracy has come from underwater exploration. Archaeologists have been diving into the sea beside the ruined city to examine and map features seen from the air. Two enormous stone banks reach out from the shore, curving round to form a big harbour. The southern one is the longer, about 480 metres/525 yards; the northern is just over half that length. Both were 60 metres/65 yards wide, on average, agreeing with the

60 metres/200 feet Josephus reported. To build the southern breakwater, blocks of stone 15 metres/50 feet long were sunk into the water, he said. Blocks like these, and even longer ones, lie under the sea.

As well as costly stones, the builders fitted timber frames underwater and poured a special concrete into them to make huge masses that would resist the pounding sea. (One is $13.5 \times 3.3 \times 1.8$ metres/ $45 \times 33 \times 6$ feet.) Tufa from Mount Vesuvius in Italy was one ingredient of the concrete. Shaped stones tumbled on the seabed are evidence of towers and other buildings once set on the breakwaters. Harbours often face the problem of silting. At Caesarea a sluice was specially devised to flush sand out of the harbour.

A temple to Augustus, a theatre, an amphitheatre, and immense warehouses made the city as impressive as the harbour. The temple is no more. The theatre, many times renovated and reshaped (see *Pilate's Own Monument*), is once more in use. The amphitheatre lies unexcavated. Near the harbour, vaulted halls grouped in blocks are parts of the warehouse and storage system. The temple of Augustus may have stood on top of them. A great arched sewer beneath the later main street is a witness to the thorough planning of Herod's city. Another is the noteworthy aqueduct. Fresh water had to

From the air it is possible to see the lines of Herod's quay walls as black masses stretching far beyond the modern harbour.

Herod's new city at Caesarea needed a reliable water-supply, so his engineers constructed a great aqueduct. Its last stretch was carried on arches to the city. The part still standing was partly rebuilt by Roman soldiers in AD 132–35.

Later builders took stone pillars from the ruins of Caesarea to build new breakwaters.

flow through 10 km/6 miles of tunnel from springs in the flanks of Mount Carmel, and along an equal length of aqueduct, to supply the city.

Founding new cities, or remodelling old ones, was a good way to increase employment. Thousands of labourers and craftsmen could be put to work, if there was money to pay them. Indeed, when the Temple was finally completed, King Agrippa II set the jobless workmen to re-pave the streets of Jerusalem with fine white slabs. Herod's large income (see *Money and Coins*) covered the expense, drawing on the profits of his estates and businesses, but also on the taxes he extracted from his subjects. Although he cut taxes by a third in 20 BC, then by a quarter seven years later, and went so far as to melt down his own gold and silver plate to buy grain from Egypt to feed his people in the famine of 25–24 BC, the ordinary citizens felt the tax burden so harsh that they burnt the record offices after Herod's death. They were the ones who paid the price for his self-advertisement.

HEROD'S SONS

On Herod's death, only the Emperor Augustus could bring his will into effect. So Herod's sons, the three claimants, hurried to Rome. A party of Jewish nationalists went also, separately, and envoys from the Greek cities in Herod's kingdom. The nationalists wanted no kingdom at all; Herod's reign had been so cruel and oppressive that to be an ordinary Roman province would be better. The Greek cities wanted no king at all. They wanted freedom to rule themselves within the province.

Augustus listened to them all, then divided Herod's kingdom, but not quite as his will set out.

Archelaus was put on probation as ethnarch of Judea, Samaria and Idumea. If he did well, he would become king, Antipas was given charge of Galilee and Perea (in Transjordan) as tetrarch, and Philip the north-eastern territories. Three Greek cities were added to Syria. One was Gadara, which Augustus had given to Herod in 30 BC. Its people had always resented the change of control, for they had suffered under Jewish occupation earlier. By giving Gaza the same standing, Augustus took away from Archelaus an important source of income through trade.

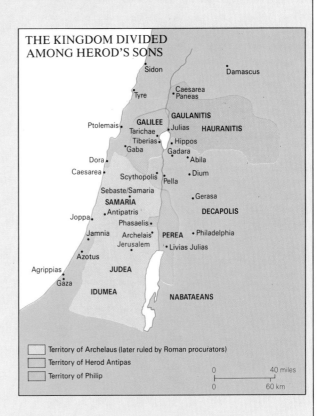

THE KINGDOM DIVIDED AMONG HEROD'S SONS

Sidon
Damascus
Tyre
Caesarea Paneas
GAULANITIS
Ptolemais
GALILEE
Julias
HAURANITIS
Tarichae
Tiberias
Hippos
Gaba
Gadara
Dora
Abila
Caesarea
Scythopolis
Pella
Dium
Sebaste/Samaria
Gerasa
SAMARIA
Antipatris
DECAPOLIS
Joppa
Phasaelis
Jamnia
Archelais
PEREA
Philadelphia
Jerusalem
Livias Julias
Azotus
Agrippias
JUDEA
Gaza
IDUMEA
NABATAEANS

☐ Territory of Archelaus (later ruled by Roman procurators)
☐ Territory of Herod Antipas
☐ Territory of Philip

0   40 miles
0   60 km

Herod Archelaus
(4 BC–AD 6)

Archelaus failed his probation. Even before he went to Rome he had killed a crowd of rioters in the Temple. After he left, the governor of Syria had put down more revolts and, when he returned, he found the country cowed. His rule was harsh. Something he had heard about it prompted Joseph, on his return from Egypt, to take his wife and the young Jesus to Galilee rather than into Archelaus' realm, according to

Matthew's Gospel (2:22).

Archelaus changed the high priests as he wanted. He upset many of his subjects by marrying the widow of his executed half-brother, Alexander. She had borne a son to her husband, so there was no question of Archelaus carrying out a levirate marriage to provide an heir for his dead brother. The marriage was illegal in Jewish eyes.

Archelaus' conduct grew so unbearable that a joint delegation of Jews and Samaritans complained to the emperor.

Augustus removed Archelaus from his position, sending him into exile in Gaul, and turned his domain into a Roman province (AD 6).

Archelaus made small coins like his father Herod's. Instead of the Greek words 'of king Herod', these carry the words 'of ethnarch Herod'. The bunch of grapes on the obverse and the helmet on the reverse continue the style of inoffensive designs used by Herod and earlier rulers.

Herod Antipas
(4 BC–AD 39)

Ancient graves, making the site 'unclean', might halt some building work, but it took more than that to stop Herod the Tetrarch! He was going to build his new city where he wanted to. So Tiberias grew up, with its harbour on the edge of Lake Galilee. Today it still has the name Herod Antipas gave it, to honour the Emperor Tiberius. If religious Jews would not live there because of the graves, Antipas could bring in others by force or by promises of land. Building his palace there would attract many who wanted work, and the courtiers and men who needed or wanted his favour. 'That fox', Jesus called him, according to Luke's account (13:32)—a name well earned by Herod's cunning.

Herod Antipas' territory of Galilee was fertile and well populated, the right place for his capital. He also rebuilt the town of Sepphoris, his first capital, to guard the region. Perea, the other half of his realm, was rough and thinly occupied. There he fortified a town and called it Livias, in honour of Augustus' wife. His father's castle at Machaerus was important, as it guarded the frontier with the Nabateans and, like Masada, it was splendidly furnished.

In both regions the people were thoroughly Jewish, forcibly converted a century before. Antipas was happy to follow his father's behaviour, and so adopted the Jewish calendar, taking part in the festivals in Jerusalem. (Luke 23:7 records that he was there at Passover time.) When Pontius Pilate set up the shields in Jerusalem which so offended the Jews, Antipas joined his brothers in writing the petition to Tiberius for their removal (see *Certainly not a Saint!*). A distinct party supported him, the Herodians, made up of those who benefited from the family's rule. They saw it as better than having a Roman governor. At the same time they

Philip (4 BC–AD 34)

Philip received the north-east part of his father's kingdom. This was former bandit country and had fewer Jewish inhabitants. That meant he could put the emperor's head on his coins without causing an uproar. His thirty-seven-year rule was peaceful; his conduct won him the reputation of being the most just and moderate of Herod's ruling sons.

Philip, too, was a builder. His major town was Paneas, by the sources of the Jordan. Herod had built a temple to Augustus there. Now Philip developed the city. He called it Caesarea, to honour Augustus; the addition 'of Philip' (Philippi) distinguished it from the city Herod founded on the coast. The other notable place he rebuilt was Bethsaida, which he named Julias after Augustus' daughter. Set where the Jordan flows into Lake Galilee, Philip's city watched the frontier.

Recent exploration strongly suggests that it is the ruin-mound known simply as 'the Tell', on the east side of the river, a mound not yet excavated. Possibly a settlement on the other bank was the Bethsaida of Galilee mentioned in John 12:21.

recognized the need for Rome's protection, and so apparently expected to pay tribute and to uphold her power (see Mark 3:6; 12:13; Matthew 22:16).

As Tiberias had shown, Antipas was not one to let Jewish feelings obstruct his wishes. According to Josephus, when Antipas was visiting his half-brother Herod (who lived as a private citizen), he fell in love with his sister-in-law, Herodias. She left her husband for him. The only other ancient sources of information, the Gospels, say that Herodias was the wife of Philip (Mark 6:17; Matthew 14:3).

Was Herod the same man as Philip?

Herod the Great certainly had two sons named Herod, and one named Philip. Was one Herod known as Herod Philip to distinguish him? The son named Philip was not called Herod, according to the evidence. Archelaus and Antipas did add Herod to their names, but only when they became rulers. Most scholars assume that the Gospel record is wrong and Josephus right. An argument that Josephus is partly wrong maintains that Herodias was wife of Herod first, then of Philip the Tetrarch, then of Antipas!

When ancient sources disagree like this, it is unfair to all of them to label one as wrong without very strong grounds for doing so. Whoever Herodias had married, he was Antipas' half-brother and she had a child by him. For Antipas to marry her was illegal in Jewish eyes. John the Baptist criticized the tetrarch and was shut up in the fortress of Machaerus for his boldness. Antipas was afraid of John's popularity, yet to kill him immediately might have led to a revolt. Eventually the execution was ordered, at Herodias' request (Mark 6:14–29; Matthew 14:1–12).

Herodias spelt trouble. As proof of his devotion to her, Antipas had divorced his wife, whose father was Aretas, the Nabatean king. Furious at the insult, Aretas attacked, defeating Antipas' forces in Perea (AD 36). Fighting between Rome's subjects was not allowed, as Herod had learnt (see *Herod—King of the Jews*). The Emperor Tiberius ordered his governor in Syria to attack Aretas but, before he could do so, Tiberius died, so the governor withdrew.

The new emperor, Caligula, was a great friend of Agrippa, Herodias' brother. He made him king of the lands once ruled by Philip the Tetrarch (AD 37). Jealous, Herodias urged Antipas to ask Caligula to give him the title 'king'. In Rome Caligula paid more attention to messages from Agrippa than to Antipas. There was no love lost between them. Antipas was condemned for building up a huge stock of arms, which he could not explain. He was banished to the west and his lands given to Agrippa.

THE ROMAN GOVERNORS

The Roman governors made small bronze coins for the people of Judea. This one, struck under Ambibulus, has an ear of corn and the word 'Caesar's' on one side, and a date-palm tree with signs for 'year 40' (AD 10).

Archelaus failed to rule his kingdom properly, so Augustus turned it into a province of the empire. Herod had set up an effective government, all that was needed was a competent manager. The emperor found one among the equestrians, the middle-class businessmen of Italy. His name was Coponius. He answered to the emperor, but the governor of Syria was higher in rank, a senator, so sometimes took charge in Judea. There were other provinces with special local circumstances that had governors of equestrian status, notably Egypt.

'Prefect' was the governor's title until the reign of Claudius (AD 41–54) when it was changed to 'procurator'. Prefect is Pontius Pilate's title on the Caesarea Stone (see *Pilate's Own Monument*) and the Greek of the Gospels reflects that accurately.

The governor had to keep order with the troops under his command, suppressing brigands and rebels (see *Army of Occupation*). He had to administer justice, taking his seat formally in his official residence, either Herod's palace in Jerusalem or the one in Caesarea. In his hands alone rested power to order the execution of a criminal. The governor of Judea had to work with the High Priest if the country was to stay calm. All religious matters went to the priests' court, the Sanhedrin. If that condemned someone to death, the case then had to go before the governor for him to order the sentence. That was why Jesus met Pilate.

Sending the province's tax to the imperial treasury was the other duty of the governor. He was responsible for having the land tax and the poll tax collected; the publicans took the customs duties (see *Caesar's Image*). Governors turned their positions to their own advantage; the greediest bled their provinces white. In AD 17 both Syria and Judea complained to Tiberius that they were too heavily taxed, asking for relief.

Both taxes were based on surveys, the one of land, the other of people. As soon as Judea became a Roman province a census was begun (AD 6). Luke's Gospel places the birth of Jesus in the context of a census: 'In those days Caesar Augustus issued a decree that a census should be taken of the entire Roman world. (This was the first census that took place while Quirinius was governor of Syria.)' (Luke 2:1,2). At present it is almost impossible to reconcile this statement with other reports. Saturninus governed Syria from 10 to 7 or 6 BC and Varus followed him. Quirinius held office from AD 6. Herod was ruler when Jesus was born, according to Matthew 2:1,22 —therefore he must have been born before 4 BC, the year Herod died. The Roman emperor would hardly have ordered a census in Judea during Herod's reign, because he was responsible for collecting the taxes in his own land. No record of Quirinius governing Syria about 6 BC exists. Each of these points, and lesser ones, have convinced scholars that Luke made a mistake. His reference to a universal tax is unexplained. But much is still unknown, and a conclusive answer can only come with new discoveries.

Governors of Judea probably also received money from the High Priests in return for appointing them. The fourth governor, Gratus, put three in office in successive years (AD 15–18), then a fourth who was High Priest from AD 18 until AD 36, Joseph Caiaphas. Ultimate control over the Temple services lay with the governor, for he kept the High Priest's ceremonial robes in the Antonia fortress, releasing them only for the few days of major festivals. In AD 36 the governor of Syria handed them back to the priests, to appease the Jews after he had sent Pontius Pilate back to Rome for misgovernment.

Apart from their names, little is recorded about the governors before Pilate. The first, Coponius, earned Jewish gratitude by repairing part of the Temple damaged in riots at the start of Archelaus' reign. One of the gateways from the Tyropoieon Valley into the Temple was named after him. Pontius Pilate gained a bad reputation (see *Certainly not a Saint!*). Later governors, such as Felix (AD 52–60), were worse, but their story does not belong here.

In the middle of each Roman army camp was a shrine. The legions' standards and the Roman eagle stood there. They were carried into battle to serve as rallying points. For any of them to be captured by the enemy was a disaster. On this Roman coin (a silver denarius) of about 31 BC, the eagle stands between two standards. Under the emperors, the roundels on the standards held imperial portraits. By allowing his soldiers to carry such standards into Jerusalem, Pontius Pilate caused a riot.

ROMAN GOVERNORS OF JUDEA

Coponius	AD 6–9
Ambibulus	AD 9–12
Rufus	AD 12–15
Gratus	AD 15–26
Pilate	AD 26–36
Marcellus	AD 36
Marullus	AD 37–41
(perhaps = Marcellus)	
(King Agrippa I ruled Judea	AD 41–44)
Fadus	AD 44–46
Alexander	AD 46–48
(nephew of Philo)	
Cumanus	AD 48–52
Felix	AD 52–59
Festus	AD 59–62
Albinus	AD 62–65
Florus	AD 65–66

PILATE'S OWN MONUMENT

The town theatre was old. King Herod had built it over 300 years before. Others had changed and rebuilt it, and now there was major remodelling to be done. The architects redesigned the orchestra area so that it could be filled with water for spectacular displays. Extra walls were needed and new arrangements for the entrances.

Cutting new stone blocks for such work was costly, so the builders looked for old or ruined buildings where they could find an easy supply. One they went to was almost as old as the theatre. There was a fine slab of stone there which would fit neatly at the top of some steps they had to build. A small problem was overcome with a few hammer blows. The slab was slightly too thick—people coming up the steps might trip on it—so workmen knocked away part of the surface to make a slope. What they did destroyed some letters cut into the face of the stone, but that did not matter to them. Now anyone coming up the steps would have a smooth passage.

In 1961 a team of Italian archaeologists from Milan were excavating at Caesarea, north of modern Tel Aviv and its suburb Herzliya. For the third year they were concentrating on the theatre which they had decided to clear. Moving away the sand and stones, they found the steps and the stone.

It is a limestone block 82 cm/32 ins high, 68 cm/27 ins wide, and 20 cm/8 ins thick. The right half of four lines of writing was still engraved on one part of it. They had survived the tread of countless theatre-goers' feet and were still clear. To find an inscription was a major event for the archaeologists—not many had come to light in Caesarea. As soon as this one was uncovered it made headline news. This is what can be seen on it:

STIBERIEVM
TIVSPILATVS
ECTVSIVD . . . E

There was no difficulty in completing the second and third lines as:

PONTIVSPILATVS
PRAEFECTVSIVD . . . E

Here is a monument of Pontius Pilate, the Roman governor of Judea who gave his consent for the death of Jesus. It is the first one ever to be found.

King Herod built the theatre in Roman style at Caesarea. It was re-modelled several times over the following centuries until a fortress was erected over it in Byzantine times.

To the Italian archaeologists excavating the theatre at Caesarea this battered stone slab was the greatest prize—it is the only known inscription from his life-time naming Pontius Pilate, the Roman governor who ordered the crucifixion of Jesus. Part of his name can be seen in the second line.

Pilate apparently built a temple or shrine in honour of the Emperor Tiberius, called a Tiberieum, and wanted everyone to know it. Exactly what the missing words of the text were is debated. From the point of view of New Testament studies, the surviving parts of the wording are the most important. If they had been the ones hammered away, the other letters would have given less information. The PON of PONTIUS and the PRAEF of PRAEFECTVS might have pointed to the sense, but with less certainty, for the words could be completed in other ways.

A battered stone naming Pontius Pilate may not seem especially important at first, but this is the only one. No other inscription or document written in the first century AD actually mentions him. This is the only contemporary evidence for the existence of Pontius Pilate.

CERTAINLY NOT A SAINT!

The Samaritans worshipped on Mount Gerizim for centuries before Pontius Pilate broke up their pilgrimage. On one part of the mount foundations of a temple built by Hadrian in honour of Zeus have been uncovered. Beneath them are ruins of an earlier building, perhaps the Samaritan temple destroyed by Alexander Jannaeus in 128 BC.

Christians traditionally call outstandingly faithful men and women of the past 'saints'. Among the saints are famous men and women, such as Augustine and Theresa, whom everyone can admire. Other 'saints'—like George who killed the dragon—survive in stories which have little claim to be true, and almost nothing is known of them. There are also people whom some Christians call 'saints', but who do not qualify as saints in most people's minds. King Charles I of England, executed in 1649, is one of them. The most surprising of all is Pontius Pilate, listed as a saint by the Ethiopian Church.

In the fourth and fifth centuries stories were told about the trial of Jesus which put Pilate in a rather

better light than the Gospels do. He was made to seem more reluctant to condemn Jesus. In some quarters there was a report that Pilate committed suicide, supposedly realizing what a terrible thing he had done. Stories like these perhaps grew in the face of pagan attacks, and gave rise to views of Pilate which led the Ethiopians to rank him with the saints.

To the rest of the world, Pontius Pilate was weak, perhaps a villain, certainly not a saint. What sort of man was he really?

The stone from Caesarea is his own declaration of loyalty to the Emperor Tiberius who had appointed him. Nothing less would be expected of any Roman governor. That stone is the only first-hand statement we have from Pilate. Roman, Jewish and Christian writers of the first century tell more about him.

Tacitus is the only Roman author whose surviving books mention Pilate, and the reason is simply to give the date when Jesus was crucified. Jewish authors present a fuller picture.

Philo, the philosopher from Alexandria, spoke about Pilate when he was trying to persuade the mad Emperor Caligula not to set up his statue in the Temple in Jerusalem. He told how Pilate had set up gilded shields in Herod's palace in Jerusalem. They were plain, except for a short notice saying that Pilate had made them in honour of Tiberius. It may have been similar to the inscription from Caesarea.

Something about them offended the Jews. They asked Pilate to take them away. No other Roman official had treated the Jews with so little respect; they were allowed to practise their religion as they wanted to. At length Pilate gave way. The Jews threatened to appeal to the emperor if he did not, and that, Philo asserted, made Pilate change his mind. He was afraid Tiberius would learn of abuses in his rule.

Pilate had begun his period in office by showing the attitudes he would take. He had a fresh garrison march into Jerusalem at night with its military standards covered. Next day people saw them in place, with portraits of the emperor on them. The soldiers paid divine honours to these standards, so they were, in effect, idols. To have those in Jerusalem, near their Temple, was more than devout Jews could bear. They followed Pilate back to Caesarea and demonstrated outside his residence. His reaction was to summon them to the stadium. There he encircled them with soldiers and threatened to kill them all. Their reaction pulled the carpet from under his feet. They would die, they said, rather than see their Law flouted in Jerusalem. Pilate ordered the garrison back to Caesarea.

The books of the Jewish historian Josephus record this episode. They also tell of two other actions by Pilate which resulted in the deaths of many people. The first one started well. Thanks to Herod's prosperous rule, and the protection of Rome, the city of Jerusalem had grown. One thing essential for the growing population was water. The Virgin's Fountain was the only constant supply, so most houses had their own cisterns to collect rainwater, but there was never enough. Some time earlier an aqueduct had been made to bring water from Solomon's Pools, south of Bethlehem, to the Temple in Jerusalem.

Pilate decided to build a new one. Surely Jerusalem would be grateful! There were funds to pay for it, too. Large sums of money were stored in the Temple treasury, offerings from all over the world, so Pilate took some of it to pay for his project. Although Jewish teachings allowed spare funds from the Temple to be used for the good of the city, it was unthinkable for a Roman to take them, however good his purpose. In addition, the Emperor Augustus had decreed that no one should interfere with the Temple tax.

When Pilate went to Jerusalem, big demonstrations were held. The governor dressed his soldiers in civilian clothes and sent them into the crowds, with clubs hidden in their garments. On his order, they drew their clubs and broke up the crowds. Some people died from clubbings, others in the panic.

This occasion may be the same as one Luke's Gospel mentions: 'there were some . . . who told Jesus about the Galileans whose blood Pilate had mixed with their sacrifices' (Luke 13:1). The people of Galilee were very patriotic, although the inhabitants of Jerusalem looked down on them as provincials (see John 7:52). Pilgrims from Galilee could easily have become involved in the protest against Pilate's action. Their fervour would mark them out in the crowd, bringing them to the soldiers' notice. However, Luke may have known of another occasion which no other writer has reported.

Pilate's governorship ended with trouble in a different place. His authority extended over Samaria as well as Judea. There the people worshipped God on Mount Gerizim, maintaining that Jerusalem was the wrong place (see John 4:20). In AD 36 one Samaritan led a crowd to the hill where he said he would show them furniture from the Tabernacle, buried there by Moses.

Pilate heard that the men were going armed, so he sent his forces to stop them. A battle took place, men were killed and the leaders captured. Pilate executed them. He seemed to be doing the right thing, but he soon found it was wrong. The Samaritans protested very strongly to Pilate's superior officer, Vitellius, the legate of Syria. Their people were not rebels, they claimed, rather they suffered so much under Pilate's rule that they planned to emigrate. Their case appeared so strong to Vitellius that he ordered Pilate to leave for trial in Rome before the emperor. Pilate embarked, but it was winter, and when he arrived in Rome three months later Tiberius was dead (March AD 37). That is all Josephus records.

In the fourth century, the church historian Eusebius quoted an earlier writer who said that Pilate killed himself two years later.

Philo, Josephus and the Gospel writers were all naturally opposed to Pilate. Jews did not want Roman rule; Christians knew the part Pilate played in the crucifixion of Jesus. Their stories about him would be likely to show him in a bad light. If his own account were found, what would it reveal?

The Caesarea Stone proclaims his loyalty to Tiberius. One other source of evidence about him does exist, in the coins minted for the land under his control.

CLUES TO PILATE'S CHARACTER

Shiny new copper coins were changing hands in the market-place. They were the small change of Palestine. People were used to them, the Jewish priest-kings had made them as signs of their independence in the first century BC. So had Herod and his sons. The Roman governors had done the same, minting coins with the emperor's name on them, a picture of a tree, a bunch of grapes, or another plant, and the date. They proclaimed Rome's rule, irksome to nationalistic Jews, but accepted.

The new ones issued in AD 29, with three ears of corn stamped on them, looked the same until people turned them over. There on the back, in place of the palm-tree or ear of corn, was a pan or ladle. It was not an ordinary kitchen utensil, but the bowl Roman priests used for pouring wine in honour of the pagan gods.

These were the first coins Pontius Pilate supplied for Palestine. There was not much the Jews could do about it. They had to handle the money with its heathen design. Perhaps they protested to Pilate. If they did, they probably looked carefully at the new coins of AD 30 and 31, and became even more dissatisfied. On the back was a harmless wreath

In a handful of coins issued by the Roman governors of Judea, those made under Pilate stand out from the rest. He issued the coins with a curved staff (at left and right) and a ladle (left). Both were pagan objects, contrasting with the ears of corn and palm branches on the other governors' coins!

with the date in it; on the front was a curling rod, something like a shepherd's crook. One objectionable design was changed for another. This was the mark of office of the Roman augur, the expert who foretold the future. When an animal was sacrificed, the augur would inspect its entrails to tell whether the worshipper should carry out his plans that day or not. By putting such a device on the coins, Pilate could not but offend the Jews.

Out of the five Roman governors who struck coins in Judea, only one other put anything on them which could upset

the Jews. He was Felix, ruling from AD 52 to 60, the man who kept Paul in prison for two years (Acts 24:22–27). Felix was a thoroughly bad governor. He was the brother of the Emperor Claudius' influential freedman Pallas, and, according to Tacitus, when in Judea he 'believed himself free to commit any crime'. Even so, while he was in power the coins made in AD 54 and 58 carried ears of corn or palm branches, and the Emperor Nero's name in a wreath. One type, which was issued in AD 54, was apparently meant to assert Rome's control. On one side it shows military equipment, crossed shields

and spears.

As people spent their money, the coins themselves would remind them how the power of Rome affected their lives. Yet, despite Roman rule, the Jews were free to follow their own religious rules and ceremonies. Pilate's coins, unlike those of all the other governors, could be seen as threatening interference in that exclusive religion. Those coins, Philo, Josephus, and the Gospels, all tell the same story: Pontius Pilate had no concern for Jewish feelings. The coins he issued give their first-hand evidence.

MONEY AND COINS

Enormous numbers of coins made 2,000 years ago still exist. On Mount Carmel in 1960 a hoard of 4,500 silver pieces was found. Most of them are shekels and half-shekels of Tyre, the rest are hundreds of denarii bearing the images of Augustus and Tiberius. Who hid them, and why, no one knows. Perhaps they were part of the yearly tax being taken to the Temple in Jerusalem when disaster struck the caravan (see *At the Moneychangers' Tables*). Even this big hoard is only a very small fraction of the coins current. A carefully calculated estimate puts the amount taken to the Temple each year at half a million shekels.

From Herod's time onwards money was officially counted by Roman standards. Greek and Semitic names were still used, and the great variety of coins circulating gave the money-changers plenty of business. The basic unit was the silver *denarius*, equal to the Greek drachma, a good day's wage. The Good Samaritan in Jesus' story left two denarii towards the cost of the robbed man's board for several days at the inn (Luke 10:35).

For very large transactions or the savings of the wealthy, there was a gold coin, the *aureus*, worth 25 denarii.

The crowds who followed Jesus rarely saw a gold coin. For buying and selling in large amounts they had the denarius and the larger silver coins of the Greek cities, the two and four drachma pieces. The four drachma piece, also called a *stater*, was equal to the Semitic *shekel*.

Copper coins served the needs of daily life. Rome made the sestertius, one quarter of a denarius, and that was the unit for counting money in Latin, even for large sums. Augustus boasted, for example, that he bought land in Italy to give to the soldiers at a cost of 600,000,000 sesterces.

The *dupondius* was half a *sestertius*, but the ordinary copper coin was the *as*, originally named *assarion*. Four asses made one sestertius, sixteen asses one denarius. The soldiers were paid by the *as*, and the average cost of a loaf of bread was an *as*. Two sparrows sold for one *as*, or five for two (Matthew 10:29; Luke 12:6).

The smallest of Roman coins was the *quadrans*, one quarter of an *as*.

In Judea the largest copper coins were issued by Herod Antipas (see *Herod's Sons*). Herod and his sons, and the Roman governors, minted coins which were mostly quadrans size, that is to say, one sixty-fourth of a denarius. This was 'the last penny' which had to be paid in Matthew 5:26.

Mark's Gospel explains that one quadrans equalled two smaller coins, the *lepton*. That was the widow's offering (see *A Widow's Mite*). The Jewish priest-kings, and Herod and Herod Archelaus struck tiny bronze coins a little over a centimetre (half an inch) in diameter, and weighing between 1 and 2 grams (0.05 oz) which were probably worth half a quadrans each, a *lepton* in Greek, or a *prutah* in Hebrew. This was 'the last penny' of Luke 12:59.

Between the poor widow and wealthy King Herod yawned an immeasurable gap. Herod's income was measured in talents, a weight too large to be coined, containing 10,000 drachmae or 40,000 sesterces. His annual income at his death was about 1,050 talents, equivalent to 42,000,000 sesterces. Cicero said an annual income of 600,000 sesterces was needed to lead the life of a gentleman in Rome about 50 BC. That amounts to about 60 talents, or 150,000 denarii, something like one thousand times the income of a Palestinian peasant farmer at the same time! In the parable of the unjust steward recorded in Matthew's Gospel (18:23,24), the ten thousand-talent-debt which the king cancelled was an unimaginably large sum—Herod's income for ten years!

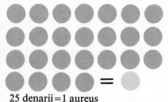

25 denarii = 1 aureus

d.19.05mm/0.75in

This aureus was issued by Augustus in Ephesus about 20 BC to celebrate the addition of Armenia to the empire. On the reverse the figure of victory is cutting a bull's throat.

4 drachmae = 1 stater (Greek)
or 1 shekel (Jewish)

d.26.67mm/1.05in

A silver four-drachma (shekel) coin from Sidon, 31–30 BC. It shows the turreted head of Fortune, and an eagle with its foot on the prow of a galley.

4 sesterces = 1 denarius (Roman)
or 1 drachma (Greek)

d.20.3mm/0.8in

The lost coin of the parable in Luke 15:8,9, was a drachma or denarius. This one was issued by Augustus to celebrate the conquest of Egypt, 28 BC.

4 asses = 1 sestertius

d.35.56mm/1.4in

This sestertius of AD 22–23 carries the letters S.C. 'by permission of the Senate' and Tiberius' titles on the obverse; on the reverse is a text advertising his generous aid to cities in Turkey damaged by a great earthquake in AD 17.

4 quadrans = 1 as (assarion)

d.30.48mm/1.2in

Tiberius had coins struck in honour of Augustus as a god. His bust wears a divine crown and the words mean 'Divine Augustus, Father'. On the reverse is a panelled altar. This is an as.

---

2 lepta = 1 quadrans

d.16.5mm/0.65in

This is a quadrans of Augustus, 9 BC. On the obverse are the emblems of Augustus as high priest, the ladle and staff which Pontius Pilate put on coins he issued. The inscriptions name the officials in charge of the coinage.

---

1 lepton (Greek) or
1 prutah (Jewish)

d.12mm/0.5in approx.

On tiny coins minted near the end of Herod's reign appears an eagle which may be the one he had put up in the Temple (see Herod's Great Temple).

CAESAR'S IMAGE

All governments tax their subjects, and Rome was no exception. Wherever Rome ruled, taxes were imposed. There was a tax on the produce of the land, there was a tax on imports and exports, and there was a tax on each person.

Even where King Herod ruled, his kingdom had to pay a tribute to Rome each year in return for her protection and as a sign of subjection. This was the land tax (*tributum solis*), probably amounting to about one eighth (12.5 per cent) of the annual yield of the crops. The well-to-do paid this to the king or,

after Judea became a Roman province in AD 6, to the governor.

All over the Empire there were tax collectors at ports and frontier towns. They had to levy tax on goods passing from one place to another. The rate of this tax is uncertain; it may have been quite low, about one fortieth (2.5 per cent) of the value of the merchandise. Collecting it could be very profitable, for it would be the tax collector's task to estimate the value, and he could easily over-estimate it. The men who did this work were not government

officials but businessmen (*publicani*) who bought the rights to collect in specific areas. They paid the amounts which the government had set as appropriate for each place, then recouped their outlay and made as much extra profit as they could from the merchants who travelled past their posts. (When tax collectors asked John the Baptist what they should do, Luke 3:13 records that he told them bluntly, 'Don't collect any more than you are required to.')

Within any area the actual collecting was done

by employees of the concessionaire. Levi, or Matthew (one of Jesus' twelve apostles), was one of these. At his tax-collecting booth by Lake Galilee he probably assessed the value of goods carried across the Lake to or from other regions (Matthew 9:9–13 records how Jesus called Matthew to follow him).

Not surprisingly, people hated the 'publicans' and their agents. They worked for the occupying power, and they lined their own pockets in the process. No wonder Jesus' conduct provoked hostile comment

Tax-collecting was a part of government everywhere. On this carving from a third-century tomb in Germany, the collector sits with his ledger and piles and bags of coins.

This silver denarius, issued by the Emperor Tiberius, is the type often called 'the tribute penny'. On the obverse is the bust of Tiberius with his titles. The reverse shows Livia, Tiberius' mother, seated, with the inscription 'high priest' applying to the emperor.

when he met and shared meals with publicans and tax collectors. To the religious people the fact that they worked with non-Jews (Gentiles) made these men 'unclean'.

One customs' post was at Jericho, by a major crossing-place over the River Jordan. The river marked the boundary between the province of Judea and the district on the eastern side, called Perea. In Jericho about AD 30 one of the leading publicans was named Zacchaeus. How much these men might gain from their activities is made clear by the promise the remorseful Zacchaeus gave, after coming face to face with Jesus: 'If I have cheated anybody out of anything, I will pay back four times the amount' (Luke 19:8).

The tax that people resented most was the individual or poll-tax (*tributum capitis*). To discover how much was due, the authorities needed to know how many people lived in each part of the Empire. That was the reason why, as Luke 2:1 tells us, the Emperor Augustus ordered a census to be taken throughout the Roman Empire, at the time of Jesus' birth. To simplify the process, everyone had to register in his own home town. Collecting this tax was a job for the governor and his staff. The annual rate at the time of Jesus was about one day's wage for a workman: one Roman denarius per head.

The teachers in Jerusalem asked Jesus about this tax, to try to trap him into saying something subversive against the Roman rule. They would then have had a case against him to take to the governor. They asked: '"Is it right for us to pay taxes to Caesar or not?" He saw through their duplicity and said to them, "Show me a denarius. Whose portrait and inscription are on it?" "Caesar's," they replied. He said to them, "Then give to Caesar what is Caesar's, and to God what is God's." They were unable to trap him in what he had said there in public. And astonished by his answer, they became silent.'

The Gospel writers do not describe the coin in detail. Many silver denarii issued by the emperors Augustus and Tiberius bore the imperial portrait. One type minted for Tiberius is especially common and has become known as 'the tribute penny' by being identified as the coin shown to Jesus.

The overseers of the Sacred Gate at Aswan in Egypt issued this receipt written in Greek on a piece of broken pottery on 12 July AD 144. Pekysis had paid poll-tax of 16 drachmas.

ARMY OF OCCUPATION

Roman soldiers were highly trained and harshly disciplined. Each man was responsible for maintaining his armour and weapons. A bronze model from the second century AD shows one wearing an iron helmet and leather clothes plated with iron.

Judea was under occupation. Even in peace-time Roman soldiers were to be seen in most places, and officers had homes in small towns like Capernaum (Luke 7:2ff.; Matthew 8:5ff.).

Herod could not command Roman troops. He had his own forces, modelled on the Roman army. Augustus gave him a bodyguard of 400 men from Galatia in central Turkey. Previously they had been Cleopatra's. To garrison his castles Herod hired mercenaries. He also had a squad of archers from Trachonitis, harnessing the skills of the former bandits.

Herod settled a large body of reservists on land around his new city at Sebaste (old Samaria), and others on the Nabataean frontier at Heshbon. He took a troop of Idumeans to the north-east, away from their home area. A troop of cavalry reserves lived at Gabae on the north slopes of Mount Carmel. They were within reach of Galilee should trouble break out there. The Idumean troop could be mustered to put down troublemakers in Trachonitis and nearby areas. The men quartered at Sebaste were convenient for Judea and Jerusalem. Herod's soldiers served his sons and, after Archelaus was deposed, those in Judea and Samaria came under the command of the Roman governor.

Pontius Pilate and the governors before and after him had five infantry cohorts of 500 men each, and one cavalry cohort, making 3,000 men in all. Their main base was the governor's capital, the largely Greek city of Caesarea. None of them was Jewish, because Julius Caesar had decreed that the Jews were exempt from military service, and Augustus had upheld that position. (Military discipline would make it impossible for them to keep the Sabbath or the food laws.) Consequently racial problems arose between the soldiers and the people they had to control. When the troops were on duty at religious festivals in Jerusalem, violence could easily break out as the crowds grew excited.

The auxiliaries were not very well paid, their annual wage being perhaps 100 denarii, whereas a legionary would receive 225 denarii. But the auxiliary had one valuable reward. After twenty-five years' service he could retire with a gratuity and receive a diploma which gave him Roman citizenship. His children would inherit that status.

Authority and discipline were the basis of the army's function. The centurion who told Jesus how his men obeyed him exemplifies that (Matthew 8:8,9). It is also clear from the camps the soldiers built. From the top of Masada the lines of stones marking tent walls and streets show up plainly. Once the siege was over (AD 73), the camps were left to crumble gradually, an impressive testimony to the basis of Roman power.

On campaign, Roman troops built ramparts around their camps at night. Laying siege to Masada (AD 70–73), they built more permanent camps around the foot of the rock, but out of bow-shot. From the top of Masada the ruins of these square camps are obvious on the bare ground.

PART THREE

RELIGION

Two discoveries have added greatly to our knowledge of
Jewish religion in the first century. One gives visible, physical evidence,
the other brings books which tell of ideas and beliefs. The first is the
excavation of remains from Herod's Temple, the Temple where Jesus
walked and taught. The second is the Dead Sea Scrolls. These books
belonged to a group of religious Jews who were hoping for the Messiah
to come. They are the only Jewish books actually surviving from the
Gospel period.

The seven-branched lampstand, the menorah, *has become a symbol of the Jewish faith.*
It was first stamped on coins by Antigonus, the man the Parthians set up as priest-king
in Jerusalem about 40 BC (see Herod—King of the Jews*).*

TEMPLE TOURISTS

They stopped and stared, and shouted for joy. There across the valley stood the Temple, white stone walls gleaming, flashing with golden ornaments. That was what they had come to see! From Jericho to Jerusalem the road was steep and hard, hot and dusty for much of the year. For the last few miles a long, tree-covered hill formed the sky-line, with a promise of shade after the bare hills of the desert. As pilgrims reached the top of the Mount of Olives, or rounded its corner, Jerusalem was spread out before them.

From every angle the Temple crowned the city, but the view from the Mount of Olives was the most impressive. The east wall ran for 460 metres/500 yards along the brow of the valley opposite, and the shrine itself stood in the centre. At the corner where the south and east walls met there was a tower. Anyone standing on the top could look straight down into the Kidron Valley, a precipitous drop

estimated by some scholars at as much as 137 metres/450 feet. 'Pinnacle of the Temple' is a name fit for such a dizzy height. That name, used in the account of Jesus' temptations, may apply to this tower or to a high corner of the main Temple (Matthew 4:5; Luke 4:9).

The Temple! That was the pilgrims' goal. To see it, to walk in its court-yards, to bring sacrifices and pray there were the aims that brought them from all over the world. Herod's wide courtyard allowed them into the Temple area in their thousands, but they could not live there. Even the most devout pilgrims had normal physical needs. They had to find somewhere to sleep, to eat, and to make themselves pure for worship.

Jerusalem was always busy with visitors and traders coming and going, so there were inns and lodging houses all over the city. In springtime, when the Passover Festival came round, the whole place became a vast camp, as pilgrims flocked in to keep the feast there. The poor set up tents and shelters outside the city walls, others paid for rooms or sleeping-spaces. According to Josephus there could be as many as three million people in Jerusalem at Passover time! All agree that this figure is too high, but pilgrims could certainly be numbered in hundreds of thousands.

Near the Temple, ruins of first-century houses have remarkably many ritual baths. One excavator has explained their number as evidence that the houses were hostels where pilgrims stayed. The baths on the

The generosity of Theodotus, who built a synagogue and an inn in Jerusalem, is recorded in this inscription.

premises were convenient for them to use before they entered the Temple.

Helping pilgrims was an act of charity. Wealthy men in Judea and abroad gave money to pay for building hostels and synagogues for them. Altogether there were said to be 480 synagogues in Jerusalem in the first century. Attached to them were schools for studying the Old Testament. There the teachers explained how to interpret and apply it to everyday life according to 'the tradition of the elders'. One of these centres is known to us from first-hand evidence.

A French team digging in the City of David, the southern part of the Old City, in 1914, found a plastered cistern. In it were pieces of stonework from a fine building. One has ten lines of Greek letters on it. They announce the building of a synagogue by Theodotus,

a priest and synagogue-ruler. His father Vettenus was also a synagogue-ruler, and his father had been, too. This meant that he was in charge of the affairs of the synagogue, including the choice of those who would read the Scriptures. The Gospels tell us that a man called Jairus held this position in Capernaum (Mark 5:22; Luke 8:41). Theodotus' inscription states that he built the synagogue 'for reading the law and teaching the commandments'. The buildings included an inn for overseas visitors who needed lodgings, with rooms and baths. The style of the letters and the place where the stone was found show that the inscription belonged to the city destroyed in AD 70. Who Theodotus was there is nothing to say. His father's name, Vettenus, was the name of a large Roman family, so he may have been a Jewish prisoner,

The only example of Herod's buildings still standing high above ground is the wall of the Tombs of the Patriarchs in Hebron.

bought as a slave, who took the family name when he was set free. If Theodotus and his father lived in Italy, their concern to help visitors in Jerusalem is easy to understand.

Ruins of synagogues from later centuries often display, engraved on the stones or laid out in mosaic pavings, the names of people who paid for parts of them to be built. Fragments of other Greek inscriptions found near the Temple indicate that the custom was well known in the first century. The names of the donors lived on, and worshippers and pilgrims were grateful.

Even without the gleaming Temple of Herod, the view of Jerusalem from the Mount of Olives enthralls the visitor.

HEROD'S GREAT TEMPLE

'Do you see all these great buildings?. Not one stone here will be left on another; every one will be thrown down.'

That was Jesus' reply to the disciple who was amazed at Herod's magnificent Temple (Mark 13:2), and it has proved to be true. Although part of the platform still stands, there is nothing left of the 'great buildings'.

Happily, Josephus wrote a description of them, and the rabbis remembered a lot of details which were written down in the Mishnah at the end of the second century. Now recent discoveries can join those ancient reports to give a clearer picture of this magnificent place.

Clearing away rubbish and the ruins of later buildings outside the south end of the enclosure and round the corner on the west side, archaeologists reached a paved street that ran along the foot of the walls. About 8 metres/26 feet of rubble and stones had to be moved to reach it, among them great blocks tumbled from the Temple walls. They were beautifully squared, just like those still in position in the lower parts of the platform. Others had fallen from the building on top of the platform at the southern end.

The written records tell that a great columned hall or portico stood there, open on the north side, like a cloister. This was called the Royal Portico because of its size. Four rows of pillars divided it into three long aisles. Josephus reports that each pillar was 8.2 metres/27 feet high and so thick that three men standing with arms stretched out could just encircle it. The tops of the pillars were carved with rows of leaves and the ceiling with leaves and flowers. Pieces of these pillars and decorations were found in the fallen rubble.

It was in this splendid porch that the moneychangers' tables stood, and the traders had stalls to sell animals and birds for sacrifices. To some religious Jews, carrying out such business inside the area of the Temple was objectionable—it seemed irreverent. Jesus dealt with the problem one day: 'Jesus entered the temple area and began driving out those who were buying and selling there. He overturned the tables of the money changers and the benches of those selling doves . . . he said, "Is it not written: 'My house will be called a house of prayer for all nations'? But you have made it a 'den of robbers'"'' (Mark 11:15–17).

Using the Royal Portico as a market-place was bad enough. But there was worse. Many of the traders charged very high prices, taking cruel advantage of the pilgrims who came from the countryside and from foreign lands. The traders had to pay for permission to have their stalls in this area, and is seems they had to pay the leading priests.

Later Jewish tradition remembered one place as 'the Bazaars of the sons of Annas'. One Annas was High Priest from AD 6 to AD 15, when he was deposed. After him five sons, one of them also named Annas, and a son-in-law, Caiaphas, also served as High Priests (see Luke 3:2; John 18:13–24;

Acts 4:6). The bazaar was called after one of these, and he and his family no doubt took a fat commission from the sales. Both Josephus and the rabbinic writings portray the family of Annas and other priestly families as greedy, extorting money from other priests and beating up ordinary people. Jesus had every reason to be angry at what was done in the Royal Portico! Others grew angry, too, and a mob swept away the whole bazaar a few years before the Roman army took the city in AD 70.

Other colonnades lined each side of the Temple area. The one on the east was Solomon's Porch. When Herod began to make the Temple courtyards bigger, his men found that the old platform wall above the side of the Kidron Valley was sound, so they did not replace it. Solomon's Porch was also left, standing on top of it. Exactly how old that wall was is uncertain, and so is the age of the Porch. In spite of its name, it probably belonged to the time when the Temple was rebuilt under the Persian kings Cyrus and Darius. The Jewish priest-kings of the second and first centuries BC may have altered and repaired it. Piles of earth were removed from the wall in 1965, revealing a junction between Herod's stonework and another style, evidently the older wall.

These covered walks provided shelter from the sun's heat and from chilly winds. People could meet each other and stand and talk in them, as the first Christians did (Acts 3:11; 5:12). Teachers and students would gather there to learn and debate, as Jesus did with the rabbis when he was young, and later with his disciples (Luke 2:46–50; John 10:23ff.).

Glistening in the middle of the courtyard was the gilded Temple itself. A big wall surrounded it, so the Jewish rebels were able to make it their last stronghold against the forces of Rome in AD 70. Like the porticoes, all this has disappeared. Everything we know about it comes from Josephus, who had been inside as a priest, and from memories handed down by the rabbis.

Foreigners were not allowed to enter the Temple courts: notices, written in Greek, forbade entrance on pain of death. In 1871 one of these notices was found intact in Jerusalem. In 1936 a fragment of another was found, showing that the letters were originally painted red.

HEROD'S TEMPLE

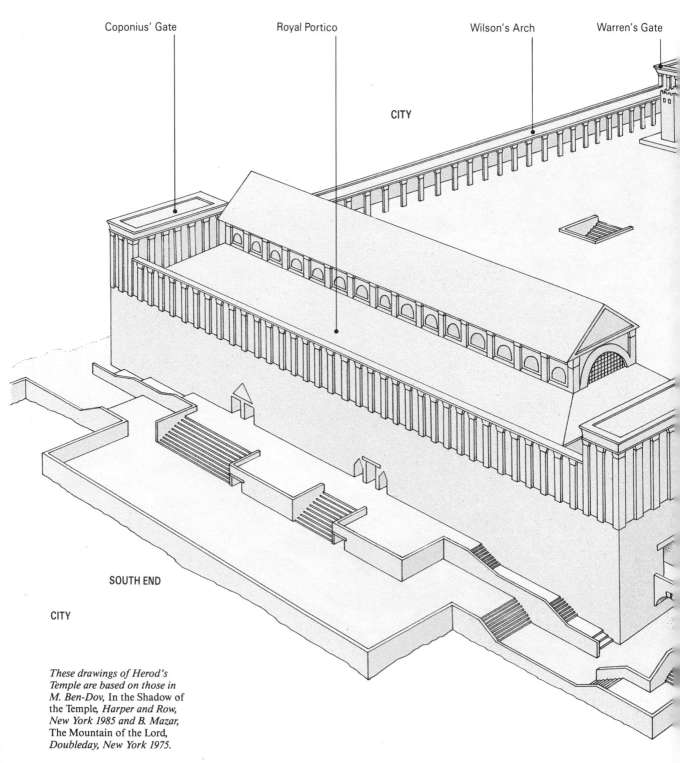

Coponius' Gate

Royal Portico

Wilson's Arch

Warren's Gate

CITY

CITY

SOUTH END

These drawings of Herod's Temple are based on those in M. Ben-Dov, In the Shadow of the Temple, *Harper and Row, New York 1985 and B. Mazar,* The Mountain of the Lord, *Doubleday, New York 1975.*

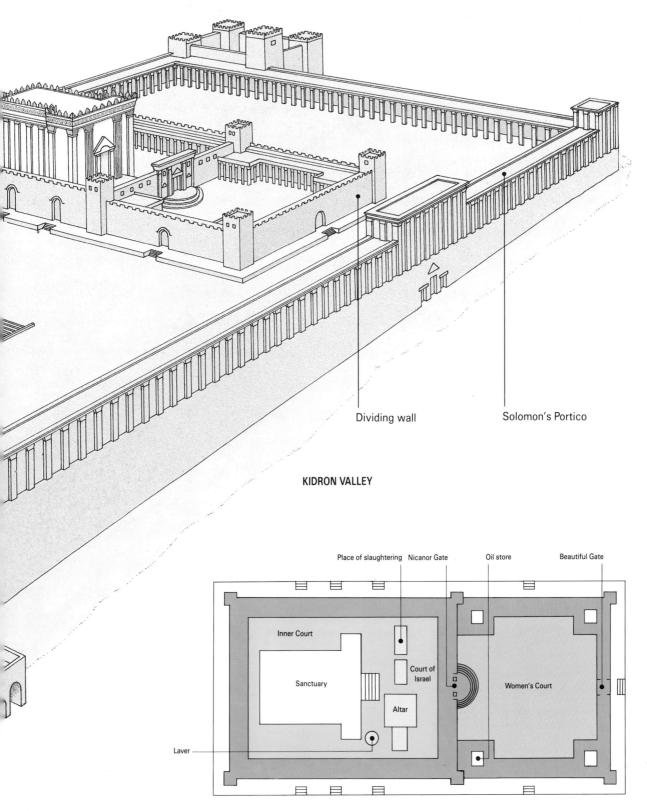

Dividing wall

Solomon's Portico

KIDRON VALLEY

Place of slaughtering | Nicanor Gate | Oil store | Beautiful Gate

Inner Court

Sanctuary

Court of Israel

Altar

Women's Court

Laver

OCTATWNTOVNEIKA
NOPOCΔΛΕΖΔNΔρεωσ
ΠΟΙΗΣΔΝΤιΣΤΔΣΘΥρΔ

ΝΟΊϳΝ 7. ΓϳϤ

This stone ossuary from a large tomb was found at the north end of the Mount of Olives in 1902. The Greek writing on the end says, 'Bones of the sons of Nicanor the Alexandrian who made the doors.' The names of the sons, Nicanor, Alexas, were added in Hebrew letters.

A few details help to suggest the grandeur and glory of it all.

Only Jews could go into the central buildings. A stone barrier about 1.3 metres/4½ feet high divided them from the outer court. Notices written in Greek and Latin warned everyone who was not Jewish to keep out. A foreigner who crossed the line was likely to be lynched. One stone block carrying the Greek version of this notice was found in Jerusalem in 1871, and is now in Istanbul. Part of another was discovered in 1936; it had red paint in the letters to make them stand out.

Steps led up to a platform and on it the high wall around the inner courtyards. More steps led up to gates in the wall. There were four on the north and four on the south. Each one was 13.5 metres/45 feet high, covered with gold and silver plating. Alexander, brother of the philosopher Philo (see *Philo—a Philosopher of Alexandria*) presented them to the Temple. Another Alexandrine Jew, named Nicanor, gave the pair of gates which stood at the east end, the main entrance. Although its decoration was only bronze, it was a superb example of Corinthian workmanship, which Josephus asserts made it even more valuable than the other gates. They were so heavy, twenty men were needed to push them shut. This 'Corinthian Gate' was probably the 'Beautiful Gate' referred to in Acts, chapter 3, where a beggar sat when Peter and John went into the Temple to pray.

Through the Beautiful Gate worshippers went into the Court of Women, 67 metres/222 feet square. At each corner was a building for storing Temple supplies. Thirteen collection boxes stood there. They were shaped like trumpets turned upside-down. This is where Jesus saw a widow make her humble offering and commended her for giving to God not just what she had to spare, but all she possessed (see *A Widow's Mite*).

Only the men were allowed to climb a flight of steps from the Women's Court and pass through another gold-decorated gate, also a gift of Alexander, to the place where they could see the altar for burnt sacrifices, and beyond into the actual Temple. That had an enormous front 50 metres/164 feet wide and equally high. King Herod put a golden eagle on top of it.

'You shall not make for yourself an idol,' said the Ten Commandments, and in the eyes of two rabbis, at least, the placing of the eagle broke the law. When they heard Herod was dying, the rabbis urged their followers to pull it down. They cut it to pieces before the crowds in the Temple. They acted too soon; Herod was not dead. His soldiers arrested the men and took them to the king. Furious, in spite of his illness, the king went out to harangue the crowd, then had the eagle-breakers and their teachers burnt alive.

The golden eagle fell. A different golden ornament was happily accepted. Curling along the top of the entrance to the Temple hung a golden vine. Bunches of grapes dangling from it were as high as a man, Josephus claimed. Worshippers could add a leaf, or a grape, or a bunch of grapes as a gift to God.

Herod redesigned the Temple, as far as he could, to make room for as many people as possible. He dared not change the shape of the holy shrine. He had it rebuilt on the same plan and to the same size as Solomon had built the first one, and just as richly. The walls inside shone with gold, and outside golden spikes kept birds from perching along the edges of the roof. Within the shrine were the golden table for holy bread, the golden lampstand with seven branches (the *menorah*), and the altar for burning incense.

The innermost room, the Holy of Holies, was empty. The Ark of the Covenant, which had stood there in Solomon's day, disappeared when the Babylonian army of Nebuchadnezzar burnt the first Temple. When Pompey, the Roman general, pushed his way into this sacred place he was surprised to find it empty (see *There's no God There!*).

All this magnificence was reduced to ashes and rubble in AD 70. According to Josephus, the Roman commander Titus, whose father was now the Emperor Vespasian, wanted to preserve the Temple. But Jewish resistance groups frustrated any attempt to save it. As the fighting moved from one part to another, fires were started and put out, until a soldier threw a flaming torch through the inner gate and set the shrine ablaze.

So the Temple was destroyed. All the great buildings were thrown down —not one stone was left upon another.

WHAT MASSIVE STONES!

Where two kinds of stonework meet, on the east side of the Temple platform, it seems Herod's builders added their larger stones (left) to an older building.

'Look, Teacher! What massive stones! What magnificent buildings!'

Those were the amazed exclamations one of Jesus' disciples made as they left the Temple in Jerusalem (Mark 13:1). Most of their houses were built of stone. They were used to seeing stone walls and arches. But the stones of their houses were simply fetched from the fields or the hillsides. They were stones a man could carry on his own, one at a time. To build a wall, he would pack the stones together, fitting them according to their shapes, and packing smaller stones and mud into the spaces. The wall could then be covered with mud plaster to give a smooth surface, and whitewashed. For doorsteps and lintels two or three men might have to carry larger, flat stones. A man with a good eye could split some stones to make a flat face, or a square block. Houses of rich people in Jerusalem were built of stones cut more carefully, but not usually very large ones. They, too, were plastered, at least on the inside.

Walls built entirely of cut blocks laid against each other are stronger than walls made of rough stones packed together. They could be taken higher without greater width, and they could carry a heavier load of floor or roof timbers or arches. That sort of building first appeared about the time of David and Solomon. Remains of palaces and other buildings of the tenth century BC at Megiddo show this style of masonry. The stones were so good that later generations took them from the old walls to make new ones. At Samaria the same style of fine stonework can still be seen in the ruins of the palace of Ahab and the kings of Israel who followed him in the ninth and eighth centuries BC. Obviously kings could afford to build in the best way.

That was what King Herod set out to do, with the Temple in Jerusalem. He wanted to make the Temple as magnificent as it had been in King Solomon's time, or more so. When the Jews came back from their exile in Babylon, they rebuilt the Temple which Nebuchadnezzar's army had destroyed (see 2 Kings 25:9ff.; Ezra 1,3). That Temple did not reach the splendour of Solomon's, so Herod declared that he would rebuild it, all at his own cost.

The work began about 19 BC, possibly two or three years earlier. It was made difficult by the need to carry on the services and sacrifices, and by the rule that only priests could go into the inner court and enter the Temple building itself. Herod wanted to do the right thing and not upset the people of Jerusalem. He hired 10,000 skilled workmen and had 1,000 priests trained in stonemasonry, so that they could erect the sacred building. One thousand wagons were needed to cart the stone from the quarries. Jerusalem's hills are all limestone of various qualities, so the material did not have a long way to travel. With everything made ready beforehand, the priestly masons managed to construct the new Temple within eighteen months. Celebrations were held on the anniversary of Herod's accession to the throne, the king himself providing a sacrifice of 300 oxen.

After that central part was finished, the work went on for a very long time. In a discussion with Jesus some Jews told him: 'It has taken forty-six years to build this temple' (John 2:21). That was about AD 28–30. Josephus reports that the whole of the Temple and its courtyards were finally completed in AD 62–64. Herod's plan was to outdo Solomon in the surroundings of the shrine.

Solomon's Temple stood on top of a hill. In order to have a level space around it, Solomon's masons probably put up walls on the east and west slopes of the hill, to hold a stone terrace. Whether or not any of this still existed in Herod's time is disputed. At the eastern side of the Temple, part of a wall can be seen which has stones cut in a different fashion from the stones of Herod's work. Most experts think this is part of the rebuilding after the exile, perhaps as late as the days of the Hasmonean kings in the second century BC, although one or two argue that it is a relic of Solomon's original wall.

The platform these terraces made seemed too small to Herod. His architects designed a much bigger one. At the north end that meant cutting away part of the rock to make the level area larger. At the south end the job was much harder. To raise the platform above the slopes of the hill, Herod's architects designed a series of vaults one on top of another, within a thick wall. At some points the wall was as much as 50 metres/165 feet high because of the unevenness of the rock. The weight of the stonework was so great that the builders had to rest the foundations on the bedrock itself.

In this way the Temple platform was made 32 metres/105 feet longer at the south. How much wider Herod made it has not been discovered. The overall dimensions of the whole enclosure are: east wall 470 metres/1,550 feet long, west wall 485 metres/1,620 feet, north wall 315 metres/1,050 feet, south wall 280 metres/930 feet. That is space enough for thirteen full-size football pitches, or nearly 200 baseball diamonds. It is about two and a half times as long as St Peter's Basilica in Rome, and nine and a half times its area—or five times the area of the Acropolis at Athens.

Parts of these great walls still stand. The most famous is the Wailing Wall, now called the Western Wall or Kotel, where several courses of the

The massive stones of Herod's Temple are visible today in the 'Wailing (Western) Wall'—a place of prayer.

Herodian stones rise above the modern pavement. Along the western side and at the south end excavations made since 1967 have uncovered a lot more of the walls and buildings which stood outside them.

Visitors who saw the blocks of stone in the Wailing Wall realized how well cut they were. Now, with much bigger stretches of wall uncovered, the impact of the massive stones is even more awe-inspiring. The average blocks are a metre or more high/3–4 feet and 1.25–3 metres/4–10 feet long and weigh from 2,000 kg/2 tons upwards. Some stones were much larger. There are many at the south-western corner, where the foundations were particularly deep, almost 12 metres/40 feet long and weighing 50,800 kilos/50 tons or more. The most enormous one was revealed in a tunnel dug illegally under the buildings against the northern part of the west wall. It is reported to be almost 12 metres/40 feet long, 3 metres/10 feet high, and 4 metres/13 feet thick, and the estimate of its weight is about 400,000 kg/400 tons.

Each stone was hewn out of a quarry near Jerusalem. ('Solomon's Quarries', shown to visitors, beneath the north wall of the Old City may have been one source.) Then teams of oxen or men would pull it in a cart to the building site. Some of the bigger stones may have been moved on wooden rollers or even had wooden wheels built around them so that they would roll. Careful organization and understanding of the principles of balance and leverage, coupled with muscle-power, were the means of bringing the stones to the walls and setting them in place. Roman engineers had developed simple gears and pulleys which would have helped to hoist the stones to the higher parts of the walls.

At the site, each block was chiselled square, so that it would fit tightly against its neighbours without need for mortar between them. The outer side of each stone was dressed with a narrow margin, leaving the centre slightly higher. As a result, the wall did not present a completely smooth, blank face to the viewer. More interest was given to the walls at a slightly higher level by adding flat pillars to the surface of the wall, to give a pattern or relief and shadows. This is not now visible at the Temple area because of later destructions, but it can be seen in the wall of the Tomb of the Patriarchs at Hebron.

Time has proved the skill of Herod's builders. Earthquakes and destructive enemies have toppled all the Temple buildings. The upper level of the vaulted platform was damaged and had to be rebuilt when the Omayyad caliphs of Damascus turned the area into a Muslim holy place in the seventh century. All the rest still stands firm. Visitors can still exclaim, 'Look, what massive stones!'

Stone blocks at Megiddo show that the technique of smoothed margins was in use in the days of the kings of Israel.

AT THE MONEYCHANGERS' TABLES

There was a lot going on in the Temple courtyard. Pilgrims came from all over the world to offer sacrifices and worship God in his only Temple, at Jerusalem. Like travellers today, they had to change their money. Although Rome ruled much of the world, and the emperor's head guaranteed that this money was good (see *Caesar's Image*), there were other states which issued their own coins. Some rulers, like King Herod, had special rights under Rome's control; others, like the Nabataeans of Transjordan or the Parthians in Persia, were beyond the imperial frontiers.

This meant that every city had to have some moneychangers who could rate the different currencies against each other. In days before rapid communication, the rate was very much at the individual moneychanger's will. Basically it was done by weight. Silver and gold coins were standardized forms of bullion, but some places issued coins which were not quite pure silver or gold, so the changers would cut or file them as a test.

Naturally the money-changers looked for a profit when, for example, they bought Parthian coins with Roman ones. It was easy to cheat, so moneychangers were not the best-loved businessmen. Little wonder Jesus chased them from the Temple, telling them they had made it 'a den of robbers' (Matthew 21:13).

Every Jew was expected to pay a tax to the Temple each year. The amount was set at half a shekel of silver, the amount laid down in the Law of Moses for the atonement of every Israelite (Exodus 30:11–16). In the first century half a shekel was reckoned the equivalent of two Greek drachmas or two Roman denarii (see *Money and Coins*). A labourer could earn that amount in two days, according to Jesus' parable of the workers in the vineyard (Matthew 20:1–16).

The priests decreed that payment should be made in coins of the purest silver. Only one sort was acceptable, the silver coins of the city of Tyre. Although Jewish officials had occasionally issued silver coins under the Persian Empire, the independent Jewish kings of the second and first centuries BC did not. These kings, the Maccabees or, better, Hasmoneans, only struck small bronze coins for daily use in the market-place.

Silver coins were minted in large numbers by the Greek kings of Damascus, the Seleucids, but to use them for the Temple tax may have been distasteful. One of those kings, Antiochus IV, had defiled the Temple in 167 BC, causing the revolt led by the Maccabees. After 126 BC Tyre became independent of the Seleucids and started to issue its own shekels and half-shekels, without a king's name on them. The fact that they had the head of Melkart, the god of Tyre, on one side did not matter. Indeed, these coins were so suitable for Jewish use that when the Romans ended Tyre's privilege, about 20 BC, it seems that the Jewish authorities took over the minting of the coins and issued them in Jerusalem. The series only stopped when the First Revolt broke out in AD 66 and nationalistic rebels issued their own silver shekels and half-shekels with inscriptions in Hebrew.

The most common coin from Tyre is the shekel (stater or tetradrachm— four drachms); half-shekels are less often found. This suggests that Jews paid the Temple tax in pairs. That is what happened on one famous occasion. The Temple tax collectors were travelling the country and were in Capernaum when Jesus arrived there with his friends. Asked if Jesus would pay, Peter impetuously answered, 'Yes'. Jesus explained to him that there was no need to pay, but that they should do so to avoid giving offence. Peter was sent to catch a fish and take from its mouth the shekel he would find there to pay for both of them (Matthew 17:24–27).

Everyone who felt it a duty to pay the tax had to obtain the Tyrian coin. The exchange could be made anywhere, but for many it was convenient to be able to do it in the Temple. That is why there were moneychangers there, besides people selling animals suitable for sacrifice, when Jesus visited the Temple (Matthew 21:12).

A silver shekel of Tyre bearing the head of the city's god Melkart on one side and an eagle with the inscription 'Of Tyre, holy place and sactuary'. The date is AD 52, which may imply that the coin was made by the Jewish authorities. Such coins may have been given by the priests to Judas Iscariot (Matthew 26:15; 27:3–10).

When the Jews rebelled against Rome in AD 66 they made their own coins in silver and bronze. This silver half shekel was now the coin for the Temple tax. On the obverse the old Hebrew letters read 'half a shekel (year) 2', and on the reverse 'Jerusalem is holy'.

WHERE THE SAINTS HAVE TROD

'This is where Jesus was kept in prison . . . this is where the soldiers dressed him up . . . this is where they crucified him.'

Guides take tourists to all sorts of places, some likely, some unlikely. Not one of them carries a guarantee that it really is the place. None has a first-century sign, 'Jesus stood here!'

It is almost impossible to identify any place where Jesus, or any other famous person, stood in first-century Jerusalem. The Romans destroyed the Jewish city, and buildings have risen and fallen, century by century, ever since. A strong tradition guided the search for the tomb of Jesus, but no one can be certain the right tomb was found (see *Can We See the Tomb of Jesus?*). Other 'holy places' have far less evidence to support them. Thanks to archaeological excavations, visitors can now go to one site where they can be sure they are walking in the footsteps of Peter, John and Paul, of Jesus himself, and of the great rabbis Hillel and Gamaliel.

These famous people were a few of the thousands who came each year to worship at the Temple. Most would go in by the main entrance at the south end, where Herod built up his great platform on the sloping hill. Its wall rose over 19 metres/60 feet from the street at the south-west corner, and the Royal Portico on top of it made an overall height of over 30 metres/ 100 feet. Two gateways in the 280 metre/ 300 yard-long wall led into the Temple courtyard. A flight of steps led up to each of the gateways, and part of these steps has now been uncovered. The

three arches of one gateway have always been visible. A later building set against the wall hides most of the other, western gateway. The area in front of the gates lies largely outside the city wall, where no buildings have stood for over a century, so it was easy to excavate there.

After digging away a heap of rubbish, Benjamin Mazar's team of archaeologists soon came to the top steps. Following them down the slope, they unearthed the whole length of the flight—thirty shallow steps. The bedrock had been cut to form a series of steps as the bedding for fine stone slabs which made the staircase. Some of the original slabs still lay in their places; masonry falling from the wall had smashed some; and other builders took some for their work. Now new stones have been laid to fill the gaps, so that visitors can climb the stairs just as people did in the first century. Chips and cracks mark out the old slabs from the modern ones—so standing on those stones is truly to step 'where the saints have trod'.

The steps led up, across a paved street that ran along the wall, to the gateways. In ancient times they were known as the Hulda Gates. At present only one edge of the western gateway can be seen, because a tower was built against it when the city walls were redesigned 900 years ago. The only original part of the eastern gateway is the lowest row of stones above the street level. Muslim masons rebuilt both gateways when they took over the Temple area, building the Dome of the Rock and the Al-Aqsa Mosque in the

A wide flight of steps rose up to the gates leading into the south end of the Temple courtyard. The broken ancient stones have been restored so that visitors can climb the steps again.

seventh and eighth centuries. The gateways served as entrances to the sacred enclosure until they were blocked when new defences were put up to keep out the Crusaders. (These new walls proved to be too weak: the Crusaders captured the city in 1099.)

Despite destruction and rebuilding, quite a lot can be learnt about the gateways. The western, double one, was 12.8 metres/43 feet wide, the eastern one was about 15 metres/ 50 feet wide. Inside, the gateways and corridors had domed ceilings. The stone domes were carved with elaborate patterns in low relief, flowers, grapevines, and geometric figures. Behind the rebuilt double gateway these domes remain in place, although they are rarely accessible. Nothing of the three-arched gateway is in position except for one stone of the western-most doorway.

Outside, the excavators recovered scores of broken pieces of carved stone which had belonged to its ceiling. These fragments illustrate the richness of the decoration of the gateways and point to the splendour of the whole Temple. Today the stones are creamy or grey. Freshly carved, they were whiter, and details were probably painted,

making a colourful canopy over the pilgrims' heads.

People could go into the Temple through other entrances. Josephus listed four on the western side. In ancient times the Valley of the Cheesemakers (the Tyropoeian Valley) divided the Temple hill from the hill to the west. Here Herod's architects had to deal with the same problem they faced at the south end, but with less space. Instead of great flights of steps straight up the hill-slope to the gateway, they made different designs.

Excavations since 1968 have made clear what they did where the platform rose high above the valley, at the south-west corner. In 1838 the American pioneer Edward Robinson noticed the stump of an arch sticking out high up in the platform wall. He saw that it was the end of a bridge which led on to the platform near the end of the Royal Portico. Josephus spoke about a bridge across the valley, so scholars thought this was part of it.

When the excavators began to dig opposite the piece of arch in 1968, they thought they would find the first support of the bridge. They did not. Stone blocks from the base of a pier were still in place, but there had not been a row of them making a viaduct. Instead a staircase had climbed up from the street in the bottom of the valley, turning at right angles over arches of ever greater height to a gate level with the Temple courtyard. 'Robinson's Arch' turns out to be part of the last and biggest arch supporting the road. Parts of the lower arches were found to prove the bridge theory wrong.

Josephus' description had been misunderstood. He spoke of the gateway being separated from the opposite part of the city by 'many steps going down into the valley and thence up again to the hill'. At the foot of the steps a paved street ran beside the Temple wall and rooms built into the bottom of the pier were shops. Another road branched off at the corner of the platform, rising by a series of steps to the Hulda Gates in the south wall.

Not far along the western wall from this staircase stood another gate. An architect named Barclay investigated it in 1855–57. It opened from the street into the platform itself, a ramp mounting up to the courtyard in the same way as the ramps of the Hulda Gates. Today only one end of its lintel can be seen, still in place, at the right end of the 'Wailing Wall'. This is an enormous stone block, more than 2.1 metres/7 feet high and 7.5 metres/ 25 feet long. Its weight is probably over 50,000 kg/50 tons.

Still further along is another arch, found in 1865 by the early explorer, Charles Wilson. 'Wilson's Arch' seems to mark a viaduct which did bridge the valley from the town to the Temple, although the existing arch was rebuilt by early Muslim masons on the remains of the Herodian one. None of the gateway itself survives.

Yet another gate, opening from street level is known. Wilson uncovered the top of it in 1866 and named it in honour of his friend Charles Warren. It has recently been cleared again. Later buildings on top prevent further digging.

Pioneer explorers of a century ago, and their successors from 1968, have found four gates in the western side. Two led at high level on to the platform and were, presumably, entrances for visitors and pilgrims. The two gates at street level were more likely service entrances through which animals, wood for fuel, oil and other supplies could be taken into the Temple. Whether or not there were other gateways on the western side is uncertain at present. A second viaduct and a gate from the castle at the north-west corner may have existed. As to gateways on the north and east, little is known. The 'Golden Gate' is an early Muslim building and the age of the archway once seen beneath it cannot be established. Near the south-eastern corner are traces of an arch which corresponded to Robinson's Arch, and apparently a similar staircase. There were, therefore, many ways for visitors to reach the Temple courtyard and its splendid buildings.

Among stones fallen from the Temple buildings, the excavators found finely carved pieces which had decorated the ceiling of one of the gateways at the top of the steps.

A SECRET TUNNEL

Matthias of Jerusalem was High Priest; King Herod had appointed him. Year by year he carried out his duties as representative of his nation. The high point of the year was the Day of Atonement. Wearing a linen tunic, he would go through the heavy curtain, the veil, into the holiest part of the Temple, to sprinkle the blood of a sacrificed bull and goat on the ground. When he came out, the people knew God had forgiven the sins of the previous year.

In 5 BC it all went wrong. Matthias became unclean; he dreamt he was in bed with his wife, and that was forbidden to him in the days before the ceremony. He could not carry out his duties, he could not perform the ritual. Someone would have to stand in for him — and a close relative who was also a priest was called to do so.

Religious laws ruled everyone who wanted to worship in the Temple (see *Cleanliness is Next to Godliness?*). Priests had to be even more particular. Every part of their lives fell under special rules, from marriage to mourning to cutting their hair, and many things could make priests unclean. Touching a person with a discharging sore or a wound, or a woman with bleeding, or a corpse, or certain insects, caused uncleanness. If that happened, the priest had to bathe himself and could not take up his duties until sunset. In Jesus' story about the Good Samaritan, the priest and the Levite who would not go near the wounded man were more concerned to keep themselves ritually pure than to help a fellow human being, and that was Jesus' point (Luke 10:30–32).

Priests living in towns and villages could clean themselves in ritual baths to wash away such impurities, like anyone else. When they were serving in the Temple that was more difficult, for the Temple proper was also pure. Jewish tradition tells of tunnels leading below the Temple to a ritual bath outside the Temple walls. A priest could immerse himself, dry off by a fire, and go back inside without the risk of infecting other priests or the holy place and its furniture.

Deep in the rock outside the south end of the Temple the excavators almost fell into a tunnel high and wide enough for one man to walk along it upright. Spaced along the walls were little shelves hollowed in the rock. When the archaeologists put candles in them, they saw at once that that was what they were for. Stones blocked the inner end of the tunnel where it ran under the Temple wall, so its route inside the area is unknown. Part of a second tunnel joined the first one, and apparently both led to a ritual bath. Only a precise description or an ancient notice could prove the purpose of these tunnels, so, as with other archaeological discoveries, the most one can say is that the link with the written tradition is likely to be right: these were the tunnels by which the unclean priests could reach the bath.

ZECHARIAH—
PRIEST OF THE ORDER OF ABIJAH

Zechariah's heart beat faster. He had come to the greatest moment of his life: he was the priest chosen to go into the holy place to burn incense. Every day the priests drew lots to pick the man who would carry out this duty. He could only do this once in his career, and some might never have the chance. The chosen priest stood there inside the Temple after the morning or evening sacrifice. He represented the people, and the incense rising from the altar was the symbol of their prayers going up to God.

Wherever they could, the priestly authorities kept to the rules laid down in the Old Testament. According to the First Book of Chronicles, King David arranged all the Temple staff. He divided the priests into twenty-four courses, each named after a leader (1 Chronicles 24:1–19). One course would do the duties in the Temple for a week, then the next course in order would take over. By this rota every course stood twice a year, taking the priests' share of the sacrifices for those weeks. At the three great festivals, Passover, Pentecost and Harvest (Tabernacles or Booths), members of all the courses shared the ceremonies. In Herod's Temple the rota given in Chronicles was carefully followed.

Jerusalem was home for many priests, and a large group lived in Jericho, but most were scattered through the towns and villages of Judea. Zechariah and Elizabeth lived in one of these hill-towns. Zechariah had made the journey to Jerusalem many times, and had waited for years, hoping his turn would come. He was no longer young, and perhaps was thinking he would never have the honour of burning the incense. He belonged to the course of Abijah, which was eighth in the list. At last his moment came, and Luke 1 records Zechariah's vision in the Temple and the extraordinary events that followed.

Even after Herod's Temple ceased to exist, the priests kept their list and orders. In some of the synagogues built during the third and fourth centuries, copies of the list were engraved on stone slabs fixed on the walls. Excavations at Ascalon and Caesarea have uncovered fragments of two of them. Beside the name of each course of priests is the name of the place where it had settled after the fall of Jerusalem. Course eighteen, named after Happizzez, made its home in Nazareth. One of the fragments from Caesarea has the name of that village on it, and that is the earliest record outside the Gospels of this then unimportant place.

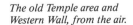

Among the stones fallen from the southern wall of the Temple, Israeli archaeologists uncovered this stone block nearly 2.5 metres/8 feet long. It had tumbled from the top of a wall, perhaps at the south-west corner. The Hebrew inscription says 'of the trumpeting place' (or 'To the . . . ') and may relate to the blowing of a trumpet to signal the beginning and the end of the sabbath, a duty of the priests in their rotas.

The old Temple area and Western Wall, from the air.

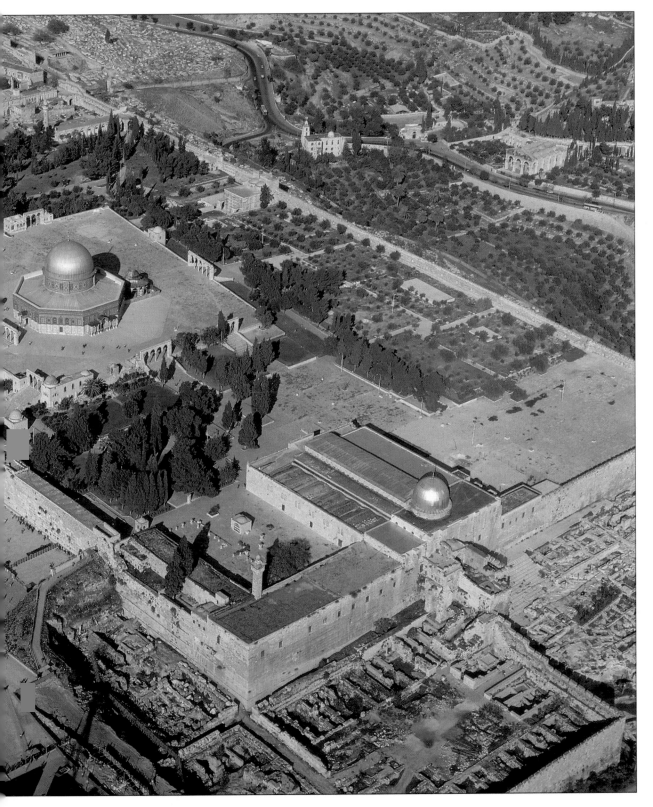

A WIDOW'S MITE

Among many small bronze coins minted by Herod the Great, this type is common. On the obverse is an anchor with the words 'of King Herod', and on the reverse two horns of plenty with a messenger's staff between.

A good day's wage for a workman in Palestine was one denarius, the Roman silver coin. It was the same value as the Greek drachma. One or other of these was the lost coin the woman hunted for in the parable of Luke 15:8–10. It was also half the tax each Jewish man paid yearly to the Temple (see *At the Money-changers' Tables*). Although a denarius was a day's wage, a labourer would not earn 365 denarii a year, because there was no pay for Sabbath days and other holidays. Jesus' parable of the grape-pickers who were each paid the same, one denarius, at the end of the day, assumes that there were workmen waiting for jobs, so some may not have found work every day (Matthew 20:1–16). Not surprisingly, cripples who could not hold a job often became beggars.

If a workman died, his widow could find herself in dire straits. Left alone (her parents also having died), perhaps with no close relatives or adult children and little or no property, she would have no income. All through the Bible, the widow is marked as one of the members of society most at risk. The story of how Jesus raised to life the son of the widow of Nain indicates the desperate state she was left in by his death (Luke 7:11–15).

The worker might receive a silver denarius as his pay, but for daily needs he would change it for smaller coins. They would be bronze pieces minted by the Jewish priest-kings in the first century BC, by Herod and his sons, and by the Roman governors (see *Money and Coins; Clues to Pilate's Character*). Sixty-four of them made one

denarius. Their Latin name, *quadrans*, was borrowed in Greek and Hebrew (see *Money and Coins*). Even these were not the smallest coins in people's pockets. The *lepton* was half a *quadrans*—a thin, tiny coin issued by the Jewish kings and Herod. Their value was very small; 128 of them were worth one denarius.

Beside the Temple tax, people made other presents of money to the Temple. Collecting boxes stood in the courtyard to receive them. As worshippers came by and threw in their offerings, Jesus was watching. He noticed a widow and drew attention to the size of her gift (Mark 12:42–44; Luke 21:2–4). She had given something more valuable than others, he said. She had put in all she had: that was two *lepta*, one sixty-fourth of a day's wage!

A TREASURE FROM BURIED BOOKS

'They're coming! Run for your lives! The Romans are coming!'

The message came at last to the edge of the Dead Sea. A commune of religious Jews lived there, isolated from everyone else. Their centre was well built, but it was not a fort where they could hold out against a strong enemy. Packing some food and other essentials, they left.

These people were devoted Bible students, owning hundreds of books. Although they could slip one or two books into a bag or a fold of a tunic, a whole Bible was too awkward to take away—it would be two dozen leather scrolls at least. To leave their holy books, and others, for the Roman soldiers to spoil was unthinkable. They would hide them.

Near the central building was a cave, and in it the people piled their library, 400 or more scrolls, books of the Bible (the Old Testament) and all sorts of others. Some of the people had been living in caves a little further away, and they left scrolls there. In one

cave there was time to wrap the scrolls in linen and put them in jars covered with lids, to protect them better. The people hoped that, when the Romans had gone, the books could be rescued.

If anyone did go back to save some of the scrolls, they left a lot of them behind. Some may have suffered at Roman hands. Among those in the main cave, a few show signs of being torn deliberately, and all were broken or damaged in some way. Winds blew dust and sand into the cave and, even in so dry a place, some damp also crept in. Worms burrowed and bored through the piles of leather. Gradually the crumbling scrolls disappeared under the dirt.

Yet they were not entirely lost to sight. About the year 200, some books of the Bible were found in a jar at Jericho, according to the great early scholar Origen. From 600 years later comes a report of another discovery of scrolls in a cave near Jericho, scrolls which played a part in the rise of a medieval sect of Jewish reformers.

In 1967 Israeli authorities confiscated the largest of all the Dead Sea Scrolls from its owner in Bethlehem. This is the Temple Scroll, 8.15 metres/ almost 7 yards long. It claims to present laws given by God to Moses about building the Temple, its worship, and the conduct of the king. The owners of the Scrolls probably hoped to bring these laws into effect when God gave them victory over their enemies.

The cliffs along the edge of the Dead Sea are riddled with caves. In the foreground of this picture is one close to the ruins of Qumran, Cave Four. About 400 scrolls were hidden here, but the ravages of time had reduced them to tens of thousands of fragments. Ever since their discovery in 1952, scholars have continued to study and fit them together.

After that, the scrolls lay undisturbed for over 1,000 years. In spite of their eagerness to find old manuscripts, neither Tischendorf (see *The Oldest Bibles*) nor any of the hunters like him saw that these stories might lead them to long-lost scrolls. No one thought that very old books would survive underground in Palestine. Only after the discovery of the Dead Sea Scrolls did the meaning of these early reports become clear.

Three shepherds were looking after their goats near the edge of the Dead Sea. Behind them were the crags of the desert cliffs. One of the Arabs saw a small hole in the cliff, and threw a stone into it. He was surprised to hear a sharp clattering noise. It was too late to explore that day, but he told the others about it. After a while, the youngest of them went off on his own and wriggled through a hole next to the first one. He dropped into a small cave, and saw what the stone had hit. An old pot was lying smashed on the floor. More pots stood in the cave. Lifting the lid off one, he found it full of red earth. In another were two small bundles wrapped in cloth, and one not wrapped. Each was a long roll of leather with small black letters all over the inside. The leather was thin and crumbly, not much use for anything. It was the winter of 1946–47 when they found the scrolls. During March 1947 they decided they might be worth some money. They took them to Bethlehem, to a carpenter who also bought and sold antiquities. He kept them for a while, then the shepherds came back.

'How much will you pay for them?'

'Nothing, they're not old!'

They took the scrolls away and arranged with another dealer to try to sell them. They agreed he could take a third of the price as his commission. A few weeks later he was able to give them their money: the three scrolls brought them £16—$65 at that time.

One of the shepherds had gone back to the cave meanwhile, and found some more scrolls buried under stones fallen from the roof. A different dealer bought these, for £7 ($28). For the effort of throwing a stone into a cave, the shepherds found themselves with more money in their pockets than they'd ever had from breeding sheep and goats. Yet that was not the end of the story for them: they had struck a gold mine, without knowing it!

An archbishop belonging to the Syrian Jacobite Church in Jerusalem had bought the first group of scrolls. Fighting in Jerusalem caused him to move to America. There he exhibited the scrolls at museums and universities, trying to find a buyer for them. Seven years after he had obtained them, he advertised them in *The Wall Street Journal*. They were for sale at a price to be agreed.

Someone showed the advertisement to Yigael Yadin, a leading archaeologist from Jerusalem who was visiting New York. He contacted a rich American friend who put up the money to buy them—a quarter of a million dollars. So it was that these scrolls returned to Jerusalem in 1954. There they were reunited with the second group, which Yadin's father, Professor Sukenik, had bought for £80/$324.

By the end of 1948 newspaper reports had told the world about the discovery and its importance—Hebrew books from the time of Christ had never been found in Palestine before. News that the scrolls were very valuable reached the shepherds and their friends. They went hunting for more caves with scrolls in them until, by 1956, they had located eleven with the same sorts of books in them. One cave, Cave 4, had had about 400 scrolls in it. Falling stones, wind-blown dust, insects, and possibly enemies, had torn them into 40,000 fragments. Each one had to be bought from the Arabs who found them, at an average price of £1/$4 per square centimetre.

Museum funds were soon exhausted in Jordanian Jerusalem. The government of Jordan produced a considerable sum of money, and more was raised from museums and academies and wealthy benefactors abroad. In 1967 the last of the scrolls to come to light was confiscated from the shepherds' Bethlehem agent by Israeli authorities. Afterwards they paid him compensation of $105,000. He and the tribesmen for whom he acted had grown rich because of one idly thrown stone!

A MONASTERY IN THE DESERT

Who were these very religious people? Why did they live in such an uncomfortable, out-of-the-way place?

The shore of the Dead Sea is bare, the cliffs behind are rugged crags. The terrace between, where the buildings stood, is flat and dry. The summer sun makes the rocks so hot it is impossible to stand still on one spot for more than a few seconds. No trees grow there to give shade. Water ran down the cliffs after the winter rains and snow, otherwise fresh water lay 2.4 km/ 1.5 miles way, at the spring of Ain Feshkha. Yet people built quite an elaborate settlement here, in the place now called Qumran.

A small farm had existed there for a short time, about 700 BC. After that the place was abandoned until the middle of the second century BC. The newcomers cleaned out a big cistern and added new ones, leading water to them from the cliffs along stone-walled channels. They set up a pottery kiln and other workshops. Soon major rebuilding began, on a much larger scale.

A strong tower looked over a square of rooms, including a kitchen and a large cistern. Outside were workshops for potters, laundrymen and others, and a long hall where people gathered to eat and talk. Many more people used the new building, so the water system was made much bigger. A dam, a rock-cut channel, and new cisterns were made. Special waterproof plaster stopped the precious water from leaking away. In the tower a staircase led to the first and second floors; another went to an

upper storey over some of the ground-floor rooms. The occupants may have slept upstairs.

Josephus reported that an earthquake did a lot of damage in the Jordan Valley in 31 BC. A line of cracks through walls and cisterns at Qumran was the result of the ground at one side sinking by 50 cm/20 ins, most likely because of that tremor. At the same time, fire burnt part of the buildings. Only a few people, if any, went on living there. About 100 years of use came to an end.

After the death of King Herod (4 BC), the whole centre came back to life. Derelict rooms were cleaned, walls strengthened, workshops re-established and the vital water-system renewed. The community was thriving when the Romans attacked it. They shot their arrows at anything that moved and set the buildings alight. Coins from years two and three of the Jewish Revolt, but not later, suggest this happened in AD 68.

In that year General Vespasian reached Jericho. From there he made a visit to the Dead Sea to conduct an experiment. He had heard that no one could drown in the salty water, so he had some non-swimmers thrown in, with their hands tied, to see if the report was true. Of course, they floated on the surface!

The attack at Qumran may be related to that visit. A small Roman garrison made its quarters in the building. From the tower they could watch the road along the shore.

Archaeologists traced the history of the site by excavating in the ruins from

1953 to 1956, under the direction of the French scholar Roland de Vaux. They concluded that the buildings had formed the headquarters of a community. Not everyone who belonged to it lived there. Caves in the cliffs showed signs of occupation. Wooden poles found in them show that tents were used too.

South of Qumran there are several springs, Ain Feshkha being the strongest. There were small oases of palm-trees where the water ran down to the Dead Sea, and ruins of quite a large farm were uncovered beside Ain Feshkha. The produce from this region, and the animals they herded, supplied a large proportion of the people's needs. They could not grow enough grain, however, and had to bring it from other places.

The community's life is clearly seen in the large hall. At one side of it was a small room. This was the china cupboard. Neatly stacked on the floor were over 1,000 pottery vessels; among them were 210 plates, 708 bowls and 75 goblets, the 'dinner service' of the community. In the hall at various points were stands for jars. Clearly the hall was a dining-room, where a large number of people would eat together.

It could also be a place for the community to meet.

Near the ruins was a cemetery with about 1,100 tombs. They lie in tidy rows, with a heap of stones over each burial. The bodies were laid neatly on their backs at a depth of 1.20– 2 metres/2–7 feet, the heads pointing to the south. Only a few graves were excavated and each one held a single male skeleton. In an extension of the cemetery the remains of a few women and a child were uncovered. Few of the people buried had lived more than forty years. This was, beyond doubt, the burial place for the community.

Keeping themselves alive took a lot of the members' time and energies, and the workshops show how busy they were. One large upstairs room had a special purpose. When the buildings fell into ruin, things from the upper storey dropped into the room below. Among them were some unusual pieces of smooth plaster. These were taken to the Rockefeller Museum in Jerusalem, and when fitted together they made up a bench 5 metres/16 feet long and about 0.5 metres/18 ins high. Two other objects, one bronze and one pottery, were found with these pieces. They are ink-pots of a shape common

The ruins of Qumran in the desert at the edge of the Dead Sea proved to be the centre of a Jewish sect from the second century BC until AD 68.

This is part of the Commentary on Habakkuk, one of the first of the Dead Sea Scrolls found. The author identified figures in the biblical prophecy with people of his own time. In this section Habakkuk 2:15 is said to refer to the 'Wicked Priest who chased the Teacher of Righteousness to swallow him up'.

throughout the early Roman Empire. One still had dried ink at the bottom! The room was evidently a writing-room or *scriptorium*.

Exactly how the scribes worked is not certain, because ancient pictures and carvings represent scribes sitting cross-legged with the scroll stretched across their knees. At Qumran, probably, scribes squatted in front of the bench, resting the scrolls on it as they wrote on them.

Did the scribes who worked in this room write the scrolls found in the caves? There is no way to prove that they did, yet there is no good reason to doubt it. By comparing the scrolls, scholars have recognized the handwriting of particular scribes, and so which texts one or another copied. The scrolls show that a large part of their work was to copy important books like those of the Old Testament. But sometimes they produced books which were unique. Since these are unknown outside the Dead Sea Scrolls, and are known only in single copies, they are almost certainly the products of the writing-room. Commentaries on books of the Old Testament are the chief examples.

Prophecy come true

The commentaries the scribes wrote are very revealing. The people who

wrote them read the Bible as if it was written about them. That is a very common attitude. Daniel had already told how a promise made by the prophet Jeremiah would come true in his time.

'In the first year of his reign, I, Daniel, understood from the Scriptures, according to the word of the Lord given to Jeremiah the prophet, that the desolation of Jerusalem would last seventy years' (Daniel 9:2).

So the authors of these commentaries identifed themselves, their leaders, their enemies and foreign powers with figures in the biblical prophecies.

For example, Isaiah promised the Jews, in God's name, 'I will build . . . your foundations with sapphires' (Isaiah 54:11). A commentary on Isaiah interprets the sentence as follows: 'this concerns the priests and the people who laid the foundations of the Council of the Community . . . the congregation of his elect will be like a sapphire among stones.'

These people had no doubt that God had chosen them. Through them he would work out his purposes. In the end, all their enemies would be defeated and they would enjoy the kingdom God would set up. A Messiah like David would be king, and another would be a priest like Aaron. All this they learnt from their study of the Old Testament. As they read their Bibles they found verses here and there which seemed to reflect their history. Through the comments they made about those verses, we too can learn about it.

They called themselves 'the Community' and looked back to a great leader whom they called 'The Teacher of Righteousness'. He did not found the movement but shaped its rules and gave it purpose a few years after it began. His leadership roused others against him. Chief of them was a man the commentaries call 'the Wicked Priest', who could not permit the Teacher to proclaim his very different ideas freely. He chased him to his refuge, perhaps at Qumran, and interrupted him and his disciples in their worship. What happened then is not related, the commentaries make only brief remarks. There is no hint of the Wicked Priest killing the Teacher. In fact, what happened to him is not stated clearly anywhere; he probably died a natural death, perhaps brought on by his enemies' persecution.

The riddle of the Teacher

Who were the Teacher of Righteousness and the Wicked Priest? There was no mystery about them to the readers of the scrolls, so there was no reason to give their names. Two thousand years later that knowledge is lost, so there *is* a riddle for modern scholars. Over the past forty years they have spun various theories. Some of these have collapsed as more documents are published and bring new facts to light.

A badly preserved commentary on Nahum altered the picture. It names a 'Demetrius, king of Greece' who tried to enter Jerusalem. He was invited by 'those who seek smooth things', but failed to reach the city. The writer says no 'king of Greece' came into Jerusalem 'from the time of Antiochus until the time when the rulers of the Kittim came'.

Josephus' history book gives the clue to this riddle. By 88 BC the Pharisees and other patriots were so outraged by the conduct of the Jewish priest-king, Alexander Jannaeus, who had been ruling from 103 and died in 76 BC, that they asked the Greek king of Syria to help them fight him. When Demetrius II (95–88 BC) came and defeated Jannaeus, some of the rebels who had invited him changed their minds, fought on Jannaeus' side again, and drove out the Syrian army. Alexander Jannaeus was not a forgiving man. He had 800 of the rebels crucified in front of his palace, and their wives and children slaughtered before their eyes.

'Those who seek smooth things' were evidently the Pharisees, disguised by a code-name. Whether they got this name because they kept the Old Testament laws less strictly than the Community, or because they were prepared to put up with foreign rule as long as they were left in peace, we cannot say.

Antiochus could be the arch-enemy Antiochus IV Epiphanes (175–163 BC), who set up a pagan image in the Temple in December 167 BC, causing the Maccabean revolt, or he could be Antiochus VII Sidetes (139–129 BC), who pulled down the walls of Jerusalem in 133 BC.

Finally, the Kittim, who occur often in the scrolls, are clearly the Romans. Under Pompey they first marched into Jerusalem in 63 BC.

None of this identifies the Teacher of Righteousness. What the commentary on Nahum reveals is the interest its author had in the events of the second and first centuries BC. Other commentaries seem to point in the same direction. Some time in the second century BC seems a good time to look for the Teacher of Righteousness, after the rise of the nationalist Jewish priesthood. None of the religious leaders whose careers can be traced fits the picture of the Teacher in the scrolls. This man, who inspired others to lives of hardship, devotion, and possibly martyrdom, is still

A few miles down the coast from Qumran is the strong spring of Ain Feshkha. Two thousand years ago a farm and workshops stood nearby. Then, as now, the water also refreshed the herds of the bedouin.

nameless to the twentieth century.

On the other hand, an enemy who could pursue and attack him was clearly in a powerful position, and so may be easier to identify. Two men are particularly suitable candidates, although theirs are not the only names proposed.

The first is Alexander Jannaeus, enemy of the Pharisees and other devout Jews. In his long reign as king and high priest he expanded his kingdom by military conquest, and made his family rich on the loot. Soon after he died, following a long illness, Pompey ended the power he had built

up. The history of Jannaeus accords well with references in the commentaries, and many scholars believe he was the Wicked Priest.

However, the case for the second candidate is even stronger. After Judas the Maccabee had rid the Temple of the pagan idol in 164 BC, he was killed in battle (160). His brother Jonathan took his place as nationalist leader. For some years there was peace and quiet, until a man called Alexander Balas landed at Ptolemais (Akko), aiming to win the throne of Syria. He promised to make Jonathan the high priest in return for his support (152 BC). When

Balas was killed in 145, his conqueror, Demetrius II, confirmed Jonathan's position. Finally, a Syrian general, Trypho, who was fighting Demetrius, took Jonathan prisoner and executed him (143 BC).

This history agrees very well with the hints the commentators give. The Wicked Priest started well, they say, then went wrong. He became High Priest, yet he was not a descendant of Aaron, and he accepted the post from a foreigner. His death, too, occurred at the hands of others, 'they took revenge on his body', in a way which might echo Trypho's deeds.

If Jonathan was the Wicked Priest, another description may apply to Jannaeus. In the commentary on Nahum we read of the raging lion who 'hung up alive' the 'seekers after smooth things', a description that fits his treatment of the Pharisees.

Even though Jonathan seems the better choice at present, as the process of piecing together and translating the fragments goes on, the case for him may improve, or it may disappear entirely, leaving the field to another man.

THE RULE OF THE COMMUNITY

Life in first-century Palestine was rougher than it is for most people in twentieth-century cities. There were none of the modern services. Water had to be carried from a river or pool, a spring or a well. It might not be clean, and proper drainage was rare. Food could not be kept for long unless it was dried or pickled, because there was no refrigeration. Houses could be draughty and damp in winter, dusty in summer. Snakes and scorpions lurked in cracks and under stones, ready to attack the unwary. Insects and parasites of all sorts burrowed into food stores, or made their homes on animal or human hosts.

Most towns and villages stood close to a water supply, with fields, orchards and pastures beside them, providing shade and refreshment. Yet the Qumran people left even that to live in a harsher place, far from ordinary society. What took them to their uncomfortable settlement beside the Dead Sea?

Religious faith can take people to extremes, can spur them to extraordinary acts. The Dead Sea Scrolls speak of those who

trust the Teacher of Righteousness. That was the secret. These people were sure their leader was right, so they would follow his teachings and keep them alive at any cost. One day, they believed, God would demonstrate to the world that they were the faithful ones who had kept his laws correctly. All their enemies would be punished.

The men of Qumran were Jews. They shared their basic faith with all other Jewish patriots. As descendants of Abraham they were God's chosen people, ruled by the laws

God gave by the hand of Moses at Mount Sinai. What made these people distinctive was their conviction that they alone were the 'remnant', they alone knew God's way.

The Teacher of Righteousness was probably the one who started this idea. Before he began to take the lead, the movement was one of several groups that grew up after the revolt of the Maccabees, calling on their Jewish brothers to follow the laws of Moses faithfully. They were 'back to the Bible' missions. Other groups

went along their own paths, one becoming the Pharisees.

They had to resolve the problem all 'back to the Bible' movements face. How does the Bible apply to us today? The Teacher persuaded his group that he had received the answer. God 'made known all the mysteries of his servants the prophets' to him, the commentary on Habakkuk states. His special knowledge divided him and his followers from the rest of Jewry.

If he had drawn vast crowds to his ideas, he might have created a party

The picture shows the opening columns of the Rule of the Community, or Manual of Discipline, which regulated the life of the people of Qumran. This copy was written on a leather scroll soon after 100 BC.

which carried weight in the Jewish commonwealth. He did not succeed in that, so his group naturally became more exclusive. When all the world is wrong except you, it is better to withdraw. For that reason, it seems, the community settled at Qumran. There they could study the Scriptures in peace.

That peace was highly organized, for everyone had his place and his duty. One of the first scrolls to be found is a rule-book, now called the Rule of the Community. It sets out the conditions of entry to the Community, guidelines for conduct in the assembly, and instructions for the leader.

To join the Community a recruit had to pass an examination by the members under their leaders. Before that there was almost certainly a probationary period when an inquirer could learn about the way of life and the rules before committing himself. Josephus says he spent some time in such a state, though not at Qumran. Membership involved total commitment, whole-hearted obedience to the rules, and putting all one's possessions at the Community's disposal. (That does not mean they gave up all their property to live in a form of communism, but they no longer did business with anyone outside.)

Growing food and working to supply communal needs took a lot of the members' time, but their most important task was workship and study. A special time was set for that. The Rule of the Community lays down that 'for a third of the night all through the year the congregation shall stay awake together to read from the Book, to study Law, and to pray together' (VI:7,8).

Some of the normal festivals were held—such as the Feast of Weeks—but not those which involved sacrifices. The men of Qumran had cut themselves off from the Temple and its services by their own exclusivism. They also made any common worship impossible by following a different calendar. Instead of the normal Jewish one, based on a moon cycle of a year of 354 days with an extra month added every three years to keep in line with the seasons, the Community had a sun-based calendar of 364 days, with leap years at intervals. As a result, they did not keep the Day of Atonement, for example, on the same day as other Jews.

The rules for life in the Community were strict.

Three priests and twelve laymen were apparently the leaders, and everyone had to respect them. They controlled the meetings at which every kind of business was discussed. Even then, order was rigidly kept. Everyone could speak, but only in order of rank, and only when called upon. No one could interrupt. The rules of conduct set a penance of ten days for anyone who did interrupt. Other offences drew heavier punishments: thirty days' penance for foolish laughter, or for sleeping during the meeting; six months for deception, bearing malice, or going about indecently dressed. Disobedience to the Community could result in expulsion; so too would the greater offence of speaking the holy name of God, even by accident.

WHOSE VOICE IN THE DESERT?

'God's kingdom is near! Repent, repent!'

Crowds flocked to hear the new prophet preach in the desert. Every few years, it seemed, another man came along with a new message. There was Theudas who was supposed to be the Messiah. He wasn't, the soldiers killed him, and his 400 followers soon disappeared. There was Judas of Gamla, too. He tried to stir people up against the Romans. They made short work of him!

The new man everyone was going to listen to was a strange, wild fellow, wearing camel-hair clothes and eating what he could find—the locusts that landed in the desert with their stomachs full of the farmers' crops, and the honey he took from the wild bees' nests.

'It's time to change,' he told them, 'time to stop cheating, to help the poor, and to be content. It's time to turn to God from evil.' If they did that, he said, they should show they meant it by being baptized in the river. Scores of people were baptized. They liked what John taught. They agreed with his attacks on their religious leaders, for some of them were double-dealers, and the endless rules and regulations they laid down grew tiresome and meaningless. It was time for a new start. People should be ready because God's chosen king, the Messiah, was on his way.

Where had John learnt his message? 'He lived in the desert until he appeared publicly to Israel,' Luke declares, and it was there God spoke to him (Luke 1:80; 3:2). All through the Bible God speaks to people and gives them tasks to do which use their experience and knowledge. Although no one should think John never left the desert to visit his family or talk with others, the desert was his home. How could he learn there, except by his own thoughts?

Before 1947 John's

110

life in the desert was a mystery. Then, when the Dead Sea Scrolls were discovered, some scholars suggested John had belonged to the group of people that owned them. The settlement at Qumran certainly stood in the desert. Its rule ordered baptisms or bathings to make the members pure for their assembly and meals. At the same time, the rule-book made it clear that such washings were no use unless there was a real determination to follow God's ways. This sounds rather like John's call to repent and be baptized. Also, the men of Qumran were looking forward to the arrival of God's Messiah. Did John live there for part of his life? Did he take over some of the ideas that were in the air?

There is no definite answer to these questions. If John did meet the Qumran people or stay with them for a while, when he began to preach he was not saying things which would have pleased them. He called people to repent and be baptized once, because God's kingdom was coming. At Qumran the bathing was done often, as the carefully-made pools show. There may have been an introductory baptism when people joined the group, as in other parts of Judaism, but there is nothing to show it was a baptism 'for the remission of sins', like John's.

Clearly John disagreed with the lifestyle of Qumran, because he did not tell his converts to leave their homes or obey such strict rules. John attacked the priests in his speeches. But as far as the records tell he did not attack the Temple and its worship in the way some of the Scrolls do. And the ultimate difference is obvious in the Messiah whom John pointed out to the crowds around him, Jesus of Nazareth. So different from the current hopes was he that even John became a little uncertain later, and had to be reassured (Matthew 11:2–19).

Whatever ideas John had heard, wherever he had lived, what he taught was not an imitation or an echo of other men's thoughts. John was independent, knowing that his work was to prepare the way for the Messiah by warning that he was coming. This warning was for everyone, not for a chosen few, as the men of Qumran believed.

People from the villages of Judea and from Jerusalem travelled across these hills and down to the Jordan to hear John the Baptist preach.

THE SCROLLS AND THE TEACHING OF JESUS

No one in modern times had ever seen the actual books people were reading in Palestine when Jesus was there. News of the discovery of the Dead Sea Scrolls led to all sorts of hopes and guesses about what they would be. Perhaps they would bring new knowledge for the history of the Old Testament books. They would certainly pull back the curtain which hid large areas of first-century Judaism, for no other Hebrew writings had survived from those days. Above all, the Scrolls might throw new light on the beginnings of Christianity. No wonder thousands of dollars were paid for these unique documents, even though most are only scraps.

Forty years after the discovery, have those hopes and guesses been realized? As far as the text of the Old Testament is concerned, the Scrolls have brought valuable new knowledge, although it is not as clear as many wished! First-century Judaism has gained a wholly new scene, a life-style not suspected before (see *The Rule of the Community*).

As for the Scrolls and the Gospels, scores of books and studies on the subject have been published. A few writers have made sensational, even outrageous, claims, and other writers have quickly shown that those claims have no foundation in fact. Yet once fanciful, wrong ideas are broadcast, they linger and are hard to destroy, so it is worth repeating some facts.

The Dead Sea Scrolls do not mention Jesus or John the Baptist. They show no links with the New Testament. When the owners of the Scrolls hid their books and ran away from Qumran, they were still waiting for the Messiah to come. They did not recognize Jesus as the Messiah, and would have needed as strong a conversion as anyone to do so. In their view the Messiah would be a warrior, leading them to victory over all their opponents and setting up his kingdom in Jerusalem. Another, priestly, Messiah would then re-establish the correct forms of worship and sacrifice in the Temple. Neither Messiah had any atoning function. Rather, the people who wrote the Scrolls saw their Community and especially its leaders, twelve laymen and three priests, as atoning for sin by just deeds and through suffering. They remained to the end a thoroughly Jewish community which, as far as can be seen, never thought of people from other races joining them.

Essenes at Qumran looked back to their Teacher of Righteousness and followed his teachings. He had died, perhaps naturally, and was not expected to reappear, except in the general resurrection when all the righteous would enjoy God's presence. Christians looked to their Teacher, who had been executed and had reappeared on the third day after he had been buried. They proclaimed him then, not just as a man but as God.

A great gap divides the teachings of the Scrolls from those of the Gospels. No one can justly claim any direct link between them. Even so, they share a lot of common ground, because both have their roots in the Old Testament. The revelation God gave to Abraham, the election of his descendants as the people of Israel to be the special nation of God, with the laws conveyed by Moses, the oracles of the prophets, the history and the psalms—all these were basic to both of them.

Prophecy reached its fulfilment in their own time, both for the Teacher of Righteousness and for Jesus. Each of them viewed the dominant parties in Judaism as mistaken in their teachings and practices. However, where Jesus relaxed religious rules, the Essenes tightened them.

The prime example is in the approach to the Sabbath day. If an animal fell into a pit on the Sabbath, it was not wrong to help it out, according to the Pharisees. In Matthew 12:11 Jesus answers the question, 'Is it lawful to heal on the Sabbath?' with these words: 'If any of you have a sheep and it falls into a pit on the Sabbath, will you not take hold of it and lift it out? How much more valuable is a man than a sheep! Therefore it is lawful to do good on the Sabbath.' At Qumran the animal could not be helped. A man must not even lift his hand to hit a stubborn animal on the Sabbath.

The common ground between the Scrolls and the Gospels was more than the inheritance of the Old Testament. In the Gospels are some expressions not found in the Old Testament which are found in the Scrolls. Here the hope that the Scrolls would shed light on the beginnings of Christianity is met in a small way. Coming from the same time, background, and country, and concerned with the same subjects, they were likely to use similar language. When the angels voiced their hymn of praise at the birth of Jesus, they called for 'peace to men on whom God's favour rests' (Luke 2:14, see *What Did the Angels Sing?*). A scroll of hymns from Qumran, possibly composed by the Teacher of Righteousness, has the phrase 'sons of good will' in two places.

Another hymn, put in the mouths of the victorious 'sons of light' after they have defeated the 'sons of darkness', proclaims 'Among the poor in spirit [there is power] over the hard of heart.' This is not the same as 'Blessed are the poor in spirit, for theirs is the kingdom of heaven', the first of Jesus' 'Beatitudes' (recorded in Matthew 5), but the phrase 'poor in spirit' is. Evidently it was current among pious Jews to denote people who were spiritually humble (compare the Pharisee and the tax collector—Luke 18:13).

When Jesus taught his followers to love their enemies and pray for their persecutors, he commented that others had said 'Love your neighbour and hate your enemy'. He may have meant the teachings of the Essenes. Several times in the Scrolls the faithful are told to hate the 'sons of darkness', an attitude not so clearly stated elsewhere.

Both Jesus and the Scrolls warn those who oppose God's will that they will end up in a place of everlasting fire (see *Gehenna—The Everlasting Bonfire*).

In John's Gospel one of the distinctive themes is light. Jesus is 'the light of the world', who offers light to mankind, although most reject him, preferring darkness (John 8:12; 3:19–21). The Dead Sea Scrolls speak of 'the children of righteousness' who 'are ruled by the Prince of Light and walk in the ways of light.' The 'children of deceit', on the other hand, 'walk in the ways of darkness', and they are contrasted with those who 'do the truth', another term applied to Jesus' followers in John's Gospel (3:21).

The Scrolls correct a common impression that John's Gospel has strong Greek influences in it. Light and darkness, truth and falsehood were equally at home in the thought-world of Palestinian Jews. Thus the possibility of its preserving authentic memories of Jesus' teaching grows a little stronger. The Scrolls underline, at the same time, the novelty of Jesus' teaching which would have struck his hearers; he called for faith in himself first, and flowing from that a life which followed the Law in its principles, whereas it was joining the Community that made someone a 'son of light' according to the Scrolls, and that brought with it a sincere and minute obedience to every part of the Law.

In the ruins of the fortress at Masada, where the last Jewish rebels resisted the Romans until AD 73, pieces of one scroll were found which duplicate a scroll from Qumran. They are part of a hymnbook belonging to the Qumran Community. Their presence at Masada suggests that someone from Qumran fled there, perhaps expecting to take part in the last battle which would see the victory of the righteous.

A GOSPEL AT QUMRAN?

Surprise after surprise has come from the Dead Sea Scrolls, and none more unexpected than a Spanish scholar's announcement in 1972. Tiny scraps of papyrus, he said, come from a copy of Mark's Gospel in Greek, from Paul's letter to Timothy, and from the letter of James.

The pieces of papyrus came from Cave 7 at Qumran. When archaeologists explored this badly eroded cave they found twenty-one minute fragments of papyrus scrolls and the 'negatives' of three others which had been pressed against lumps of mud leaving their ink letters on it, although the papyrus itself had rotted away. The fragments came from thirteen or more scrolls, all in Greek. Enough writing was left on one piece to identify it as part of Exodus, and on a second piece to show it came from a copy of the apocryphal *Letter of Baruch*. Studying the other pieces, José O'Callaghan found he could fit the letters on one of them (numbered 7Q5) into Mark 6:52,53.

If this claim is true, it is an astonishing one. The handwriting of the papyri places them in the middle of the first century AD. Pottery found in the cave belongs to the same time, and is like pottery from other caves where Hebrew manuscripts lay. It would be hard to argue that these scrolls were left behind by people who had no connection with the owners of the scrolls in the other caves. Therefore the presence of New Testament manuscripts would mean that people were reading Christian books at Qumran before the place was abandoned in AD 68.

Numerous people, including the author, would be delighted if a genuine Gospel manuscript of the mid-first century came to light in Palestine, or in Egypt. Many cherished theories would collapse, most histories of Gospel writing would be changed. Arguments for the reliability of the Gospel records would gain strength. Just because the effects of so sensational a discovery would be so far-reaching, the claims of O'Callaghan and of a German scholar Carsten Peter Thiede who has supported them, need to be treated with great caution.

Small scraps of papyrus books can be identified even though the number of words on them is few. The Rylands papyrus of John (see *Oldest of All*) has several whole words (among them 'the Jews' and 'signifying') and distinguishable parts of others arranged on both sides of the page in such a way as to leave no doubt that it comes from a page of John's Gospel. The Qumran piece is smaller and does not contain as many distinctive words.

Two points favour its identity with the Mark passage. In line 4 three letters and remains of a fourth could be the middle of the name Gennesaret (a term for Galilee). The previous line has a space before the word 'And', indicting that it starts a new paragraph (otherwise Greek scribes did not leave spaces between words). These two lines could be part of Mark 6:53, 'When they had crossed over, they landed at Gennesaret', which starts with 'And' in the original. Following this, it is possible to read the letters in the other lines to fit the adjacent sentences in Mark 6:52,53.

An astonishing claim needs an unshakeable foundation if it is to be accepted as fact, especially if other arguments are to be built on it. Statistics count against finding more than one book with exactly the same sequence of letters and spacing over five lines on a page, so the identification seems strong. A computer search through Greek literature found no other passage which showed the pattern of letters O'Callaghan read on the papyrus.

Are his readings satisfactory?

Some of the letters are far from clear, notably in line 2 and after 'And' in line 3. Read differently, the pattern is changed, opening the door to doubt. The letters which fit 'Gennesaret' could equally

The tiny piece of a papyrus scroll which two scholars claim contained Mark's Gospel. Mid-first century AD.

be part of a verbal form. With other letters reconstructed in alternative ways the fragment could come from a completely different book. No one knows how much Jewish literature in Greek from the period 200 BC to AD 70 has been lost to us. Some of these writings are quoted by Josephus, or mentioned by name, others survive in translations into Latin, or Ethiopic. The Hebrew and Aramaic manuscripts from the other caves disclose more books whose existence was previously unsuspected.

With regret, we have to conclude that the fragment is too small, its letters too uncertain, to warrant the label 'A piece of Mark's Gospel from the first century'. And the same verdict applies to the other fragments claimed as New Testament scrolls.

Although it is possible, the identity is not proved. Even if some people at Qumran did read the Gospel, there is no sign of it affecting the teachings of the people living there.

PART FOUR

DEATH AND BURIAL

From earliest times people have laid the dead to rest in the ground with reverence. Jesus' friends did that for him. Christians often ask what sort of tomb his body rested in, and where it was. The study of tombs around Jerusalem and burial customs of the time, together with recent explorations in the city, now bring clearer answers than could be offered before. As a result the Gospel descriptions grow more vivid.

The bones of the dead were collected into stone boxes or ossuaries, sometimes ornately carved.

TOMB FASHIONS

Cemeteries and tombs—the town-planner's headache, the property-developer's nightmare—often lie in the path of a motorway, or the site of an apartment block.

What to do with the bodies of the dead has been a problem ever since people began to live in towns. Some buried the remains in their houses, perhaps keeping their families together in that way. Others made graveyards just outside the built-up area and buried the dead there. Cremation, which saves space, was rare in the biblical world until Roman times. For the Jews it was not acceptable because they believed in a resurrection related in some way to the physical body. Over the centuries the number of tombs and cemeteries grew. Sometimes new ones destroyed or re-used the old ones, sometimes builders dug through old burials without care.

Where the soil was deep enough, people could dig simple graves and bury the bodies without fear of wild animals disturbing them. In much of Palestine the spade hits rock just below the surface of the ground, so proper burial was more difficult. One way was to place the person on the ground and pile stones into a cairn, or build stone slabs into a small 'house'—like the dolmens of Celtic lands. That was not very secure. If a robber thought there might be something very valuable in the tomb, he could make his way into it.

What became the usual thing was also the more expensive one, to make a room in the rock big enough to hold at least one corpse. There are plenty of caves in the limestone hills of Israel and Judah, so the smaller ones that could be closed were natural tombs. Already before 2000 BC groups of tombs were cut in the ground near towns like Jericho. A narrow shaft one or two metres/a few feet deep would open into a chamber like a small cave, with enough room to allow the body to be arranged and a few pots and pans put beside it. After the burial, a stone might be used to close the entrance, then the shaft would be filled with earth and stones.

To hollow out a new tomb like that for everyone who died probably cost more time and labour than many families could afford. Often, by making the tombs larger, they could create a family vault. Husbands and wives, aunts and uncles, children and grandchildren could all be laid together, the tomb being reopened whenever one died.

At Jericho Dame Kathleen Kenyon opened several tombs made about 1800 BC. They held up to twenty bodies each, occasionally more. As the later ones were added, the older remains were pushed aside to make space, so that the excavators found only the last burial neatly arranged with its equipment.

This was the time of Abraham, Isaac, and Jacob in the Old Testament. They followed the same custom. The cave Abraham bought in order to bury his wife Sarah later received his body, then those of his son Isaac and his wife Rebecca, and later of Jacob and his wife Leah (Genesis 23;49:31—33). That tomb—so Jewish tradition claimed—

Kings and noblemen of Judah had spacious tombs hollowed in the hills around Jerusalem in the eighth and seventh centuries BC. This chamber in the grounds of St Stephen's Monastery north of the city has benches on either side for the bodies to rest on, and further space beyond. At a lower level is a repository for the bones of earlier burials— only the most recent lay neatly on the benches.

could still be seen at the town of Hebron, south of Jerusalem, in the time of Jesus. King Herod built a great wall around it to mark it as a holy place, a wall which still stands after 2,000 years.

Tombs from the days of the kings

In the centuries of the kings of Israel and Judah forms of burial changed very little. Example of tombs from that time have been found all over the country. Particularly well-made ones can be seen outside the Old City of Jerusalem. One row has been known for a long time. It faces the eastern slope of the original town, now known as the City of David, in the village of Silwan.

Wealthy families paid for chambers to be cut square in the rock face of the valley. Some were even cut as free-standing blocks, to look like houses. Over the doorways, Hebrew letters gouged in a smoothed surface told the names of the dead and, in one case at least, cursed anyone who would open the tomb.

Another row of tombs was made along the southern edge of the Valley of Hinnom, beside the modern St Andrew's Church. Archaeologists excavated them between 1975 and 1980. They had a long history. Dug in the rock in the seventh century BC, they went on being used as tombs until late in the sixth century BC. Then more bodies were buried in them in the first century BC and the first century AD, above the earlier ones. In the second and third centuries pyres were built on the site for cremations. Cooking-pots found buried there held ashes and burnt bones. Other cremations discovered around Jerusalem belonged to the Tenth Legion, the Roman garrison stationed in the city after AD 70—so these may also be theirs. Further burials were made during this time, too.

In the fifth century, parts of the rock walls of the tombs were quarried away when a church was built nearby. The most recent relics were dozens of rusty rifles, army buttons and oddments left by Turkish soldiers who watched the road to Bethlehem from a guard-post beside the tombs, probably during the First World War. They were lying on the rock bench of one of the seventh-century tombs.

These tombs were single rooms

In the first century BC leading families of Jerusalem had grandiose tombs cut for themselves in the Kidron Valley. The pillared entrance leads to tombs which belonged to priests of the Hezir family (1 Chronicles 24:15) according to a later inscription. The solid square tower with a pyramid on top is part of this monument; its traditional name 'Tomb of Zechariah' has no foundation.

about 3 metres/10 feet square with a step down from the entrance. On either side and at the end were benches over a metre/3 feet high, cut in the rock. On the benches in two of the tombs the stone had been carefully carved to make resting-places for the heads of the corpses. One tomb had three rooms opening off the entrance hall, and on one bench six head-rests were cut in a row.

All this laborious cutting in the rock, done to a high standard, allowed a few bodies to be laid neatly in each of the tombs. Space was too precious to devote one expensive tomb to a very small number of people. Underneath a bench in several of these tombs were smaller hollowed spaces. All of them were empty except one.

In the largest tomb the roof of this space had fallen in, saving what was in it from robbers. As well as scores of pots, pieces of jewellery, and two precious silver amulets, there were lots of bones. Bones of nearly 100 people were collected there. Evidently once the places on the benches were full, the first burials were taken up and bundled into these cellars. Here is a physical illustration of the biblical phrase 'gathered to his fathers'.

A third group of tombs created for rich citizens of Jerusalem in the eighth or seventh centuries BC lies to the north of the Old City. They have the same basic plan as those of the Hinnom Valley, but are much bigger. Rooms with benches for burials and repositories for bones open out of an entrance hall. Seven rooms belong to one tomb, with another larger room that has no benches and may have been a place where the bodies could be prepared for burial. Like the Silwan tombs, these display the work of skilful masons. Near the ceilings, the rock was carved to make a cornice. The doorways were nicely squared with, in one case, sockets for the hinge posts of a pair of double doors. On the walls shallow recesses seem to imitate wooden panelling. Here was truly 'an eternal home' of the highest quality.

Tombs of Jesus' days

Tombs made 600 years before Christ may seem too old to help us understand tombs of the first century, yet they are important. They reveal an attitude to the remains of the dead which was almost the same in the New Testament period. The idea of burying many people in one tomb did not change either. The problem of space grew more acute. Tombs from the first century BC and the first century AD illustrate these points, as well as making clear what sort of tomb the Gospels describe at the burial of Jesus.

To be buried in a rock-cut tomb was no doubt expensive, so only fairly well-to-do people would have afforded them. In the Gospel period the tomb-cutters of Jerusalem made simple tombs, fine tombs with carved entrances, and elaborate tombs with monuments marking them above ground. Simple tombs have a small doorway, 1 metre/3 feet high, closed by a boulder which fitted like a plug, or by a stone slab. It was essential to close tombs tightly, otherwise wild animals, dogs, jackals, hyenas, which were always scavenging outside ancient towns, would enter and tear up the bodies. After stooping or crawling through the entrance, the mourners would go down one or two steps, then be able to stand upright.

Around three sides of a roughly squared room is a bench cut in the rock about waist high. From the bench short tunnels run into the rock walls. They are up to 2 metres/6 feet 6 ins long, half a metre/18 ins wide and 1 metre/3 feet high. Each could hold a human body lying flat on its back. Sometimes stone slabs or rough stone walls closed these tunnels.

Wealthy people might order superior tombs with courtyards in front of the entrances. Plants and shrubs may have been grown in them. The entrances themselves were neatly carved in the rock face to look like the doorways of noble mansions, decorated in some cases with flowers and leaves in low relief. These were full-

The tomb of Queen Helen of Adiabene dates from the Gospel period. Tombs had to be tightly closed lest dogs or wild animals should creep inside and disturb the dead.

Hidden at the back of the Church of the Holy Sepulchre is the 'Tomb of Joseph of Arimathea'. Here are the tunnels and bench typical of a first-century tomb. (Visitors enter on the level of the bench and the grille prevents them slipping down on to the original floor.)

sized doorways, closed with wooden, or occasionally stone, doors. Beyond was a large room opening into other rooms with the short tunnels in the walls for the burials. In one tomb there are eighty of these tunnels. Occasionally these fine tombs were designed for burials in coffins. A shelf was cut in each wall, up to 2 metres/ 7 feet long, with an arch in the rock above it (termed an *arcosolium*). Very rarely the bench under the arch was hollowed out to form a coffin.

Most elaborate of all is the burial place called today 'the Tombs of the Kings'. A royal family from north-eastern Iraq was converted to Judaism and had this large tomb created north of Jerusalem.

An impressive flight of steps leads down to a large courtyard dug out of

the rock. At one side was a pillared entrance, originally crowned with three pyramids, Josephus reports. All this splendour leads to a low doorway shut by a stone which rolled from a slot, like a wheel. Inside is a large room and eight other rooms with burial tunnels.

When the French explorer De Saulcy cleared out the tomb in 1863, he found a big stone coffin. On it was written the name and title of the queen in Aramaic and Hebrew. A few people were buried in stone coffins, but this, too, was something only the rich could afford.

In most tombs the bones were not left lying neatly in the tunnels. Instead, after a year or so, when the flesh had decayed, the bones were collected and put in boxes (see *Their Names Live On*). Six or seven of the boxes could be fitted into the tunnel a single body would occupy when laid out flat, and so a lot more people could be accommodated in a tomb. When the tombs are opened, the boxes are also found on the benches and even on the floor. Although the boxes were made to hold the bones of one person, the remains of several may be in a single box. An inscription on one says, 'Simon and his wife', and on another was scratched, 'The wife and son of Matthia'.

In the light of all this, the accounts in the Gospels of the burial of Jesus and the circumstances of the first Easter Sunday morning can be read more intelligibly. Joseph of Arimathea was a wealthy man, with a new tomb in a garden. He took the body of Jesus to it and laid it there quickly because of the Sabbath. To keep the body safely, everyone was content to close the tomb with a heavy stone. As soon as possible after the Sabbath, some of Jesus' women followers went to anoint the body with spices, to give it the attention the Sabbath had prevented. They expected the stone would be an obstacle, and when they found it had been moved they saw quickly that the body had gone. A figure sitting inside, on the right, told them Jesus had risen.

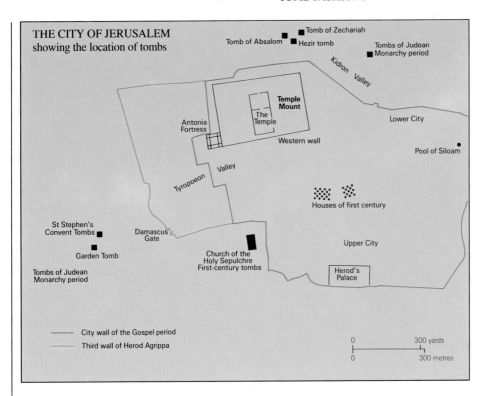

THE CITY OF JERUSALEM
showing the location of tombs

Tomb of Zechariah
Tomb of Absalom Hezir tomb
Tombs of Judean
Monarchy period

Kidron Valley

Temple
Mount
The
Temple

Antonia
Fortress

Lower City

Western wall

Pool of Siloam

Valley

Tyropoeon

Houses of first century

St Stephen's
Convent Tombs

Damascus
Gate

Upper City

Garden Tomb

Church of the
Holy Sepulchre
First-century tombs

Tombs of Judean
Monarchy period

Herod's
Palace

City wall of the Gospel period

Third wall of Herod Agrippa

0   300 yards

0   300 metres

Jesus' disciples went to the tomb: one peered in, Peter actually went in, and both saw the graveclothes lying there. Then Mary peered into the tomb and saw two angels sitting where the head and feet of the body had been.

The Gospel writers evidently describe a tomb with a small entrance and a rock-cut bench, of the sort now well known as the fashion in the first-century Jerusalem. Jesus' body was not placed in one of the tunnels, as would be expected, because it was brought into the tomb hastily and left without full preparation. It was laid on the bench. After the resurrection, the clothes were left there, easily seen, and the angels could conveniently sit on the bench.

A very elaborate tomb was built to the west of Jerusalem with a monument above ground and four chambers dug in the rock. Some of Herod's family may have been buried there. The entrance was closed with a large round stone slab.

THEIR NAMES LIVE ON

The bones in this ossuary belonged to a man named John, who spoke Greek.

'They have no known grave' are the sad words said of many soldiers killed in battle. They are also true of thousands upon thousands of men, women and children who lived in times past. These people have literally disappeared. Their bones have been scattered, or have completely decayed, or lie in the ground with nothing to mark them. Quite often old burials come to light in the course of farming or construction work, yet they are only a few of those made over the ages. Sometimes things the dead had used in their lives lie with them. They range from a ring on a finger, or a few beads with a child, to the thrones and chariots of Pharaoh Tutankhamun.

In the tombs of important men and women, kings like Tutankhamun, their names may be carved or painted on the wall, or the coffin, or pots and pans. But even very rich tombs may not disclose the names of their dead. A noteworthy example is the group of magnificently furnished burial chambers opened in 1977 at Vergena in Macedonia. The excavator claims that Philip of Macedon, the father of Alexander the Great, was interred there, but not one of the treasures bears a name. It is not surprising, therefore, that the graves of the less important people, the majority of ancient society, are usually anonymous.

Some cultures have had fashions for recording a dead person's identity. Greek citizens set up tombstones, and Romans carved names and other details on stone urns or slabs that covered them. In Palestine during the first century BC and through the first century AD some burials had names on them which give valuable information about Jewish society.

A year after the body had been laid in the tomb the bones were often collected in stone boxes long enough to hold the leg-bones easily. These boxes occupied much less space than a skeleton needed when laid out flat, so more bodies could be put into one tomb. Ossuaries, as the boxes are called, could be plain or decorated. There are patterns of lines and circles on some, scratched with a sharp point, or carved with a chisel. A few have floral decoration and one or two carry carvings imitating stonework.

Hundreds of ossuaries are now in museums, especially in Jerusalem. The majority are plain, but scores of them, plain and decorated, bear names. The letters may be carefully engraved, or roughly scratched, or scribbled in charcoal. They were not public memorials to the dead people, but labels to identify their remains. Usually they give the name of the dead person, often the father's name which served the purpose of a modern surname (many of which, e.g. Johnson, Robinson, Jameson, were formed in just this way), and occasionally a title. There are 'labels' for a rabbi, for priests, for a temple builder, for a scribe, a potter, and for various others. Women's names appear as well as men's, with a description sometimes added, 'daughter of X', or 'wife of Y'.

The Greek, Aramaic and Hebrew languages were all used to give this

The Hebrew inscription states that the remains of Shitrath daughter of Yehohanan lay in this ossuary. (Yehohanan is ultimately the same name as John.)

information. Greek was the least common, and in several cases there is a Hebrew or Aramaic translation of a Greek text. From this it is clear that all three languages could be understood by people living in Jerusalem in the first century (see *The Languages they Spoke*).

The names of the dead reflect this variety. There are Greek names like Andrew and Alexander, Aramaic ones, for example Abba and Yithra, and Hebrew, among them Gamaliel, Isaac and Levi. They show the sort of names parents were giving to their children at that time, and how they were written. What is interesting to see is that the commonest of them all occur in the New Testament. John, Judas, Jesus, Mary, Martha, Matthew are all found, and Lazarus or Eliezer and Simon are among the most frequent.

These were not the same individuals as those in the New Testament, simply others who shared the same name. Finding bones in an ossuary inscribed in Aramaic for Jesus son of Joseph does not affect the Christian belief in the resurrection of Jesus. It shows the same thing—that these names were common at the time. All this is helpful for evaluating the Gospels. As far as the personal names are concerned, there is a striking correspondence; the Gospels reflect well the first-century fashion in names. These simple marks of identification on the stone chests bring us into contact with a few of the people in Jesus' day. Even though scores are named in this way, there were very many more whose tombs bore no names or of whom all trace is gone. They were among the crowds who stood in the Temple or thronged the streets, eager to see Jesus.

CAN WE SEE THE TOMB OF JESUS?

'Jesus was buried here!'
'No, Jesus was buried here!'

Two places are shown to visitors in Jerusalem, each by people who believe this was the tomb where Jesus was buried. The fact that there are two rival sites upsets some pilgrims; others are convinced one is right and take no notice of the second. Is either of the two—the Church of the Holy Sepulchre and the Garden Tomb—the right place? Growing knowledge about the way tombs were made and the fashions in tomb designs around Jerusalem during the centuries (see *Tomb Fashions*) helps to explain why one place may be the right one, and the other not.

The Garden Tomb

In 1883 General Charles Gordon, a famous leader of the British army in the Crimean War, in China and in Egypt, reached Jerusalem. Gordon understood the Old Testament by means of the New Testament. The rites for worship in ancient Israel he saw as pointers to the life and work of Christ. He went to a small hill north of the Turkish wall of Jerusalem. Two caves in the sheer face opposite the city look something like the eye sockets of a skull, so it was called Skull Hill.

Gordon reckoned the priests killed the animals for sacrifice in the Temple there, north of the altar (on the basis of Leviticus 1:11). It would therefore have been the appropriate place for Jesus, the 'Lamb of God', to be killed. In this way he identified the hill as Golgotha or Calvary, and many today still call it 'Gordon's Calvary'. His

notes were not printed until 1885. In 1884 Gordon was killed at Khartoum, trying to end the rebellion of the Mahdi.

Quite near the edge of the hill is a tomb in the rock. Forty years before Gordon's visit someone had suggested it might be the tomb of Jesus. Another tomb, not far away, was put forward by a different explorer. With Gordon's idea about Calvary, the first tomb gained favour. A lot of rubbish and Crusader buildings were taken away to reveal the large flat space, cistern and vertical rock wall with a doorway which are visible today.

Inside the doorway is a small room leading to another on the right. This one has two troughs hollowed out of the rock on either side of the doorway, and a smaller one between them at the end. Slots in the rock show where stone slabs made sides and lids for these troughs. Painted on the walls are crosses and Greek letters standing for Jesus Christ, the First and the Last. The paintings belong to the early Byzantine period, the fifth or sixth century AD.

Why should this tomb be identified as the tomb of Jesus, rather than one of the others in this area? The nearness of Gordon's Calvary is one reason. Another is its position—outside the city wall but quite close to it. Emotions also play a part. European Protestants going into the Church of the Holy Sepulchre can feel uncomfortable. The lamps and candles, the gaudy colours, and the black-robed priests are alien to their ways of worship. In its simplicity this tomb, with its well-tended garden, has an immediate appeal; the visitor can imagine the events of the first Easter Sunday morning without difficulty.

Yet there is no real evidence in favour of the Garden Tomb. General Gordon's idea about the hill being the slaughtering-place for the Temple has no historical or geographical facts on its side. He added to his idea the suggestion that the outline of a human figure can be drawn with its skull on the hill, its seat on the Dome of the Rock, and its feet at the Pool of Siloam. When he set out this theory, Gordon himself called it 'fanciful'.

Everyone can see that the Garden Tomb lies outside the city wall, the Holy Sepulchre stands inside it. Where the city wall ran at the time of the crucifixion is something scholars have argued about for years. Of course, the feelings of modern visitors cannot affect the arguments in favour or against the identification.

In recent years archaeological evidence has grown to the point where it can decide the question. Fashions in tomb design are well attested and clearly dated by the objects found in undisturbed burials. Trough tombs were mostly the work of Byzantine masons. However, the Garden Tomb is certainly older than that. Marks left by the stone-cutters' tools are the clues that point to changes inside it. The troughs are not original. Those who first made the tomb left a rock-cut bench around three of its walls, and probably one in the outer room, later chiselled away. Tombs of the first century have rock benches, but running from them in most cases are short tunnels which received the bodies.

The marks left by the stone-cutters' tools are still visible on the walls of the tomb. They are not all the same. Around the upper part, where the walls and ceiling meet at carefully cut angles, they are single long strokes. In contrast, tombs of the first century were normally worked with a toothed chisel which left groups of small parallel lines in the stone. None of these is evident on the walls of the Garden Tomb.

The conclusion is unavoidable: the Garden Tomb is not a first-century tomb. More and more discoveries point to it being much older, as old as the eighth or seventh centuries BC, the days of Isaiah or Jeremiah. Very near to it, on the same hill, are the third group of large tombs from that age, and others lie close by. Here was a burial area at the end of the Monarchy. The Garden Tomb seems to have been part of it. Over a thousand years later, Christians remodelled the inside in order to bury their dead in their own way.

Later still the outside was changed. Perhaps it was the Crusaders who lowered the ground level outside, dug a large cistern with a channel running in the rock to it, and put up some buildings against the rock. All these changes have left their imprints on the Tomb, and now they do seem to make sense: what is missing is any sign of first-century use. The Garden Tomb was not the tomb of Jesus.

This verdict should not upset anyone who has found it a peaceful or inspiring place in which to meditate and worship, for the nature of the place is unchanged, and so is the message of the resurrection. That the angel actually announced the news in a different place is unimportant.

The Church of the Holy Sepulchre

Ropes and crowbars strained at stones, picks and spades thudded into the earth, as gangs of men pulled down an old temple and dug away the soil below it. The year was 326, and the Emperor Constantine had ordered an excavation in Jerusalem. He wanted to build a church in honour of the resurrection. Christians said they knew where the actual tomb of Jesus lay, and obviously that would be the ideal site for the church. They pointed to a rather unexpected place, underneath a temple in the middle of the city.

After the Jews failed to free themselves from Roman rule in their

For over a century Protestant Christians have preferred the simplicity of the Garden Tomb, north of the Old City of Jerusalem, to the ornate tradition of the Holy Sepulchre. Although much research has concluded that the Garden Tomb is not a first-century burial place, the peaceful gardens make it an attractive retreat for thought and prayer.

Second Revolt (132–35), the Emperor Hadrian rebuilt Jerusalem as a completely Roman city. It had a new name, Aelia Capitolina, and no Jews were allowed to enter it. In his new city Hadrian had a temple built for the goddess of love, Venus. That was the one which hid the tomb of Jesus. Hadrian's builders took a lot of trouble to lay a firm foundation. They carried tons of earth to make a level platform over very uneven ground, kept it in place with a huge wall, and set the temple itself on top.

Now, less than two centuries later, this was all being demolished in order to uncover the old tomb supposed to be below it. The Bishop of Caesarea at that time was Eusebius. He wrote a long history of the Christian church, which is his most important book, and some shorter works, among them a Life of Constantine. In that he tells how the tomb was found:

'The Emperor ordered that the stone and wood from the ruins (of the pagan temple) should be carried and dumped as far away as possible, and that a large amount of the foundation earth . . . should be dug away very deeply . . . The task was put in hand at once, and as the subsoil appeared layer by layer, so did the venerable and sacred evidence of the Saviour's resurrection, beyond all our hopes, brought back to life, like our Saviour.'

Constantine's masons chopped the rock away all round the tomb so that it stood free from the hillside. A shrine was put up to protect it, and eventually a ring of pillars and an outer wall supported a dome above it. Next to the shrine was a garden with porches at the sides, and beyond that a large church. At one side another rocky outcrop was trimmed, to be kept in the area as the site of Calvary. Enemy attacks, fires and earthquakes damaged these buildings on many occasions, more or less severely. The rock of the tomb was totally demolished by the mad Caliph Hakim in 1009. As a result, the Church of the Holy Sepulchre is a conglomerate of designs and styles from the fourth century onwards, the greatest part being the Crusaders' work. Pilgrims have prayed at the same place ever since Constantine's workmen discovered the buried tomb.

Is it really the tomb of Jesus?

Did Constantine's men find the right grave? Could the fourth-century Christians who told them where to dig be sure they would uncover the right tomb?

Until the reign of Constantine the Christians were an unpopular and often persecuted minority. Most of those who lived in Jerusalem when the first Jewish revolt broke out in AD 67 left the city. After the Second Revolt, Christians who did not have Jewish connections apparently could live there. In the new city plan the main street ran south from the present Damascus Gate. Hadrian placed the Forum or market-place to the west of the street and attached to it the temple of Venus. The position of the temple was probably just the most convenient one, rather than being chosen to obliterate a Christian holy place. Almost 200 years later, Christians were so certain the tomb was buried there that they persuaded the emperor to order, and pay for, the demolition and excavation needed to clear it. If they had not known a tomb was there, they would hardly have dared suggest the

work. What would the Emperor have said if his men had found no tomb? To be safe, the Christians could have pointed to one of the many other tombs outside the city.

Outside the city wall?

The Church of the Holy Sepulchre presents one glaring contradiction. Calvary, the hill where they crucified Jesus, was outside the city walls (see John 19:20), and so was the tomb, for Jewish law did not allow burials inside the city. Yet the Church of the Holy Sepulchre was built, and has always stood, well within the city walls.

The walls that surround Jerusalem today are not the walls of the New Testament period. They were erected between 1537 and 1540 at the command of the Turkish Sultan Suleiman the Magnificent. For a lot of their route they follow the line of older walls. The question that was open until recently concerned the line of the north wall. Supporters of the traditional site of Jesus' tomb, the Church of the Holy Sepulchre, have always argued that there was a change in the shape of the city after the crucifixion, so that the tomb was then included. Others have asserted that the present line of the north wall has not altered in that time, and so the tomb lay north of it.

Archaeological excavations in recent years have ended this debate. The British School of Archaeology in Jerusalem dug at the present-day Damascus Gate from 1964 to 1966. Over 7 metres/24 feet down, beneath old roads and ruined buildings, the excavators reached road surfaces of the first century. Very careful study was made of the different levels and the objects found in them.

Covering the natural rock was soil of farm fields, with a few burials in it. On that the first road was laid. In its plaster make-up was a coin of King Herod Agrippa I, made in AD 42–43. Before the road was put down, foundations had been laid for a magnificent new city wall and gate. As

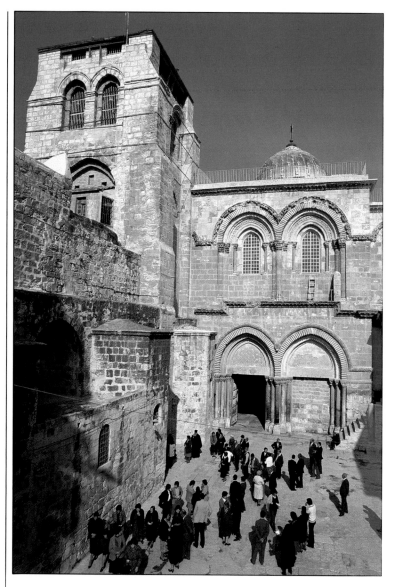

Ever since Constantine the Great built his church in the fourth century, Christian pilgrims have come to the Church of the Holy Sepulchre. Most of the building which stands today, including the entrance, was put up by the Crusaders in the twelfth century.

so he stopped when he had laid only the foundations. The coin found in the road surface agrees with the witness of Josephus.

If the north wall of Jerusalem was not on that line until Herod Agrippa's time (AD 41–44), where was it before? No one can give a definite answer. No traces of the wall which defended the north side of Jerusalem at the time of the crucifixion have been identified. Josephus indicates part of its route near the Temple. Excavations near the Church of the Holy Sepulchre have added to his information. What they add are clues, not direct evidence. Within the present city walls not many places are free for digging, so only small areas have been explored. One of them is in the market-place to the south of the church (the Muristan).

In 1963, Kathleen Kenyon sank a trench deep into the ground and eventually hit bedrock, 15 metres/ 49 feet below the modern street. She found that the rock had been cut and quarried in the days of the kings. Dumped into the quarry was soil containing pottery from the seventh century BC and the first century AD. A few years after that excavation more digging was done, beneath the Lutheran church nearby, finding the same things. Then repairs to the Church of the Holy Sepulchre made it possible to investigate under its floors. Again there were signs of quarrying, dated by pottery lying on the rock to the seventh century BC or earlier. Vergilius Corbo, the Italian expert in charge of this work, argued that part of the quarry was used as a garden in the first century BC.

Taken together, these discoveries imply that the area was outside the city as long as the quarries remained open (the north wall would have run south of them). Filling up the quarries with earth can be seen as the work of Hadrian's builders, preparing the site for the centre of his new city in 135.

Even so, someone might say that the quarry could have lain within the city walls, and so this could not be the

far as can be deduced from the existing stones, the building of the wall and gate at this point was never finished on its original design. Everything suggests this was part of the new north wall Herod Agrippa began to build. Josephus described this wall. It was planned on so huge a scale that, had it been finished, it would have been pointless for the Romans to lay siege to the city. But Agrippa had second thoughts. When he saw the size it would be, he was afraid the emperor would think he was plotting to revolt, place where Jesus was buried. But stronger evidence rules out any doubt. For years visitors who have known about it have taken candles or torches to go into the Tomb of Joseph of Arimathea. Opening off a chapel in the wall beyond the 'tomb of Jesus' is a dark cave. Although Constantine's builders cut away a lot of the rock, they left enough to show what had been there before.

Part of the rock bench and four of the short tunnels typical of first-century Jewish tombs prove that this was one of those burial places. Two other tombs of the same type are known to have existed quite close to this one, although they cannot now be seen. (One was found a century ago under the Coptic monastery; the other was turned into a water reservoir in the entrance court, but Professor Corbo has found clear traces of its original use.) Since burials had to be made outside the city, these tombs are clear proof that the city wall then stood further south. The rock walls of old quarries were ideal places for the masons to burrow the tombs.

Once again, an objector could argue that these tombs belong to the first century BC, before a city wall was built to enclose the area they occupy. That is possible, indeed it is true, although not in the sense that would

be needed. A wall was built to enclose the area, the wall of Herod Agrippa of AD 41 and after. No records or physical remains exist to indicate any city wall other than Agrippa's that followed a northerly line and was built within a hundred years of that time.

To be sure that any tomb in Jerusalem belonged to Joseph of Arimathea, and so was the tomb in which he laid Jesus' body, we would need a genuine first-century inscription giving his name. No one has found that. The names of the owners of the tombs were very seldom carved in them, so such a discovery is unlikely. With all the evidence available, the Church of the Holy Sepulchre has a very strong claim to stand on the site of Joseph's tomb. There is no way of knowing whether or not the place said to be that tomb is the right place. Perhaps Constantine's men did uncover signs or writing left by Christian visitors before Hadrian covered the cemetery with earth, or perhaps they uncovered several tombs and simply chose one as the most suitable, the easiest one to make into a shrine. Whatever it was they found, they made it into a centre which 1,650 years later still continues to attract pilgrims—pilgrims convinced that the tomb was empty on the first Easter Sunday morning.

HOW WAS HE CRUCIFIED?

An ossuary came to light in a tomb north of Jerusalem in 1968. Scratched on it is the name Yehohanan (John), followed by an unusual phrase. Among the bones in the box was a heel bone with an iron nail through it. After examining that and other bones a group of Jerusalem physicians concluded they belonged to a man who had been crucified. His arms, they said, had been nailed to the cross and his body twisted so that a single nail, driven through both feet, the right above the left, fixed him to the upright. This meant that there had to be a bar part way up the post which bore the victim's weight. A vicious blow had broken both legs.

Several years later an anthropologist and another physician examined the bones and reached different conclusions. The ossuary, they said, held the bones of three people, the crucified man, his son, and another. There was no sign of nailing the arms to the cross, nor of breaking the legs. The nail had been hammered through the heel bone from the side, so that the man's legs straddled the post, rather than one foot being on top of the other. A piece of wood was held against the heel before the nail was driven in, to act as a washer, so preventing the foot from tearing free.

Here is an example of how hard it is to interpret fragmentary remains. However, the more recent study does agree about the unusual nature of the phrase on the ossuary. It appears to describe Yehohanan as 'the one hanged with knees apart'. That suggests this was an unusual position. Written records tell how the criminal was usually stripped and laid on the ground with his arms spread out on the cross-bar. They were either tied or nailed to it, then the bar with the man hanging from it was lifted to be fastened to the vertical stake. After that, the feet were tied or nailed in place. Death came by suffocation, as the victim's chest muscles weakened.

Crucifixion was a death the Jews abhorred. In the Dead Sea Scrolls one author condemns an enemy because he 'hangs up men alive' (the Nahum commentary, see *A Monastery in the Desert*). Another scroll sets it down as the fate reserved for traitors. It horrified Greeks and Romans, too. They kept it as a punishment for slaves and any who challenged the ruling powers. It was as 'king' that Pilate sent Jesus to the cross.

DID HIS FATHER CARRY THE CROSS?

Jerusalem was a magnet for Jews from all over the world 2,000 years ago, as it is today. Pilgrims travelled long distances to attend the festivals, especially the Passover. The book of Acts gives a list of fifteen regions whose languages could be heard in Jerusalem just after the crucifixion (Acts 2:8–11). They ranged from Persia to Rome. Some of these pilgrims fell ill and died in Jerusalem; others, perhaps, came there to die.

A few of the tombs around Jerusalem give evidence that they contain the remains of such visitors. Stone ossuaries which held their bones are labelled not only with their names but also with their places of origin. One ossuary was inscribed in Greek for Judan, a convert or proselyte, from Tyre, another, also in Greek, for 'Maria, wife of Alexander, from Capua'. An unusual memorial cut on the rock wall of one tomb tells how a pious man brought another from Babylon and bought the grave for him at Jerusalem. These finds illustrate the reality behind the list in Acts 2.

In 1941 a tomb was opened in the Kidron Valley which held eleven ossuaries. Nine of them have inscriptions. Although one of the names is Simon, which is among the commonest found on the ossuaries, most of the names were rare ones, e.g. Philiskos, Thaliarchos. Such names were popular among Jews who lived in North Africa, rather than in Palestine. They are found in the inscriptions of Jewish colonies in Egypt and Libya. In fact, the tomb was a burial place for Jewish people from Cyrenaica. Their presence in Jerusalem is mentioned both in Acts 2:10 and in Acts 6:9. One ossuary was marked explicitly in Aramaic 'Alexander of Cyrene'. On the same ossuary is a notice in Greek, giving his father's name—'Alexander, son of Simon'.

Now Mark's Gospel includes a detail in its narrative of the crucifixion which Matthew and Luke do not give. All three tell how Simon of Cyrene was forced to carry the cross for Jesus (Matthew 27:32; Luke 23:26). Mark adds that Simon was 'the father of Alexander and Rufus' (Mark 15:21). Was the Alexander of Cyrene, son of Simon, whose bones lay in that ossuary, the man whose father carried the cross? It may, of course, be a coincidence, yet the identification does seem very likely.

Roughly scratched on an ossuary from the Kidron Valley is the name 'Alexander, son of Simon', in Greek (above). More neatly engraved on the lid is 'Alexander', in Greek, and 'Alexander of Cyrene', in Hebrew (below).

DO NOT DISTURB THE DEAD

'Caesar's order' were the words at the top of the stone. There it was, a marble slab standing in a Paris museum. The words caught the eye of a famous scholar looking over the antiquities. 'Caesar's order' had to be important. What did it say? He read on:

'It is my will that graves and tombs lie undisturbed for ever . . . Respect for those who are buried is most important; no one should disturb them in any way at all. If anyone does, I require that he be executed for tomb-robbery.'

Somewhere people had been opening tombs and moving the bones, and the matter had become serious enough to have the emperor's attention. Where had the stone come from? Which Caesar made the order?

In 1930, when Michael Rostovtzeff, a famous historian, saw the stone and realized it was important, it was on show in the national library in Paris (Bibliothèque Nationale). It had been sent there in 1925 with other objects from a private collection. The original owner had not let people study his treasures, and he left only a short note about this stone. But it does tell us one important thing. It says, 'Marble slab sent from Nazareth in 1878', indicating that it was found somewhere not very far from Nazareth. Otherwise it might have been thought to have come from Turkey, where large numbers of Greek inscriptions are found.

An imperial decree from northern Palestine forbidding grave robbery may not seem very noteworthy. But when the writing itself is put beside other Greek inscriptions something more appears. The shapes of the letters point to a first-century date for the engraving.

Does the inscription refer to the resurrection of Jesus? Some scholars have argued that it does. They suppose that the Emperor Claudius (AD 41–54) tried to put a stop to the Christians' preaching by making this harsh decree. If the Jewish claim that 'his disciples came during the night and stole him away' (Matthew 28:13) was right, the followers of Jesus could be punished for tomb-robbery!

Another proposal brings the Nazareth Decree even closer to the time of Jesus' death. Pilate wrote to the Emperor Tiberius, some suggest, to ask how he should deal with the Christian claim about Jesus' empty tomb. Part of the reply was set up at Nazareth, known to be Jesus' home. In either case, the inscription would be the earliest monument relating to the central point of the Christian faith. It would be evidence of the effect which the preaching of the resurrection had on the Roman administration.

Ideas like these are so attractive that they easily lead to the neglect of some awkward facts. No one knows exactly where the stone was found. Nazareth may be the place, but the finder could have carried it there from somewhere else, a few days' donkey journey away, wanting to sell it to Christian pilgrims. Since the nature of the connection with Nazareth is uncertain, no argument linking the stone with the early Christians can rely on it. Unless the stone was set up in Judea and moved northwards later, Pontius Pilate cannot have had it

The Nazareth Decree, a stone slab 60 cm/2 feet high, 37.5 cm/15 ins wide, now in the Bibliothèque Nationale, Paris. It carries a decree of Caesar, translated from Latin into Greek, ordering that tomb-robbers be put to death.

made, because Galilee was in the kingdom of Herod Antipas, where Pilate had no power (see Luke 23:6,7). Indeed, even a decree of Caesar would hardly be displayed in Galilee until after Antipas' reign ended in AD 44. That means it is possible that Claudius made the decree.

Robbing tombs has been a fact of life ever since people began to bury valuable things with the dead. In Babylonia the 'Royal Tombs' of Ur (about 2500 BC), and in Egypt the empty Pyramids and the Valley of the Kings, bear witness to the robbers' activities. All sorts of ways were tried to stop this crime. Often curses were written on the tomb to frighten intruders with the fear of the gods. Greek and Roman law ruled against anyone disturbing burials, and it was impious for the Jews. An emperor's decree could be even more effective if his soldiers were in the area to enforce it.

From the Nazareth Decree we learn about the existence of tomb-robbery on such a scale, or in so sensational a way, that it needed the emperor's attention. The stone illustrates how seriously the Roman government viewed the crime, and how severe its punishment might be. Taking into account only the facts— the erection of this decree somewhere in the Galilee region, which includes the Greek cities to the east, in the first century—we cannot find any reason to link the inscription with the teaching of the resurrection. Even so, it does underline the unlikely nature of the charge that the disciples had removed Jesus' body, disheartened as they were by his death. It also underlines the failure of both the Jewish and the Roman officials to take the action which would be expected if the disciples were accused of a crime that could carry the death penalty.

THE TOMB A PILGRIM SAW

No one can be sure that the Church of the Holy Sepulchre was built over the tomb where Jesus was buried. Today it is impossible to see the tomb the fourth-century Christians identified, because Caliph Hakim's men smashed it with hammers and picks in 1009. Among pilgrims who saw it before then was a man called Arculf, who travelled from France to the Holy Land in about 680. He reported that inside the tomb there was 'a single shelf stretching from head to foot without division, which would take one person lying on his back. It is like a cave with its opening facing the south part of the tomb, and is made with a low roof over it.'

Arculf's description fits very well a first-century tomb of the richer type, with an arched recess for a body or coffin (an *arcosolium*). The tomb of a rich man like Joseph of Arimathea might have had such a recess. Once more, the verdict on the Holy Sepulchre has to be 'possible, but not certain'.

In some grand tombs of the first century around Jerusalem the body was laid in an arched recess, an arcosolium. Rarely the floor of the recess was hollowed to form a coffin.

THE MYSTERY OF THE TURIN SHROUD

Thousands of pilgrims have gone to Turin in Italy every year to pray in the cathedral. They have gone there because they believe the shroud in which Jesus was buried is kept there. Now a scientific test has shown, almost beyond doubt, that it cannot be the shroud of Jesus. It is only 700 years old. In spite of this, the shroud deserves a place in this book, to demonstrate some of the difficulties scientists face when they study things made long ago.

In 1898 an Italian photographer was allowed a special privilege: he was to take the first photograph of the Shroud of Turin. This is a piece of yellowish linen 4.34 metres/14 feet 3 ins long and 1.09 metres/3 feet 7 ins wide. On the cloth are shadowy marks which look like the front and back of a man. When the photographer developed his plate, he was amazed to find it had a much more detailed picture than he could see with his own eyes. It was as if the cloth were a negative from which he had made a print. More photographs taken later proved this was not a freak. In fact, every photograph develops in the same way.

What is the Turin Shroud?

The history of the shroud is known from the 1350s. A French knight living near Troyes owned it then, and 100 years later his granddaughter gave it to the Duke of Savoy. A fire in the church at Chambéry, where it was kept, damaged it in 1532. Finally, the Duke of Savoy moved it to Turin in 1578, where it is housed in the Cathedral of St John the Baptist. There is nothing certain about the earlier history. Some think it had none. When the shroud was first exhibited in Troyes, the local bishop denounced it as a fraud. He knew the artist who said he had made it. A few others said the same, but they were ignored.

On the other hand, there are reports of a shroud of Jesus in Constantinople which disappeared when the Crusaders looted the city in 1203. The shroud that came to Troyes might be that one. Six hundred years earlier a cloth marked with a face was taken to be the likeness of Jesus. This relic lay in the city of Edessa, now Urfa, not far from ancient Haran in southern Turkey. A legend said that one of Jesus' disciples took it there soon after the crucifixion. Was the cloth at Edessa the same as the Shroud of Turin, folded up? No one could be sure, because there were too many gaps in the story.

For several years scientists asked for a piece of the shroud to submit to the radio-carbon dating test. (All living things contain the radioactive substances Carbon 12 and Carbon 14. When they die Carbon 14 decays at a regular rate, giving out measurable particles. The particles emitted are counted, and the amount of decay which has taken place can be calculated by comparison with the stable amount of carbon 12. Then the date when the material died can be worked out.) The sample needed would be several centimetres/inches square. The custodians of the shroud feared that cutting so large a piece would cause too much damage, and so

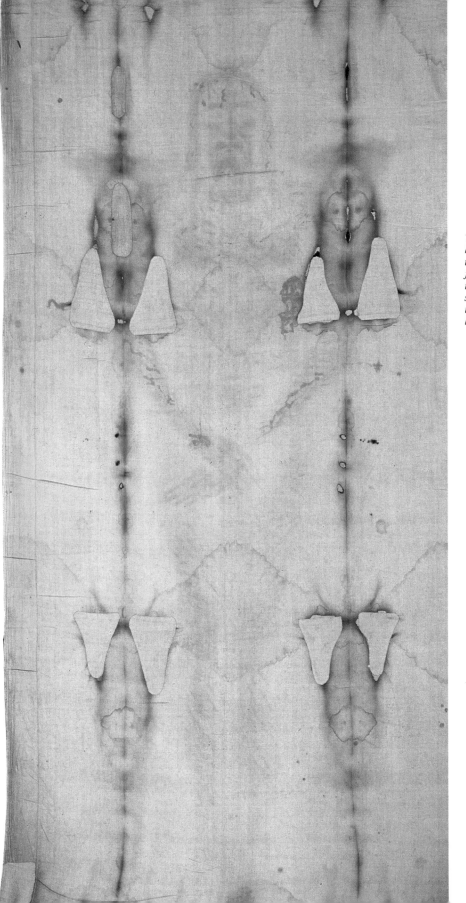

The body was laid on the lower half of the Shroud, then the upper part (shown here) was folded over the face and down to the feet. The apparent bloodstains can be seen clearly in this photograph as faint redbrown stains.

they refused permission.

When technical progress made the tests possible with much smaller samples, the authorities agreed to send tiny pieces of the shroud for examination. Samples went to three centres, in Arizona, Oxford and Zurich. With each fragment were bits of other cloths known to belong to the first century and to the Middle Ages. These were 'controls', to be tested at

When the Turin Shroud is photographed, it produces a startling image like a negative.

the same time and in the same conditions as each of the shroud samples. All of the pieces were sent to the laboratories without labels to tell the scientists which was which. Only when their tests were done could the co-ordinator reveal which pieces came from the shroud.

He made his announcement in October 1988. The results were clear, all three centres agreed. Each fragment of the shroud gave the same answer: the cloth was made from flax cut between AD 1260 and 1390. A first-century date was ruled out. This was a bitter blow for devotees of the shroud.

Could they hope the dating was wrong? There seem to be no reasons for such a hope. The dating method has been developed and improved in separate laboratories, reducing points of uncertainty. With once-living matter less than 2,000 years old there is very little room for doubt or error. The laboratories agreed on the dates of the control pieces.

Even though the Carbon 14 dates show that the Turin Shroud is not a relic from the first century, it is still a remarkable object, worthy of study.

Believing is always easier if there are things to see and touch. 'Doubting Thomas' explained this clearly, when his friends said they had seen Jesus risen from the dead. 'Unless I see the nail marks in his hands and put my finger where the nails were, and put my hand into his side, I will not believe it' he said (John 20:25). Not surprisingly, as Christianity spread, people began to produce relics of martyrs to help the devotion of worshippers. The first example may be the careful burial of the bones of the elderly martyr Polycarp in Smyrna, in the middle of the second century. The Christians would meet at the place to remember him.

The same need for a visible, physical link with heroes of the past exists in non-religious contexts, too. Businesses flourish by taking tourists to see Shakespeare's birthplace, or Napoleon's tomb, or George Washington's farmhouse. Figures of history become more real when they can be related to a place or an object they used.

Relics were almost 'produced to order' in the Middle Ages, with embarrassing results. So many churches claimed to own fragments of the cross of Jesus that it was said there was enough wood in them to build a galleon! Among the relics were more than forty said to be the shroud in which Jesus was buried.

What makes the Turin Shroud a special case?

Reddish stains scattered over the

image of the body fit the descriptions of the wounds Jesus suffered. Small marks all over the back fit the record of the scourging. For some Christians this was enough. The figure on the shroud, which the photographs show distinctly, is a man who has been crucified as Jesus was, so this must be his shroud.

Not everyone found the case strong enough on this evidence alone, and the marks on the cloth need to be explained, so various tests have been made, especially since 1978. Their aim was to find out as much as possible about the shroud. They produced some more mysteries.

Were the reddish marks bloodstains, or not? One scientist claimed they were paint, others declared they came from an organic substance, which some concluded was blood. When the back of the shroud was studied, these stains were seen to have soaked through the fabric—whereas the image of the body is on the upper surface only.

If these are bloodstains, how did they come to be on the shroud? Blood clots quickly and the flogging and crowning with thorns took place before the crucifixion. Forensic scientists and pathologists, experienced with criminal and accident victims, answered this question with two points. One is the large quantity of perspiration which pours from a person hung by the wrists. This would leave the wounds moist. The other is John's report of Nicodemus bringing a heavy load of myrrh and aloes, which he put on the body of Jesus (see John 19:39,40). Oily or greasy ointments slow down the clotting process.

Even so, the fact that the marks are so clear is almost too good to be true! When the body was taken down from the cross and carried to the nearby tomb, rubbing and movement could be expected to spread the stains much more, especially if the body was carried in the shroud. Another question not finally answered is why the stains have not turned dark brown,

as old bloodstains usually do.

Other tests made on the cloth have brought further claims. Among pollen grains caught in the fabric were some typical of the eastern Mediterranean area, and even the Dead Sea region, a Swiss scientist reported. Yet one of the pollens common there, that of the olive tree, is missing. Mineral particles in the fibres include limestone similar to Jerusalem stone, and the reaction of the hot, crucified body with the alkaline stone might produce the yellowish figure on the Shroud, according to an American crystallographer and an archaeologist. When an Image Analyzer was applied to the photograph of the Shroud, it produced three-dimensional pictures of the body, a result which a painting could not give.

The photograph of the face magnified five times revealed a round mark on each eye. One researcher says he sees part of the imprint made by a coin of Pontius Pilate, placed on the right eye. The coin is the 'crook' type described in *Clues to Pilate's Character*. Yet placing a coin on a corpse's eyes was not customary in first-century Judea, and the reproductions of the imprint are not at all convincing to the writer.

With all these points in mind, we have to ask, 'Would the Turin Shroud be anything like the cloth which Joseph of Arimathea took to wrap the body of Jesus?' To the Gospel-writers, the only interesting thing about the grave-clothes was their position in the empty tomb, where they were evidence that Jesus was not there. In the circumstances of the first Easter we may doubt whether any of Jesus' friends would have gone back to tidy the tomb, or if Joseph would have sent a servant to do it. To keep used grave-clothes would be contrary to normal Jewish habit, because they were 'unclean'.

The Gospels are not precise in describing the burial. Matthew, Mark and Luke all report Joseph bringing a piece of linen. John says he brought pieces of linen, and when Peter looked into the tomb on the Sunday he saw them 'as well as the burial cloth that had been around Jesus' head' (John 20:6,7). What John describes agrees with knowledge of the Jewish burial routine, and Lazarus was treated in the same way (John 11:44).

The body was dressed, the hands and feet tied so that they would stay in place, and the head bound with a bandage under the chin to stop the jaw sagging. But the crucified Jesus had no clothes (the soldiers took them), so Joseph's cloth could be a substitute, a shroud. John's pieces of linen might include it; they were not necessarily 'strips of linen' as the New International Version translates. If this is a correct reconstruction, signs of the bandages around the hands, feet and head ought to appear on the Turin Shroud.

They do not. If the shroud had been tied down there would be clear crease marks, which there are not. It did not fall closely over the sides of the body, and this agrees with the temporary nature of Joseph's and Nicodemus' attentions, for they expected the final burial to be made after the Passover. Then the body would have been more securely wrapped.

Who could have created so convincing a relic in the Middle Ages, and how? Future inquiries may find the answers. Perhaps the best suggestion is that a Crusader brought back this length of linen from his travels. It was a shroud which had been used to wrap the body of a badly wounded man. This suggestion fits the evidence well, even if the cause of the marks is not properly understood. Modern knowledge is far from explaining many curiosities of this world, and the Turin Shroud remains one of them.

The Roman Catholic Church never claimed officially that the Turin Shroud was the burial cloth of Jesus. Like all other relics, it should be an aid to faith, not an object of faith. The announcement that the shroud is not 2,000 years old may disappoint some Christians, but they should not allow it to shake their faith. Rather, it should help them to concentrate on the Person whose shroud it was supposed to be.

PART FIVE

WRITERS

When did that happen, and why? What sort of a man was he?
History-writing tries to report and explain the past. It is not a modern
invention. In the first century Flavius Josephus wrote books to set out
the reasons for the Jewish revolt against Rome, and to tell his Roman
friends about his nation's beliefs and past. His books, with the books
of other Jewish, Greek and Roman authors who lived in the first and
second centuries, allow us to weave the historical back-cloth to the
Gospels. They fill out the careers of the kings and rulers they name,
reflecting the opinions of intelligent observers. They clarify some
points which the first readers of the Gospels understood, but modern
readers do not. The following pages offer brief biographies of the two
most important men, describing the value of their works. They also
explain the writings of other authors mentioned in this book. The
section ends with an outline of the sources for early rabbinic traditions.

*Roman ladies liked to be portrayed as writers. This one, from Pompeii,
is thinking carefully before she writes on her wooden tablets.*

PHILO—A PHILOSOPHER OF ALEXANDRIA

Ships approaching the harbour of Alexandria were guided by the lighthouse, the Pharos. A coin of the Emperor Commodus struck in 188–89 records its appearance. One of the Seven Wonders of the Ancient World.

Alexander the Great marched from Macedonia in northern Greece in 334 BC. In 332 he conquered Egypt and the next year made himself master of the Persian Empire. Across this great stretch of land he founded Greek cities. He hoped to spread the Greek way of life and thought over as much of the world as possible, so he settled his soldiers in the new cities. Several of them were named after him—Alexandria. The one that grew into the greatest and most famous is still a major city in Egypt. Alexander himself founded that one in 331 BC, on a neck of land between a lake and the sea. It was an ideal place for a harbour and later developed into the major port for shipping grain to Rome.

Alexander died in 323 BC. His generals took charge of the empire on behalf of his son Alexander, who was born after his father's death. The boy was killed before he grew up, and three of the generals divided the empire among themselves. Seleucus set himself up as king of Syria and Babylonia in 312 BC, then Ptolemy made himself king of Egypt in 305. He took Alexandria as his capital. Ptolemy's dynasty ruled until Octavian, later Augustus, conquered Mark Antony and his mistress Cleopatra with her son, the fifteenth Ptolemy, in 30 BC. Egypt then became a province of the Roman Empire, with the governor's palace in Alexandria.

Alexandria was a Greek city. Many citizens had Greek ancestors. They spoke and wrote Greek, they watched Greek plays in the theatres, they took part in Greek sports, and they wor-shipped Greek gods and goddesses. Alexandria quickly became the greatest centre of Greek culture outside Athens. In its library were half a million books, all written on papyrus rolls. The librarians tried to collect a copy of every book in existence. There was a research centre, too, the Museum, where scholars from all over the world lived and studied at the king's expense.

Beside the Greeks in Alexandria there were native Egyptians. They learnt Greek ways, and began to write their own language (Coptic) with the letters of the Greek alphabet instead of the complicated Egyptian hieroglyphs. The city also held the largest number of Jewish residents outside Palestine. They occupied most of two of the five sectors of the city. Living in a mostly Greek society, these Jews spoke Greek and lived more and more in the Greek way, although they kept the main rules and festivals of their own religion. As time passed, fewer and fewer of them learnt Hebrew so, when the lessons were read in the synagogue from the Hebrew Bible, they could not under-stand them. Jewish scholars began to translate the Law, the Five Books of Moses, into Greek before 250 BC, and gradually did all the other Old Testament books, producing the translation called the Septuagint.

Having their Bible in Greek no doubt helped many to keep to their religion, but the tension between Jewish traditions and Greek culture was too much for some to bear. They took up the Greek way of life, abandoning their religious practices and becoming just like their neighbours. When the Romans took control of Egypt, they allowed the Jews in Alexandria to live as a recognized community, permitting them to keep to their peculiar customs. They were not allowed, it seems, to hold the same rights as Greek or Roman citizens unless they gave up their Jewish status. There were some who did that. One who belonged to a very wealthy family actually became the Roman governor of Palestine from AD 46 to 48, and later prefect of Egypt (AD 66–69). He was Tiberius Julius Alexander, whose father gave doors decorated with gold and silver to beautify Herod's Temple.

His conduct upset the Jews who were trying to keep the faith taught in the Law of Moses. In particular it upset his uncle Philo. Philo, who lived from about 20 BC to AD 45, was a leader in the Jewish section of Alexandria, and a philosopher. His special concern was to explain the Jewish religion and way of life in ways that educated Greeks could understand. By picking ideas from Greek philosophers and knitting them to Jewish traditions he made a bridge between two very different ways of thinking about God and the world. Philo's books were partly intended to help Jews who found Greek thought attractive to reconcile it with their inherited faith, rather than abandoning it. He may have sent some of his books to his nephew, hoping to change his mind.

Philo's sixteen religious and philosophical books are valuable because they are the only Jewish writings of this sort to survive from the Gospel period. They present a way of thought that is different from the style of the rabbis, and show some of the ideas early Christians faced as they preached about Jesus to Greek-speaking Jews.

In Philo's books there are expressions which also occur in the New Testament. One is 'the Word' (*logos*), the power who links God and man. Although Philo's thinking is at

first sight like the beginning of John's Gospel, careful reading makes it plain that they are not the same. Philo's 'Word' was the image of God and the ideal human mind, yet he also identified the Word with the whole intelligible universe. The body, Philo thought, was wicked and an obstacle to knowing God. John, on the contrary, could say 'The Word became flesh and made his dwelling among us,' not as

an idea or an influence, but as the personal Son of God (see John 1:14,17,18). The New Testament Letter to the Hebrews uses language and forms of thought which have more in common with Philo, yet with them the Christian author set out a message about God's revelation which is very different from Philo's.

Philosophers like peace for thinking and writing. Philo's peace was shattered near the end of his life. It was the year 38. Flaccus had been governing Egypt for five years. The Emperor Tiberius, who had appointed

Jews living in Alexandria could not understand Hebrew well, so they had the books of the Hebrew Bible translated into Greek. These fragments are part of the oldest surviving copy of Deuteronomy found in Egypt, a scroll made about 100 BC. In the Greek text the sacred name of God (traditionally written Jehovah in the European languages) stands in Hebrew letters (e.g. line 6). It was too holy to read, so the word 'lord' was spoken instead.

The philosopher Philo was a leader of the Jewish section in Alexandria, the famous Egyptian city named after Alexander the Great. Its position on a neck of land between lake and sea made it the ideal harbour it remains today.

him, died in 37, and Flaccus felt at risk. Gaius Caligula, the new emperor, quickly executed the key figures of Tiberius' court, leaving Flaccus without a powerful friend in Rome. Worse, a Greek, whose political manoeuvres in Alexandria Flaccus had upset, won Caligula's favour. The Greek and his supporters came back to the city and offered to help Flaccus avoid the emperor's displeasure. They had a price for their aid: Flaccus was to let the Greeks of Alexandria have the upper hand over the Jews there.

Apparently the Jews wanted the advantages of Greek citizenship (one being to pay less tax), without accepting some of the responsibilities which ran against their religious beliefs. The Greeks evidently felt the Jews had enough privileges already.

Flaccus was afraid to refuse. Like Pontius Pilate, he needed to be 'Caesar's friend'. So when the Greek mob, annoyed that the Jewish King Herod Agrippa had paraded through the city, started attacking synagogues, Flaccus did nothing. In fact, he ordered the Jews to live in one section of Alexandria only, the first ghetto. His attitude encouraged the anti-Jewish crowd in their attacks, and many Jews were killed and synagogues burnt.

Suddenly everything changed. In the autumn of 38 a troop of soldiers sailed in from Rome to arrest Flaccus. He was taken aback to find that those accusing him to the emperor were the very people whose help he thought he had bought at the cost of the Jews. He was sent into exile, then executed. Philo and his friends praised God for acting to save them!

Philo's book *Against Flaccus* tells the tale. It reveals the problems Jews faced in pagan society, problems similar in some cases to those the early Christians met. It also illustrates how a pressure group could force a Roman governor to act against his better judgment, in the same way as the priests in Jerusalem did at the trial of Jesus (John 19:12–16).

Philo wrote another 'political' book, *The Mission to Gaius*, explaining how he led a party of five elders from Alexandria to put the Jewish case to the emperor, countering the claims of the Greeks. Gaius met them early in AD 40, and gave no reply. During the summer he made a decree that a statue of himself dressed as the god Zeus should be set up in the Temple in Jerusalem. The governor of Syria, Petronius, sensibly delayed obeying because he realized the trouble that would follow. Then a close friend of Gaius, the Jewish King Herod Agrippa, found out about the order and wrote a letter to him which persuaded him to withdraw it.

Philo declares that the emperor still planned to have the statue put in place in Jerusalem when he visited the east himself—a visit he never made. Later in the year Gaius heard the two parties from Alexandria again, and again failed to resolve the problem. He was stabbed to death on 24 January 41. His uncle Claudius was made emperor and quickly gave the Jews back their previous position in the city. At the same time he told them not to try to get rights which were not theirs. (Claudius' letter to Alexandria, preserved on a papyrus found in Egypt, gives this information.) *The Mission to Gaius* has lost its ending. Comparing it with *Against Flaccus* leads scholars to suggest the last part described Gaius' death, explaining it as an act of God on behalf of the Jewish people.

This book of Philo's contrasts Gaius' behaviour to the Jews with the considerate ways of Augustus and Tiberius. It preserves the letter Herod Agrippa wrote to change Gaius' mind —or Philo's version of it. In that he drew the emperor's attention to Tiberius' reaction when Pontius Pilate brought the gilded shields into Jerusalem contrary to custom (see *Certainly not a Saint!*). Although he lived in Alexandria, Philo heard of events in Judea, and the reports he gives about a few of them are valuable additions to the information preserved by Josephus and the New Testament.

Philo's books were never best-sellers—few philosophers' books are —yet they were not forgotten. As Christianity spread, the question of how to explain Greek ideas in Christian terms became important and Philo's efforts to do the same from a Jewish point of view influenced some of the Christian thinkers, including St Augustine. So it was Christian scribes who continued to copy and preserve Philo's works. Translators made versions of some of them in Latin and Armenian.

JOSEPHUS THE JEW— PATRIOT OR TRAITOR?

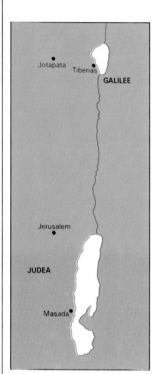

They were just a handful of patriots, facing a well-organized war-machine. What was the point of fighting so strong an army? Why not surrender and save as much as possible? These were the thoughts of the thirty-year-old Jewish commander, Joseph. It was AD 67. He was in charge of the resistance to Rome in Galilee, holding out in the town of Jotapata. He had to keep his thoughts to himself and spur his men on.

After forty-seven days under siege, the town fell. Joseph and forty men hid in a cave. There they made a pact with each other not to be taken alive; they would kill each other. Joseph managed to be one of the last two left. He persuaded the other man that they should not die, then gave himself up to the Romans. Instead of executing the rebel leader who had caused him such trouble, the Roman General Vespasian put him under close guard.

Joseph was a very shrewd and persuasive man. In a private conversation with Vespasian he forecast that he would be made emperor of Rome. When Vespasian's troops did proclaim him emperor, in the summer of 69, he released Joseph from captivity. The new emperor went to Rome to secure control, leaving his son Titus to carry on the war in Judea, with Joseph as one of his consultants. Naturally, the Jews were eager to lay hands on the man they saw as a traitor, and some of the Romans did not trust him, although Titus did. Joseph had to watch, as the Roman soldiers broke into Jerusalem and fought through the Temple courts and sacred buildings.

When they had overrun the whole city, they herded the thousands of prisoners into the Temple courtyard and Joseph was allowed to find his friends among them and set them free. When the revolt was all over, with only the rock-fortress of Masada in Jewish hands, Titus took Joseph to Rome.

In Rome he was lodged in the house the emperor had previously occupied. Vespasian gave him property near the coast of Judea and a pension, and, most valuable of all, the privilege of Roman citizenship. Joseph followed the custom of those who were made Roman citizens in this way and gave his name a Latin form, adding to it the family name of the emperor, so becoming Flavius Josephus. He spent the rest of his life in Rome, dying there about the end of the century.

Unable to return to Palestine, where he had many enemies, Josephus spent his years in Rome writing books. These were copied and published and became particularly useful to Christian writers, because they give the history of the Gospel period in detail. They are still the most important sources of information about Palestine in the first century BC and up to AD 70.

Josephus set out, first, to give an accurate account of the Jewish war against Rome. Others had written about it, he said, at second-hand and unreliably. He would tell the true story. He issued the book in his own language, Aramaic, for Jewish readers in the east. Afterwards he had it translated into Greek, and it is that version which can be read today.

Josephus' *Jewish War* is the most

extensive account of Roman warfare in the first century, so Roman historians prize it. The eye-witness reports of different stages in the war, and of the events leading up to it, make quite lively reading. Josephus relied on his own memory, perhaps his own notes, and claimed he had drawn on the reports Vespasian and Titus placed in the official archives of Rome. He submitted his book to Titus and to the Jewish king, Herod Agrippa II, who both approved it.

Naturally Josephus wrote from his own point of view. He thought the war could have been avoided and so painted the leaders of the Jewish rebels as black as he could. He did not hide his own role, for he apparently believed it was justified by the events. There are some statements and figures which are hard to accept, but most of the book is considered by all scholars as a first-class historical source.

A much bigger book followed the *Jewish War*, for Josephus felt the Roman world was badly informed about his people and their long history. He followed the biblical line from Adam to Moses, through the kings to the Exile, and on to the days of the Jewish kings, Herod, his sons and the war.

The *Jewish Antiquities*, like the *Jewish War*, is especially valuable for the later part of ancient Jewish history. Almost half the book relates events from the times of the Maccabees to the start of the Jewish War. It provides us with a lot of knowledge about the Gospel period. Some of Josephus' descriptions of Herod's buildings and other monuments have proved to be remarkably accurate when archaeologists have excavated their remains. Putting the ancient book and the physical evidence side by side brings a richer picture than either can give alone.

This long work—60,000 lines of writing in Greek, the author stated—was finished in 93 or 94. Josephus dedicated it to a man called Epaphroditus. He may have asked for the book, or stimulated the author to write it, rather as Theophilus (whose name is recorded at the start of Luke's Gospel) may have done for Luke.

Two other books which Josephus wrote survive, both defending him against his enemies. One is his *Life*. In it he concentrates on rebutting an historian from Tiberias, whose own book accused Josephus of stirring up the anti-Roman revolt in Galilee. If people accepted that view, Josephus' favoured position in Rome would be at risk. At the beginning he sets out a summary of his early life. As a young teenager, he boasts, he was so well-

The Roman Emperor Vespasian (AD 69–79) accepted Josephus' surrender and rewarded him for his help in the Jewish War with a house in Rome.

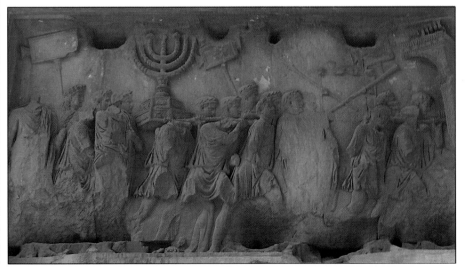

After the fall of Jerusalem, Titus brought back his prisoners and booty to Rome. His triumph was commemorated in the Arch of Titus near the Colosseum. On one wall the carving shows Roman soldiers carrying the table, trumpets and golden lampstand from the Temple.

versed in the Jewish laws that the priests asked his advice. A little later he studied the various parties of Judaism to see which he thought best, and went off to spend three years in the desert with a hermit. When he went back to Jerusalem, he joined the moderate party, the Pharisees.

In 64 Josephus paid a visit to Rome. The governor Felix had sent some priests for trial before Caesar, and Josephus wanted to arrange their release. After escaping from a shipwreck, he reached Rome in the company of a Jewish actor. This man was a favourite at court, so he introduced Josephus to Poppaea, Nero's wife. She agreed to Josephus' request.

The strength and power of the Roman Empire, and its efficiency deeply impressed Josephus, convincing him that to fight against it would be foolish. Even so, events took such a turn back home that, soon after his return to Palestine, he found himself doing just that. Most of the *Life* explains what he actually did, and why.

The fourth book is called *Against Apio*. It is a reply to a piece of anti-Jewish propaganda. Jewish religion and the Jewish race were very old, Josephus declared, and gave proof of this by quoting ancient authors from Egypt, Phoenicia, Babylonia, and even Greece. (Often their writings have

disappeared since Josephus' time, so he has preserved the only traces of them.) Further, Josephus argued, the Jewish belief in one moral God who gave just laws for mankind was far better than Greek belief in many gods who behaved disgracefully.

Josephus published his books in Rome, where scribes copied them so that they were widely available. All those copies have disappeared. One third-century papyrus containing a few paragraphs of the *War* has been found in Egypt. In the fourth century Eusebius drew heavily on Josephus' writings for historical details in writing his history of the early church. Ever since, scholars have valued these books for the same reasons.

Scribes continued to copy them throughout the Middle Ages, and some translated them into Latin. A Latin version of five sections of the *Antiquities* is preserved in a papyrus book copied in the seventh century. The oldest Greek manuscripts available, apart from the papyrus, are from the ninth or tenth centuries. They show that the earlier copyists had made a number of mistakes which were passed on uncorrected, and part of *Against Apio* survived only in Latin. The popularity of Josephus' works is clear from the fact that at least six editions of parts of them in Latin were printed between the invention of printing, in 1453, and 1500.

ROMAN WRITERS

As the second century AD began, two Roman authors were at work, composing histories of the previous hundred years. Their books are the chief sources of information about the reigns of the first Roman emperors. Tacitus' *Annals* dealt with the years from Tiberius' accession to the death of Nero (AD 14 to 68). There were eighteen books, but numbers 7–10 and 17 and 18 have disappeared. The oldest manuscript of books 1–6 now available was copied in Germany about 850. Tacitus was a very careful historian, concentrating on the emperors and their policies, which he did not like. As far as the Gospels are concerned, he makes only one direct

In this painting from Pompeii the man holds a papyrus scroll; his wife has hinged writing-tablets and a metal stylus. Painted before AD 79.

reference, commenting that the Christians persecuted by Nero began with Christ 'who had been executed in the reign of Tiberius by the governor of Judea, Pontius Pilatus'.

The Lives of the Caesars by Suetonius is rather different. His book presents biographies of the emperors, from Augustus to Domitian (43 BC−AD 96). Suetonius enjoyed scandal and gossip, yet he was able to include details from the official records of the Caesars because he was secretary to the Emperor Hadrian. Thus his writing has special value. The oldest surviving copy was made in the ninth century.

A century after Suetonius, Cassius Dio put together a long history of Rome from its foundation to AD 229. Two-thirds of his books are lost. A summary, and extracts other writers made, preserve pieces of his work, sometimes recording events other historians omitted.

One historian has left a first-hand account of Tiberius' reign. Velleius Paterculus was a soldier who had fought as an officer in the future emperor's army. Unhappily, he favoured Tiberius wholeheartedly, so that his account is seriously unbalanced. A single copy of his work, made about AD 800, was available in the sixteenth century, but was later destroyed.

Apart from the historians, a lot can be learnt about the Roman world from the *Geography* written in Greek by Strabo during the rule of Augustus. Pliny the Elder, who died observing the eruption of Vesuvius at Pompeii in AD 79, wrote works which filled over sixty books. Only thirty-seven survive, the highly valuable *Natural History*, a sort of encyclopedia of Roman knowledge.

Various other authors, poets, playwrights and philosophers have left writings in Greek or Latin which help to build a rich picture of life in the Roman Empire at the time of the Gospels.

The greatest ancient library was at Alexandria, but a hostile king forced many scholars to flee to other cities in 145 BC. They created new libraries and academies, including one at Ephesus. In AD 135 a man from Sardis built a new library there in honour of his father Celsus. Behind the façade, now partly rebuilt, was a reading room 16.76 metres/ 55 feet wide.

JEWISH WRITINGS

Someone hoping to learn about the period of the Gospels might turn to Jewish writings first. After all, Jesus was a Jew and lived in Palestine. There are large volumes of the rabbis' teachings in Hebrew and Aramaic: the Mishnah, the Talmuds, the Targums, and the Midrash. Sadly, all these books were made long after the fall of Jerusalem in AD 70. They tell stories about events before the calamity, and report teachings of the rabbis in those days, but each of these texts has to be thoroughly assessed.

The rabbis' recollections were coloured by history, and later teachers tended to combine their opinions with the views of their forebears. However, with careful sifting, these writings can supply pieces of information about early first-century life and thought. Even so, the rabbis who taught after AD 70 were almost wholly from the moderate wing of the Pharisees, so their doctrines represent only that section of early Jewish faith.

Any religion that has a sacred book must make its scriptures meaningful to its followers. All the rabbinic writings have that aim. After AD 70 the rabbis had to rethink the way they should apply the Law of Moses to daily life, for there was no Temple in Jerusalem, and after the Second Revolt ended, in AD 135, Jews were not allowed there. New circumstances demanded new interpretations.

About 200, Rabbi Judah the Prince collected the decisions, with supporting discussions, in a series of books which together form the Mishnah. He drew on some older collections in writing, but most of his material came through the traditions of the rabbinic schools. The Mishnah is written in a dialect of Hebrew which may stem from the spoken language of earlier times. It is the written form of the oral law which governed the lives of the pious, the detailed working out of every rule, and the addition of steps to ensure that the laws were not broken by accident. These were carried to such extremes that the Gospels record Jesus' condemnation. (See Mark 7:1–23; Matthew 15:1–20; and *Small is Beautiful, Cleanliness is Next to Godliness?, Did they Wash Beds?*)

As time passed, debates over interpretation continued. The Mishnah itself became a subject for study. Early in the fifth century the opinions of the rabbis in Palestine were put together as a commentary on sections of the Mishnah, to form the Jerusalem Talmud. (Talmud means 'teaching'.) Here the Mishnah text is in Hebrew, the comments in the Aramaic of Galilee. Despite the date of its compilation, this Talmud preserves some much older material.

A similar process took place in the rabbinic schools in Babylonia, ending in the Babylonian Talmud. This was finished in the sixth century. Its language is the Babylonian form of Aramaic, but with some reports in Hebrew.

Aramaic was the common language of Palestine in the first century (see *The Languages they Spoke*), and after AD 70 Hebrew declined further, so the majority of the people did not benefit from reading the Hebrew Bible.

Apart from the Dead Sea Scrolls and fragmentary books from Masada and the Bar Kochba caves, there are no copies of distinctively Jewish writings from the early centuries of the Christian era. This painting from a tomb at Abila in northern Transjordan (modern Quweilbeh) shows a woman writing in a codex. Third century AD.

made about AD 300 and revised even later, they do contain much older traditions. Their closeness to the Hebrew text varies. Some passages are literal Aramaic translations, others are paraphrases or interpretations in the light of current affairs. Agreements between the Targums and the Greek translation (the Septuagint) show that some of these ideas arose in the second or third centuries BC.

Finally, there is the wide range of books called Midrash. These are 'explanation' of Scripture, put in the form of commentaries on the biblical books. They are brief sermons and meditations, illustrating the meanings of the texts as different teachers understood them. Often they fill in the brief biblical stories with colourful details, or bring out the supposed meaning through fanciful word-play. The written books of Midrash belong to Talmudic times and later, although they, also, include much earlier material. Their methods of treating Scripture are seen in the Dead Sea Scrolls, in the Septuagint, and to some extent in the Old Testament Book of Chronicles which calls itself a midrash (2 Chronicles 13:22; 24:27—though the meaning of the word there may not be identical with its meanings in rabbinic circles).

All these writings are helpful in illustrating beliefs and customs in the Gospel period. They are most helpful to someone wanting to trace the influences of Jewish religious attitudes in the Gospels themselves, which is a separate field of study.

Aramaic translations or paraphrases had been read in the synagogue for a long time. Officially they were not to be written down. In fact, as the Dead Sea Scrolls prove, some were. Eventually the rabbis accepted some Aramaic renderings and they circulated under the name Targum ('interpretation').

There are three important Targums, Onkelos and the Palestinian Targum on the first five books of the Bible, and Jonathan on the historical and prophetic books. Although they were

PART SIX

GOSPEL RECORDS

Christianity, an illegal religious movement, spread rapidly
across the Roman Empire. Although persecuted by the government,
despised by the intelligentsia and spurned by the Jews, it grew stronger
and stronger. At its base were the books of the New Testament, and
especially the Gospels. When they could lay their hands on them,
officials burnt them. Amazingly, copies survive which were made
during the centuries before Constantine the Great legalized Christianity
in 313. They are important evidence that the Gospel text was handed
down accurately. In some verses they show where misunderstandings
took place later. No other ancient Greek books are known from such a
wide range of copies, written so close to the times when their authors
composed them.

*A scene in a Roman school. The master instructs a boy who is reading from a scroll.
From Neumagen, Germany, second or third century AD.*

THE OLDEST BIBLES

Codex Alexandrinus was a present to King Charles I of England. It dates from the early fifth century and shows the scribe decorating his work. This is a photograph of the end of Luke's Gospel.

Britain and France have often been at loggerheads, and sometimes at war. Their rivalry has reached round the globe and affected many people and many aspects of life—even biblical scholarship!

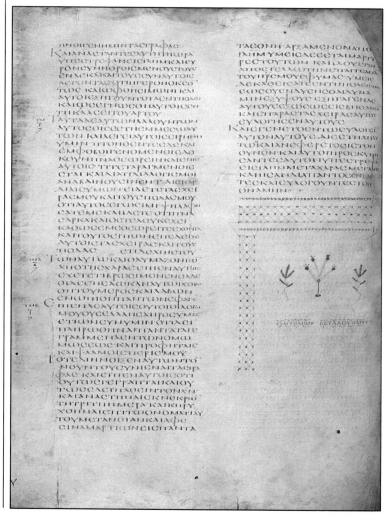

A gift for a king

In the reign of King James I (1603–1625) there was a struggle in Constantinople between the Greek Orthodox Church and the Roman Catholic Church. Who should be more important in the Turkish capital, the Greek Patriarch or the Roman primate? The English ambassador supported the Greek, the French the Roman.

The Patriarch was grateful for the Englishman's support, and helped him to collect old manuscripts and sculptures. To show his gratitude, the Patriarch offered a special present, which he thought the king of England would like. The ambassador wrote to London describing the gift. It was, he reported, a copy of the Bible written by a martyr, Thecla, 'that lived in the time of St Paul'. King James died without receiving the book. His death delayed the affair, but in 1627 the Patriarch delivered the Bible to the ambassador for the new king, Charles I.

The manuscript reached London where it became part of the Royal Library (which King George II gave to the British Museum in 1757). Scholars studied it and wrote about it quickly. Although there was nothing to uphold a date as early as the ambassador had said, it was clearly one of the oldest Greek copies of the Bible to have survived.

Today this copy is named the Codex Alexandrinus, because the Patriarch who sent it to England seems to have taken it from Alexandria, where he had been Patriarch, on his move to Turkey. It is not known where it was originally written. The fact that it includes an introduction to the Psalms by Athanasius, who died in AD 373, shows that it cannot have been written before about the middle of the fourth century. To work out the age of such a manuscript is difficult. From the style of the handwriting a date between 400 and 450 is now usually accepted. That is to say, it was copied less than 350 years after the New Testament was written.

A hidden book

Since the fifteenth century, and perhaps for long before, the library of the Vatican in Rome has owned a very old Greek Bible. The famous scholar Erasmus, who was the first to publish the Greek New Testament in print (1516), was sent information taken from this copy. A few scholars made incomplete studies during the next centuries, but it was not until it left Rome that its value was understood.

The book left Rome as loot; Napoleon carried it off to Paris in 1797. While it was there, a German professor examined it and wrote about its age and importance. When it was returned to Rome in 1815, the Vatican authorities refused to allow scholars to study it freely. The brilliant young Tischendorf was allowed to see it for six hours in 1843, and for a longer time in 1866. A great English scholar had his pockets searched and all his writing materials taken away before he was allowed to look at the book. Eventually the Vatican issued photographs of the whole manuscript in 1890, so that everybody who wanted to could read it.

This copy of the Greek Bible was made about the middle of the fourth century, so it is older than the Codex Alexandrinus. Again, the dating depends to a large extent on the style of handwriting. There is another pointer to the date which applies both to this Codex Vaticanus and to its companion, the Codex Sinaiticus, whose discovery makes a romantic story.

Saved from burning!

In 1844 a German student made a dramatic discovery. Constantine Tischendorf was on a journey round the churches and monasteries of the Near East. Other travellers had brought back valuable manuscripts from some of them, and Tischendorf hoped to find more. In due course he reached the monastery of St Catherine on the north-west slope of Jebel Musa, the traditional Mount Sinai. All sorts of manuscripts were stacked in the library to delight and occupy the young student. On 24 May, however, it was not in the library that Tischendorf experienced his great moment. He described it:

'I perceived in the middle of the great hall a large and wide basket full of old parchments which were to be burnt as fuel for the monastery's ovens. The librarian said that two heaps of papers like these, mouldered by time, had already been committed to the flames. What was my surprise to find amid this heap of papers a considerable number of sheets of a copy of the Old Testament in Greek which seemed to me to be one of the most ancient that I had ever seen.'

Tischendorf told the monks that these old pages were worth keeping, and managed to find 129 leaves altogether. He wanted to take possession of them all but, now that the monks could see they were valuable, they let him take away only the forty-three he rescued from the rubbish basket. Proud that he had made such a discovery and could bring some of the pages home with him, Tischendorf presented them to his patron, the king of the German state of Saxony. The king placed them in the university library at Leipzig, where they are still. Tischendorf printed an edition of this section of the book in 1846, and argued that it was written in the middle of the fourth century AD. He deliberately did not say where he had found it.

Several years passed—how tantalizing they must have been—

The discovery of Codex Sinaiticus was the most important of all the manuscript discoveries of the nineteenth century. The beautiful even script and spacious margins make it a noble book. When the parchment sheets were bought by the British Museum they were carefully treated and re-bound.

then in 1853 he managed to visit the monastery again. His high hopes were dashed! No one would tell him anything about the manuscript. All he found was a scrap with a few verses from Genesis. Had all the other pages he saw in 1844 been burnt? He left frustrated.

Despite that disappointment, the German scholar, now aged forty-three, was back at St Catherine's in January 1859. After a short stay, he was talking with the keeper of the library and gave him a copy of the Old Testament in Greek (the Septuagint) which he had had published. In reply the monk said, 'I, too, have a Septuagint.' He lifted a package wrapped in red cloth from a shelf over the door of his cell.

To Tischendorf's amazement, there were all the leaves he had seen fifteen years earlier, with very many more. Here was most of the Old Testament and the whole of the New Testament! That night Tischendorf did not sleep. The monk let him take the manuscript to his room to study and, in such a situation, the scholar wrote in his diary, 'that night it seemed sacrilege to sleep'. The monks refused to sell the manuscript, or to let Tischendorf borrow it. Happily, when Tischendorf reached Cairo, he met the abbot of St Catherine's monastery, who was

A NEW DISCOVERY AT MOUNT SINAI

When Tischendorf brought back the Codex Sinaiticus from St Catherine's Monastery, he obtained altogether 390 pages. They contain all of the New Testament and some of the Old Testament in Greek, but much of the latter is missing. Tischendorf's story pointed to the fate of the missing pages: they had served as fuel to warm the monks (see The Oldest Bibles).

In May 1975 another discovery was made in the monastery. A fire had destroyed a chapel and the monks were clearing the ruins. As they worked, they found an old cell. The ceiling had fallen in, burying everything inside. When the monks dug away the rubbish they came upon scores of pages from old books. Some are in Arabic, some in Syriac, and some are Greek. Many of them are 1,000 years old, or more;

others are only three or four centuries old. Why they were in the cell is not known. Perhaps they were rescued from an earlier disaster, stacked in the cell and forgotten.

Long ago, at the foot of Mount Sinai, the monks had a copy of Homer's poem The Iliad, copied about AD 800 and supplied with a translation into Greek prose of that time. They read religious books more often. There were parts of a devotional study by an early abbot of the monastery, parts of a copy of Mark's Gospel from the sixth century, and fragments of Genesis in Greek from the century before. Thirteen pages and fifteen fragments belong to another copy of the Old Testament in Greek. The monks have identified them as part of the Codex Sinaiticus. These, at least, had escaped both the flames and, to the monks'

delight, the eyes and hands of Tischendorf!

Justinian, the great Byzantine emperor ruling from Istanbul (then Constantinople) in the sixth century, founded the monastery, although monks had been living in the area before that time. Whether he gave the Codex Sinaiticus to his new establishment, or whether a monk brought it with him, no one knows. Although the new discovery may give slight hope that other pages lie hidden, no pieces of any older manuscripts have appeared there, as they have in Egypt.

Codex Sinaiticus, one of the most important Greek manuscripts, containing the whole New Testament and some of the Old Testament, was discovered in the nineteenth century at this monastery, St Catherine's, at the foot of Mt Sinai. The story makes exciting reading. On Christmas Day 1933 the British Museum bought it from the Soviet government for £100,000.

visiting the city, and persuaded him to have the book brought there for him to examine. With the help of two friends, he spent two months copying out the whole manuscript—110,000 lines.

What should happen to the manuscript? Could it be kept safely in the Sinai desert? Eventually Tischendorf persuaded the monks to offer it to the Czar of Russia, the protector of the Orthodox Church. On 19 November 1859 the Czar received the 347 parchment sheets. He paid for the text to be printed as part of the celebration of 1,000 years of the Russian Empire (1862).

There was one more journey

for this Bible. In 1933 the Soviet government decided to raise money by selling it. After negotiations in America failed, the British Museum bought it for £100,000 (over $500,000 at that time), more than half the money coming from donations made by the general public.

Tischendorf argued that this manuscript, the Codex Sinaiticus, is as old as the Codex Vaticanus. Both were copied, he thought, about AD 350. One reason for thinking this is a report given by the church historian Eusebius who died in 340. He recorded a letter to him from the first Christian emperor, Constantine the Great,

in AD 313, Christians were often persecuted and their books burnt. A complete Bible, handwritten on papyrus or parchment, would be quite a large, thick book, and so be difficult to hide. It seems likely that the books of the Bible were rarely copied into a single volume when there was such a risk of their being destroyed. Once the danger had gone, wealthy Christians or churches could order complete Bibles, handsomely written. They would be expensive. Calculations suggest that one of these copies might have cost more than half a pound in gold coins.

The survival of these manuscripts is a reminder of an important stage in the history of the church, and a major step in the history of the Bible. Although they are not the oldest copies we have of the books of the Old and New Testaments, they are very important for understanding the history of the Greek text.

Codex Vaticanus is the most important Greek manuscript of the whole Bible. Like Codex Sinaiticus, it was copied in the middle of the fourth century, but at a later date someone inked over the letters. The pages are 27 cm/10.3 ins square. The passage shown is John 5:13–37.

asking for fifty copies of the Bible to be made in Caesarea in Palestine, for use in the churches of Constantinople. Perhaps these two were survivors of those fifty.

Nowadays scholars do not believe they are part of that order. There is no evidence that either of them was in Constantinople early in their history. It is thought as probable that they were written in Egypt as in Caesarea.

These two manuscripts deserve to be called 'the first Bibles'. Until Constantine adopted Christianity

BOOKS FROM NEW TESTAMENT TIMES

A pungent smell filled the air. As the fire crackled and the flames sank, someone threw some more fuel to make it blaze again. Then it was all gone, and the fire died away.

People of every age burn or destroy some of the things they inherit from the past, whether they are buildings or furniture or papers; but this story, told about people in Egypt, is especially sad. What they were burning, 200 years or more ago, were rolls of papyrus, ancient books. The smell of burning papyrus was enjoyed by the inhabitants. The report says forty or fifty rolls were found, a merchant bought one, the rest fed the flames.

Today, when printing produces a book in thousands of copies, the loss of a few by fire or flood is no tragedy. When every copy was made by hand it was common for there to be so few copies of a book that it could easily disappear altogether. Many ancient books are known to us only by name. Every one that does survive, therefore, is precious.

Scholars eventually saw the value of papyrus rolls from Egypt, so the local people began to treat them with more care and sell them to European collectors and museums. Ancient Egyptian books were most attractive, some illuminated with coloured paintings, and there was competition to acquire them. There were other rolls with columns of writing in Greek. The majority of them deal with local government affairs, taxes and conscription. A few are copies of Greek books, in particular Homer's *The Iliad* and *The Odyssey*.

Here was the opening of a new door in the study of the classics. Until these papyri were found, that is up to the middle of the nineteenth century, the works of Greek and Latin authors were known only from medieval copies. Few of those were more than 1,000 years old, the oldest were three copies of Virgil's famous poem *The Aeneid*, made in the fifth century.

Over hundreds of years, as the scribes copied the books again and again, they made mistakes. Sometimes they did not correct their mistakes, and later scribes copied them without noticing what was wrong. If they saw an error, they might be able to correct it, or by trying to do so they might make it worse (see *Finding the True Text*). Certainly, by the time Johann Gutenberg invented printing from moveable metal type (about 1450), there were many mistakes in the texts of classical authors read in schools and colleges, and they were perpetuated in printed editions.

With much older papyrus copies to study, scholars hoped they might see the texts as they were before many of the mistakes were made. That proved to be true, although all sorts of other mistakes appeared, too. Even so, the copies on papyrus have made it possible to reach more reliable texts in many places than the medieval manuscripts could give. On occasion they support wordings in the medieval copies which modern scholars had condemned as impossible or wrong, and from time to time their evidence disproves modern theories which attacked ancient statements.

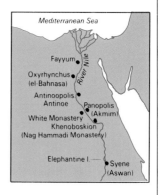

Where did the books come from?

Greek papyri are found at sites throughout Egypt south of Cairo. The biggest discoveries were made in abandoned towns standing round a small lake. Today the area is called the Fayyum. Between 300 and 200 BC, Greek engineers organized an irrigation system for the region. As long as the canals were kept clean and the whole system operated, people could farm the land and prosper. Once the organization broke down, or people lost the will to work together, the flow of water dwindled, people left, and their abandoned houses crumbled and filled with sand.

That began to happen in the fourth century AD and there were only a few towns still occupied by the time of the Arab conquest in 642. Abandoned,

Papyrus reeds growing at the edge of the Nile were stripped of their outer skin. Then layers of pith were laid horizontally on a flat surface, others laid vertically across them, and the sheet beaten flat and smoothed.

Fresh papyrus was flexible and easily rolled up.

the heaps of ruins became quite dry. Papers left in the houses or on the rubbish tips were dehydrated, too, and so survived. Circumstances like these are unusual, but ancient manuscripts have been found in other dry places, for example, near the Dead Sea and in Central Asia.

Greek-speaking immigrants had flowed into Egypt under the kings named Ptolemy, who ruled the country after Alexander the Great (from 304 to the death of Cleopatra in 30 BC). They settled in many places beside the native Egyptians, but the newly developed land in the Fayyum was especially attractive to them. There they spoke and wrote Greek, which was now the dominant language for government and business. Under Roman rule, Greek maintained its status, although Latin was needed for some official purposes.

The papyri are the archives, the collections of books and papers, of these people, usually government officials, landowners and educated men. From the enormous quantity of papyrus documents it is easy to form the impression that most people could read and write. That is false. Those who were literate were a small minority. Another misleading idea is that the papyri make up complete files of papers or libraries of books. Even when they are found in the room of a house, no one can be sure all the papers are there. Occasionally complete rolls of accounts are retrieved and, even more rarely, entire scrolls of literary compositions. For the most part, the papyri are recovered from the rubbish dumps. They were tipped there because they were rubbish, so they are torn, broken, and incomplete. As a result, the books from New Testament times that we can look at today are often very disappointing—only part of a column from this one, a few lines from a page of that.

Finding the age of the books

Greek books did not have title pages, and the scribes who copied them

Sheets of papyrus glued together made scrolls to contain books. Here is the end of Homer's Iliad *from a scroll 6 metres/20 feet long, copied in the second century* AD.

almost never signed their work. To give a date to the ancient copies, scholars examine the style of the handwriting and compare it with the writing on legal deeds and official papers which do carry dates. Although these comparisons are a good guide, we have to remember that a scribe might continue to write in the way he had learnt at school for thirty or forty years, at the same time as new fashions were developing.

Further, styles might develop at different rates in separate centres and, although the documents often state where they were written, the books do not. Taking account of all the uncertainties, expert papyrologists can usually tell the century in which a text was copied and, where there are particular characteristics, can reach an even more precise range of years.

What did people read?
Homer's great poems, *The Iliad* and *The Odyssey* were favourites among the Greek books. Between 600 and 700 copies on papyrus are known. Homer's epics are quite long—*The Iliad* is divided into twenty-four books, and one modern English translation is 459

pages long—so each would occupy several scrolls. One scroll, now in the British Museum, is 6 metres/20 feet long. It contained the last two books of *The Iliad* alone.

Writings of famous playwrights, poets, philosophers and historians are well represented. One fragment of Plato's philosophical essay *Phaedo* can be dated to the third century BC, so it was copied within a century of the author's death (348 BC).

A popular dramatist was Menander, who lived just after Plato. His name and work were mentioned by other writers, but only a few quotations survived, until the papyri yielded examples of his work. Now one play is known in full, and six others to a considerable extent.

Greek citizens of Egypt read plays of Aeschylus and Sophocles which later ages forgot, and they had books by Aristotle as well. All these books, and others whose authors are less famous or quite unknown, have been added to modern knowledge of Greek literature by the discoveries in Egypt. They also show us the literature which some of the early Christians would have read.

A reed pen of the Roman period from Egypt. The nib was cut sharp and split.

THE OLDEST CHRISTIAN BOOKS

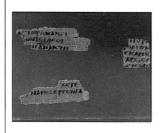

Three tiny pieces of papyrus come from one page of a copy of Matthew's Gospel made near the end of the second century. The book had two columns of writing on each page; the words on this side belong to chapter 26, verses 7, 10, 14, 15 (verses 22, 23, 31–33 are on the other side). A visitor bought the fragments at Luxor in Egypt in 1901 and presented them to Magdalen College, Oxford, where he had studied. The fact that they come from the oldest known copy of Matthew was recognized by the papyrologist C.H. Roberts in 1953. Other pieces of the same book, with parts of chapters 3 and 5, are now in Barcelona.

When the British Museum bought the Codex Sinaiticus in 1933 there was a lot of public interest, because it is one of the two oldest Bibles in Greek (see *The Oldest Bibles*). That copy was made about AD 350 or slightly before. Earlier than that, as far as we know, the books of the Bible were not collected into a single volume. One reason may have been the danger of persecution. A complete Bible would have taken a lot of pages, making a thick book, difficult to hide in times of danger. After Constantine the Great's Edict of Milan (313) it was no longer a risk to possess a large Christian book.

The earlier copies available to us include one which held the four Gospels and Acts (a third-century copy, now in the Chester Beatty Library in Dublin) and another the letters of Paul (except the 'Pastoral' letters) and Hebrews (made early in the third century, in the same library). Today we know of just over thirty papyrus manuscripts of New Testament books which can be dated before the fourth century. That number is small in comparison with the scores of copies of Homer and the dozens of copies of other famous Greek authors. But even though so few, these papyri are very important.

In the first place they show us the form of the New Testament text current in the second and third centuries AD. Each copy has its own oddities and mistakes: no two are completely identical, or the same as the Codex Sinaiticus or other later manuscripts. However, they do fall into groups or families which can be distinguished among the later copies. A single letter changes the meaning of a sentence, and it is usually just single letters or words that are in question. When all the variations have been sifted, only a few deserve closer examination. In the Gospels there are about seventy places altogether where scholars are doubtful about the original reading—that is to say are unsure whether one group of

manuscripts or another has the correct words. Few of these places impinge on any major Christian doctrine, and in no case does any uncertainty affect the Christian faith (see *Finding the True Text*). We can be sure that we read the words of the New Testament books almost exactly as they left their authors' pens.

Books of the New Testament lying forgotten in Egypt are signs that Christians were there. If the books were found only in one place, and all belonging to the same date, they might have belonged to a student of religions or an enemy of Christianity. The range of dates, the variety in handwriting and the different places of discovery weigh against that suggestion. Several of the books are represented by more than one copy on papyrus, which also makes it unlikely.

At least four examples of John's Gospel belong to the third century, and there is another in the book holding all four Gospels. John was perhaps the favourite, but all the Gospels were known. Of the other books of the New Testament, every one is to be found in a third-century papyrus copy, although the only example of Peter and Jude was made at the end of the period, or early in the fourth century. Clearly there were a number of people reading the Christian Scriptures in third-century Egypt.

Those readers had their predecessors in the second century. Parts of copies of Matthew's Gospel, one of John, and possibly fragments of a copy of Paul's letter to Titus, can be placed towards the end of the century on the basis of the writing. One well-known scrap from the Gospel of John is dated before AD 150 (see *Oldest of All*). In addition to these New

Modern Antakya on the Orontes river covers the site of ancient Antioch, where the disciples of Jesus were first called Christians (Acts 11:26) and where, it is suggested, there was a centre of Christian book production by the end of the first century.

Testament manuscripts, pieces from two 'imitation Gospels' are known which belong in the second century, and part of a book about Christian behaviour, *The Shepherd of Hermas*.

The significance of these pieces is seen when they are placed in the context of the history of Christianity. The New Testament refers to churches in Palestine, Syria, Turkey, Greece, Italy, but never in Egypt. From Egypt itself no Christian remains have come to light which are older than about AD 300, apart from the New Testament papyri. The papyri, therefore, are the only evidence for the spread of Christianity to Egypt. It follows that Christians may well have lived in other places, where papyrus books cannot survive because the soil is damp, but no trace of them will be identified.

A new sort of book

All these early copies of the New Testament are important for another reason: they are books with pages. This is a striking contrast to the copies of Greek literature on papyrus, and to the earliest Hebrew manuscripts of the Old Testament, which are all written on scrolls. Scrolls were normal for books until the third century AD. Until that time, a book with pages, a *codex*, was used only for note-taking. Only in the fourth century do we find more texts in book-form than in rolls.

Today the advantages of the codex over the roll are obvious. The roll is wasteful because it is written only on the inside, so it can contain only half as much in the same space. It is awkward to carry and use—to find a passage may involve unrolling several feet of it. These facts may have appealed to early Christian scribes and early Christian readers. They evidently did not care about the current customs of the book trade! The gradual change from the scroll for pagan literature may have had its stimulus in this Christian novelty.

In the early New Testament papyri there are some unusual features, little points which set them apart from the other papyri of the first and second centuries. They clearly have a common origin, and recent study has suggested that they began in one place. Somewhere there was a centre where a common pattern was set for copying Christian books, and for copying them as codex books. Wherever it was, and a likely guess is Antioch in Syria, it was surely operating for some time before the oldest copies we can see today were made (and they all survive by accident). That would put its date as early as 100, if not earlier.

The oldest Christian books allow us to read the New Testament as it was within 200 years of its writing—even less for some books. They show that the Greek text of the New Testament was copied faithfully, and they point to the spread of Christian literature on an organized model. They clearly demonstrate the importance the early church attached to its Scriptures.

OLDEST OF ALL

Papyri poured out of Egypt into museums and private collections. They came in such large numbers that it was impossible to study or even catalogue them all straight away. In 1920 one of the scholars who had excavated papyri in abandoned towns bought a collection of pieces for the John Rylands Library in Manchester. While he was cataloguing them fifteen years later, C. H. Roberts — an expert from Oxford — identified all sorts of interesting pieces of Greek books, and even part of a Latin speech by the Roman orator Cicero. Then, looking at smaller scraps, he came to one torn from the top of a page. Parts of seven lines of writing remain on each side. Although it is very small, 9 cm/3½ ins × 6.2 cm/ 2 ins, there are enough words to identify it. Roberts recognized that it belonged to the Gospel of John.

Other copies of John's Gospel written on papyrus had been found in Egypt, some copied as early as the third century AD. To find the age of the papyrus scrap was part of Roberts' job. By examining the style of handwriting, the shapes of the letters, he reached a conclusion. He asked senior and more experienced papyrologists for their opinion, because his conclusion was surprising. The other scholars agreed with him. The shapes of the letters are most like the writing on

documents dated in the first part of the second century, perhaps between AD 125 and 150. Fifty years later this verdict still stands. After half a century of continuing research, this little piece of papyrus is still the oldest known copy of any part of the New Testament.

What survives on this scrap comes from chapter 18 of John, verses 31–33 on the front, verses 37 and 38 on the back. The size of a whole page is calculated to be about 21 cm/8½ ins high and 20 cm/8 ins wide. And the whole book is reckoned to have occupied about 130 pages. Most likely it was complete by itself, not combined with any of the other Gospels.

Why is it important?
None of the Gospels states exactly when it was written. Clearly all come from the time after the resurrection of Jesus, but

there is nothing that shows decisively whether they were written five, twenty or 100 years after. Christian tradition has always believed that the four evangelists composed their accounts before the year 100. John's Gospel was said to be the last, written in the apostle's old age when he was at Ephesus, in the closing years of the first century.

Traditions like these came under attack in the nineteenth century, and one influential school of thought based at Tübingen in Germany argued that John's Gospel came into existence late in the second century, well after AD 150. Echoes of that view can still be heard in some anti-Christian circles today. The Rylands papyrus puts that case out of court.

If this copy of John was made towards the middle of the second century in Egypt, it is a

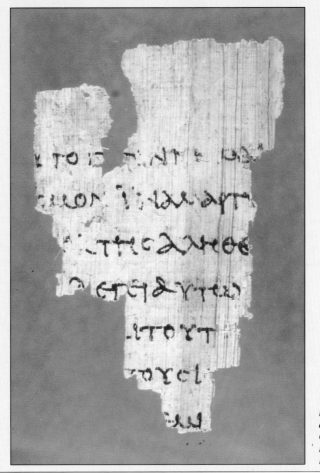

The few words on either side of this small piece of papyrus fit exactly into the text of John's Gospel (chapter 18). The handwriting is believed to date between AD 125 and 150.

sign that someone was using this Christian book at that time—probably in one of the towns of Middle Egypt 160 km/ 100 miles or more south of Cairo. Unless its owner was a personal friend of the author of the Gospel, the fragment indicates that people knew about the Gospel and that examples had spread from wherever it was composed (traditionally Ephesus), had been re-copied and become familiar. All this points to a date no later than the opening years of the second century for the writing of John's Gospel, and possibly earlier.

Early Christian tradition said John wrote his Gospel at Ephesus on the western coast of Turkey near the end of the first century. The theatre in this view was built in the third and second centuries BC and altered several times in the first century AD. The flat green area beyond the end of the road is the silted-up site of the ancient harbour.

BEFORE THE GOSPELS

If the Gospels were already being copied and circulated in a standard form by the year 100, what was their history before that? Exactly when the Gospel-writers did their work is a question scholars are always discussing. By comparing Matthew, Mark and Luke it is easy to see they share a lot of information. Perhaps there was an earlier collection of stories and sayings of Jesus which they all used. (Students of the Gospels call this collection 'Q', from the German word *Quelle*, 'source'.) Each writer added things he learnt from different followers of Jesus and arranged the material to bring out particular points. How they did that is a subject outside the scope of this book.

Another question which is part of the same study is whether the Gospel-writers reported accurately the words that Jesus spoke, or invented speeches and put them into his mouth. If they did make up some of the sayings, they probably included ideas that grew up in the church as Christians thought and talked about their new faith. It would not be easy to disentangle the actual words Jesus spoke from the later additions. This, too, is a subject that cannot be explored here.

What is important to remember in reading any study of it is that all theories about the history

For school exercises, notes and reports people often wrote on wooden tablets which could be tied together like the pages of a book. This example was used in Egypt in Roman times.

of the Gospels are speculations. The only facts available to us are the Gospels themselves and it is impossible to prove that any of their records of the life and teaching of Jesus are wrong or misleading.[1]

Clearly the Gospel-writers had sources of information, whether they were witnesses of the events they described, or were not, like Luke. Did they rely on their own memories and the memories of others who had seen and heard Jesus? One person remembering and telling another is commonly thought to have been the way the Gospel stories spread until they were collected and written down in 'Q' or other forms.

It is easy to imagine the process. Jesus spoke to the crowds, to small groups of people, and to individuals. When they went away, they would pass on to others what they had heard. With his challenging words and sensational claims, Jesus quickly caught the

attention of the Jewish religious leaders, and they debated what he was saying. A few were sympathetic, most were angry. There were foreigners who heard Jesus, too. There were a lot of men and women in Palestine, and some abroad, who lived on after the crucifixion with the words they had heard alive in their minds, ready for an inquirer to release.

Learning by memory was the usual way of education in ancient Palestine, and some of Jesus' sayings are obviously short and clear and suitable for remembering. When some of his words are translated back into Aramaic, the language he normally used, they turn out to have a poetic rhythm which also helps to make them memorable. These were some of the ways Jewish rabbis used to teach their disciples, and it is not surprising that Jesus should follow their patterns.

But was word of mouth (oral transmission) the only way the church broadcast its Master's words and works before the Gospels (or 'Q') were written? Were there some who heard Jesus' teaching and said to themselves, 'I must write that down'? This possibility had hardly any place in Gospel studies until recently. Now archaeological evidence for the amount of writing being done in first-century Palestine and new studies of other sources sets it in the balance beside theories about oral tradition.

Tombs in Jerusalem reveal the use of writing for recording the names of the dead so that relatives could distinguish them (see *Their Names Live On*). Other examples were found near Jericho. Excavations in Herod's palaces brought out jars labelled in Greek or Latin with the date and the king's name and title. Other jars found at Qumran and in Jerusalem carry names or labels of contents in Hebrew or Aramaic. There are also a few short messages scribbled on potsherds. These are all very brief, yet they are still signs of people being ready to write, although far removed from books of history or teaching.

Mainline Jewish thought was against writing and collecting the teachings of the rabbis. Although the oral law, the 'traditions of the fathers', had great authority, it was not the same as the written Law of the books of Moses. The basic collection of rabbinic teaching, the Mishnah, was not made until a century after the fall of Jerusalem (AD 70; see *Jewish Writings*). However, other Jewish teachers were prepared to have their own lessons put into writing—Philo and the apostle Paul are examples. Among the Dead Sea Scrolls is a remarkable letter which sets out the opinions of a leader, possibly the Teacher of Righteousness himself, about all sorts of questions

of ritual purity and behaviour. To introduce each opinion, the letter has the words 'About such and such, we say that . . .', which are similar to the repeated 'but I tell you' of Jesus in Matthew 5. In each case the teacher is giving his own, different, instructions.

Even though the rabbis' words were not to be collected, their students were allowed to make notes of them for private study, and we are

told some did so. What is especially interesting is that they wrote in notebooks, rather than on scrolls or potsherds. The Hebrew language had no word for notebook, so it borrowed the Greek word *pinax*. A *pinax* was any sort of board for writing, drawing or painting on. Zechariah wrote on a little one (Luke 1:63; it could also be a tray, such as the one John the Baptist's head was carried on— Matthew 14:8; Mark 6:28.)

Wooden writing tablets of Roman times have come to light in places as far apart as the fortress of Vindolanda, on the line of Hadrian's Wall, and the deserted towns of Egypt. Often they are broken and the writing has disappeared. The writing could be done in ink directly on the wooden surface, or on to a white plaster coating the wood. Alternatively, the tablet was given a shallow recess which was filled with wax.

At many places in the Roman Empire bronze and iron styli have come to light. The points were for scratching letters on wax tablets, the broad ends were for smoothing away the writing for re-use.

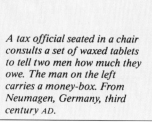

A tax official seated in a chair consults a set of waxed tablets to tell two men how much they owe. The man on the left carries a money-box. From Neumagen, Germany, third century AD.

With a pointed stylus the writer could scratch letters into the wax, and later erase them by smoothing it over with the flat end of the stylus.

Wooden writing tablets of any type could be joined with hinges or thongs to make a pair or, when a lot of space was needed, to make a group of several boards or pages. Such a group of leaves was called in Latin a *codex*, the first-century author Seneca informs us. Ordinarily these tablets were for school exercises, accounts, messages and notes of all sorts. At Rome, shorthand writers took down speeches in the Senate; a secretary slave stood by the scholar Pliny to take down in shorthand anything his master found that would be useful in his studies. Manuals for teaching systems of Greek shorthand have been found among the papyri from Egypt.

Alongside the wooden tablets, notebooks of parchment came into use in Rome by the first century BC. They were lighter to carry than wooden ones, and the poet Martial, in about AD 85, recommended to his friends that they should have the poems of Homer and Virgil written in this type of book. He gave some copies to his friends to try to convince them how much better the book with pages was than the traditional scroll. Regrettably, no books survive from the first and second centuries in Rome, so we cannot tell whether Martial was advertising a growing fashion or was an eccentric a century before his time. Papyrus books from Egypt indicate that the scroll was the more popular form of book for another 200 years (see *The Oldest Christian Books*).

The fact that the Gospels were some of the first books to be copied in the codex form, as distinct from the scroll, leads to the suggestion that they were based on notebooks. Such notebooks could have held reports of Jesus' sayings and actions put down on the day they were heard or seen, even the words of Jesus recorded in shorthand. Taking into account the fact that the places where Jesus worked were often towns, with resident government or army officers, tax collectors and religious teachers, makes this more likely than the common pictures of him on green hills or open lake-sides. (Perhaps the 'parchments' Paul asked for—2 Timothy 4:13—were such notebooks.)

No physical evidence exists to prove, or disprove, this suggestion. It came from C. H. Roberts, a scholar expert in studying Greek papyrus books (see *Oldest of All*), and deserves a place in the discussions of New Testament scholars.

[1] For an excellent introduction to these matters see Craig Blomberg, *The Historical Reliability of the Gospels*, Inter-Varsity Press, 1987

FINDING THE TRUE TEXT

How do we find the true text of something written centuries ago? William Shakespeare, for example, wrote his plays from about 1588–1613. He was both an actor and a playwright, and he wrote some parts to suit other actors in his company. Nothing is known about the way he worked, except that he produced rough drafts in the first place. These do not survive, nor do any fair copies he may have made. Obviously actors with leading roles had to have copies for themselves, at least for their major scenes. The prompter, too, would need a complete text, so that he could help the players who missed their cues or forgot their lines.

Clearly, Shakespeare's plays were not limited to the author's copy for long. As they grew popular, printers wanted to publish them. What they put on sale were sometimes 'pirate editions'. Actors or members of the audience memorized the words, or even made notes of them, and the printers made up a text from that information. This happened, for example, when *Romeo and Juliet* was printed in 1597, *Henry V* in 1600, and *Hamlet* in 1603.

Shakespeare's ideas and words were spoilt in these books, so he or his friends had new editions printed of some of them (*Romeo and Juliet* in 1599, *Hamlet* in 1604–1605, both based on the author's rough drafts).

When Shakespeare died in 1616, twenty-two of his plays were still unpublished. His friends eventually issued a volume containing thirty-six plays in 1623. They wanted to make as perfect an edition of his work as they could, and so honour his name. They used some of the earlier printings which had been corrected, but, wherever they could, they relied on the author's own copies. Even so, there are lots of printers' mistakes in this 'First Folio' edition.

The 'Second Folio' (1632) corrected some of them while making others. Ever since, scholars have tried to discover what some words and lines mean, or how Shakespeare originally wrote them, because they are unintelligible or sound wrong.

There is wide agreement over the greater part of the text, yet some passages are still hard to understand (the curious might read *King Lear* Act IV, Scene VI, lines 217, 218, or *Hamlet* Act 1, Scene IV, line 37). By ingenious guesses at the ways badly written copies could be misread or printers could make mistakes, sense can be made of some of the hard lines. In *Romeo and Juliet* Act I, Scene IV, line 42, 'we'll draw thee from the mire of this sir-reverence love' can be corrected to 'we'll draw thee from the mire of— save your reverence—love', as many editions do.

For certain plays Shakespeare seems to have added to someone else's work, notably for *Henry VI*, Part 1. There are puzzles left in the text of Shakespeare to occupy future generations of scholars. No one is ever likely to be able to print an edition which they can prove is word for word what Shakespeare wrote.

Shakespeare lived only 400 years ago, yet we cannot be sure that every

The original scribe of the Codex Sinaiticus made several mistakes as he copied. In the third column of the last page of John's Gospel a later scribe made several corrections, especially in John 21:18.

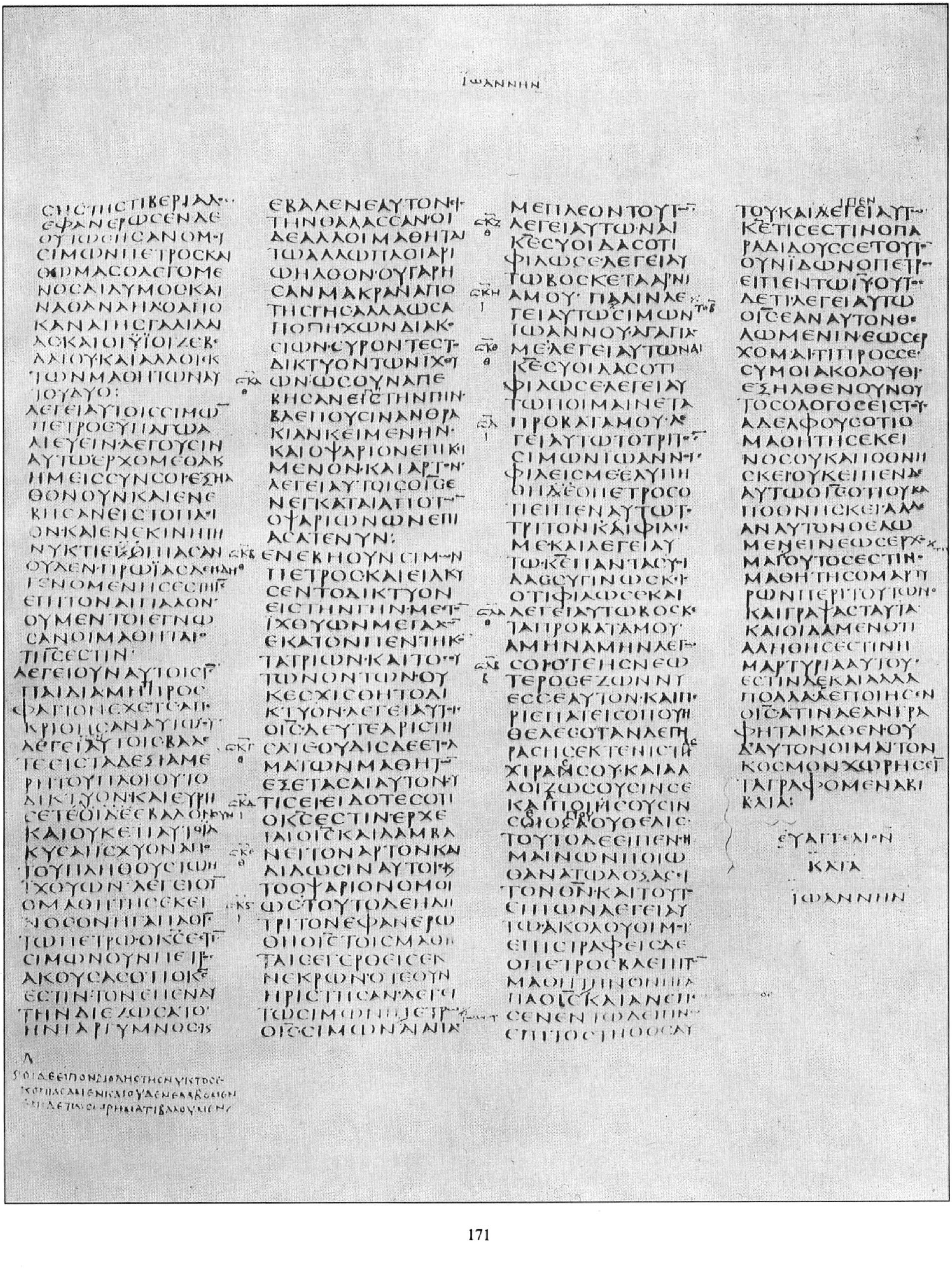
ΙΩΑΝΝΗΝ
ΕΥΑΓΓΕΛΙΟΝ
ΚΑΤΑ
ΙΩΑΝΝΗΝ

line we read of his plays is what he wrote, even though some of them were printed during his lifetime. So no one should be surprised if the same is true in the case of books such as the Gospels and books of the New Testament which were written 2,000 years ago. The authors' manuscripts perished long ago; we can read only copies of copies of them. All the Gospels were written before AD 100, a century or more before scribes made the earliest extensive copies at present available for study.

Did those scribes and their predecessors do their work accurately?

Answering that question is the task of the specialized research called textual criticism. To know a little of the facts which textual critics face, and the ways they explain them, can help anyone who reads the New Testament seriously to understand it better.

Printers may make mistakes, as Shakespeare and his friends found out, and each one is reproduced hundreds or thousands of times. Scribes copying books by hand were just as likely to make mistakes. Yet it is to their labours that we owe the preservation of the New Testament.

The copyist

Try to imagine this key figure in the history of the Gospels. His school record was average, with good marks for handwriting. A career in a government office or a big business was beyond his reach, but he could earn his living as a copyist. People wanted books, so he could provide them.

Of course, he had to borrow the books to copy, or his clients had to bring them to him. In a big city that was not difficult. There were men who had their own collections of books, and it was common to borrow from such a collection for copying. A copyist who lived in a small town might have to ask a number of people before he found the book a customer wanted him to reproduce. He might have to send away for it or travel

himself, to use a rare copy in another place.

Copying was a rather tedious job. To be faced with another hundred columns of text was not all that exciting. If the book was one that bored the copyist, or if it was one he had worked with several times before, his attention could easily wander. Then the mistakes would creep in. He might write one sentence twice, or leave out a line that began with the same word as the line before, or he might even write nonsense.

If another man dictated the book to him, mistakes might come from mishearing. If the copyist read from the exemplar himself, he might confuse the words as he transferred them to his own page.

If he was interested in the book, he might work more carefully. Then he might go beyond the limit of his task and try to improve its language. Perhaps the author did not write very fashionable Greek, so the copyist would try to make it more 'stylish'. The book done, the conscientious copyist would check it for mistakes and hope to correct them all, or he could ask another scribe to do it. Quite often the checking was slap-dash and incomplete, as surviving copies show.

The rate of pay for a copyist was apparently about the same as for a farm labourer, although he was paid for what he produced rather than at a daily rate. Naturally, he would be eager to copy as much as possible and, working fast, he would make mistakes more easily.

Late in the first century the poet Martial mentions the price of a cheap book in Rome. It was from one and a half to two and a half denarii. The labourer's daily wage, according to Matthew 20, was one denarius. That was half a century earlier, so perhaps the lower price was about the worth of a day's work. In Egypt during the second century there was a rate of twenty denarii for 10,000 lines, or one denarius for 500.

Very rough calculations suggest

that a copy of John's Gospel would have about 2,000 lines, and so would cost four denarii. Copying would probably have taken three or four days.

Clearly, copying could earn a man his bread and butter if he had regular orders. In a small town it is unlikely that he would. That might mean that someone wanting a book would either have to copy it himself or pay an ordinary scribe to do it. The results of this can be seen in some of the papyrus books recovered in Egypt.

Book copyists were trained to set out their work in a certain style which other scribes did not always follow. When a man who usually wrote accounts and legal deeds copied a book he might easily write numbers as figures and abbreviate common words, just as he did in his daily routine. These things occur in some of the early examples of Christian books, very rarely in others. Evidently some Christians could not obtain or afford the books professional copyists made, or some Christians who could write made their own copies. They read them privately, but the large writing in certain copies may show that they were made for reading aloud to groups of people. Here is more evidence for the need they felt to have the Gospels and other New Testament writings available for study.

Spotting the mistakes

Some of the mistakes the copyists made are easy to see, and often the scribe himself or a colleague corrected his work. The famous Codex Sinaiticus (see *The Oldest Bibles*) has many places where the man who made them put his faults right. After him several other people also made corrections to it at different times.

A scribe copying the Gospel of John shortly after AD 200 slipped fifty-four times by leaving out words when his eye jumped from one word to a similar one (Papyrus Bodmer II). He also repeated words mistakenly twenty-two times. On the other hand, a scribe who put Luke and John into one book

about the same time worked very carefully, making fewer mistakes (Papyrus Bodmer XIV–XV).

When one copy is set beside another these errors are obvious. Two scribes would not always miscopy the same words. Less obvious faults might go unnoticed and so be passed on from copy to copy. These are more serious because they can result in the loss of the original words. One faulty manuscript may spawn dozens of copies perpetuating its error. If that faulty copy was kept in an important library or school, it would be more likely to be the ancestor of many copies than a carefully made copy lying on a shelf in an out-of-the-way town. A single copy made from that one would have much greater value than all the others in preserving the more correct version of the book.

In the same way, there might happen to be copies of the faulty manuscript which are much older than any copy of the careful one. Were that the case, the oldest copies would not necessarily be the best. Neither the number of copies of a text in one form, nor the age need always be weighty arguments in deciding whether that text is better than another one that is slightly different.

Over 5,000 Greek manuscripts of the New Testament survive. They are grouped into families according to their characteristics. A series of family portraits will reveal a large nose or red hair prominent in several generations, yet each person possessed features which made him or her an individual human being. In the same way, each manuscript has both its own features and the marks of its 'family'. The usefulness of any copy depends on an analysis of all the copies. Such an examination, copy by copy, allows scholars to identify these characteristics and to weed out many of the mistakes.

It is reckoned that there may be over a quarter of a million manuscripts of the New Testament books, if translations are taken into account.

That means, inevitably, that the number of differences is enormous. The majority are unimportant. After sifting them, the editors of standard editions of the Greek New Testament give 10,000 or so in their footnotes. Of these, about 1,400 were selected as sufficiently significant to be included in the Bible Societies' Greek New Testament of 1966. Does this mean we cannot be sure that we are reading the words the authors of the Gospels wrote? How does it affect translations of the New Testament?

A THEOLOGICAL DIFFERENCE

Occasionally a change in translation changes the teaching of a verse. Obviously every case deserves careful thought, and such changes are not made without good reason. When a major doctrine is involved, a change in one verse does not alter it, for every important teaching rests on several pasages.

One case is in John 1:18. The Authorized Version translated the traditional Greek text. It has, 'No man hath seen God at any time; the only begotten Son, which is in the bosom of the Father, he hath declared him.' The Revised Standard Version has almost the same, and the New English Bible does, too. The Good News Bible is similar. On the other hand, the New International Version offers, 'No-one has ever seen God, but God the One and Only, who is at the Father's side, has made him known.' A footnote states that 'some manuscripts' have the other version.

Why does this translation differ? The first papyrus copy of John in the Bodmer collection was published in 1956, followed in 1961 by the second. Both of these were copied early in the third century. Both have the text which the NIV translates, and it is also in Codex Sinaiticus and Codex Vaticanus. Some of the Fathers of the church also knew it.

All depends on one word. Is 'Son' or 'God' the one the author wrote? Nowadays the majority of scholars think it is 'God', because the phrase 'the One and Only God' is harder to understand. 'One and only Son' is found in John 1:14 and 3:16, so a copyist faced with the other phrase might have made this one agree with it, consciously or unconsciously. A change the other way, from the known phrase to a strange one, is less likely. There is no question of an attack on teaching about the deity of Christ here. The opening verse of John and the whole passage make that crystal clear.

SIMPLE MISTAKES

A phrase left out

John 13:31 and 32 read, 'Now is the Son of Man glorified and God is glorified in him. If God is glorified in him, then God will glorify the Son in himself . . . '

Some Christians long ago did not read quite the same words. One of the two copies of John now in the Bodmer Library, made soon after AD 200 has, 'Now is the Son of man glorified, and God is glorified in him. God shall also glorify him in himself . . . ' Both Codex Sinaiticus and Codex Vaticanus agree. Yet this is not a real difference. The copyists' eyes simply slipped from the first 'glorified in him' to the second, jumping over 'If God is glorified in him.' This sort of mistake is common in copies of ancient books. (Textual critics give it the technical name *homoioteleuton*.)

A phrase repeated

The opposite mistake is equally easy to make, repeating a word or phrase unnecessarily. In Codex Vaticanus the copyist did that at John 17:18, producing, 'As you sent me into the world, I have sent them into the world, I have sent them into the world.' This common error is called 'dittography'.

'Infection'

There are many chapters in Matthew, Mark and Luke which tell of the same events or speeches in almost the same words. When he was working on one Gospel, a copyist familiar with all of them might unconsciously make it agree with another, because that one was fresh in his mind. Others might deliberately make one Gospel agree with another.

Finding early manuscripts of the Gospels has made it clearer how this happened. Recent translations of the Gospels often draw attention to these places by putting the additions in the margin. When he was warning, 'how it will be at the coming of the Son of Man', Jesus said, 'Two men will be in the field; one will be taken and the other left. Two women will be grinding with a hand mill; one will be taken and the other left', according to Matthew 24:39–41. In Luke's report there are other pictures, then the one about the women grinding. Following that, in the traditional text, is a sentence about two men working in the field, one of whom is taken, ending the speech (Luke 17:30–36).

However, the oldest copy of Luke's Gospel, Bodmer Papyrus XIV, written early in the third century does not have this last sentence. Codex Sinaiticus, Codex Vaticanus, Codex Alexandrinus and other early manuscripts agree. Possibly the scribes who wrote all those copies missed it out accidentally, because it ends with the same words as the sentence before. More likely, a scribe familiar with Matthew added this verse to Luke to make the two reports of Jesus' prophecy more alike.

Examples of harmonization in the same way are plain in Luke's version of the Lord's Prayer. Comparing Luke 11:2–4 with Matthew 6:9–13 in the Authorized Version and in a recent translation shows this clearly.

Copyists made mistakes in various other ways, but these cases are enough to illustrate the value of studying the different manuscripts in order to obtain as accurate a text of the New Testament as possible.

The copyist of Codex Sinaiticus left out the words 'If God be glorified in him' from John 13:32. A later scribe added them in the margin.

175

DELIBERATE CHANGES

When copying, a scribe who was thinking about his work, and had time to do so, might occasionally alter the text or add to it. One working from dictation would hardly be able to do so until after he had written the text. His alterations might stand in the margin. That was a place where any scribe or reader might put notes of all sorts. A careless writer might then copy those notes into his text, as if they were part of it.

An explanatory note, perhaps based on knowledge of local traditions, seems to have entered the text of John 5. The traditional text relates that at the pool of Bethesda 'a great number of disabled people used to lie—the blind, the lame, the paralysed—and they waited for the moving of the waters. From time to time an angel of the Lord would come down and stir up the waters. The first one into the pool after each such disturbance would be cured of whatever disease he had.' The oldest copies of John do not contain this verse, and it has words in it

Some Greek manuscripts of Matthew 27 name the bandit in whose place Jesus was executed Jesus Barabbas. Codex Vaticanus does not have the name Jesus here, but its wording indicates that it was copied from one that did. This page contains Matthew 26:70—27:24.

which are not expressions found anywhere else in the Gospel.

Sometimes a scribe thought he knew better than the text he was copying from. One making a copy of John soon after AD 200 (Papyrus Bodmer XV) was puzzled by 'I am the gate for the sheep' in chapter 10, verse 7, so he wrote, 'I am the shepherd for the sheep' instead. Although this is one of the oldest manuscripts of the Gospel, no one wants to

adopt its reading here. It is an obvious case of simplification by the copyist.

Changes of religious outlook could also lead to changes in the text. Growing devotion to Jesus as God apparently caused scribes deliberately to leave out a word in Matthew 27:16,17. The name of the brigand whom Pilate released in place of Jesus was probably not just Barabbas but Jesus Barabbas. Codex Vaticanus

implies the two names, and Origen knew of them in the third century. Jesus was a common name in the first century (see *Their Names Live On*), so there is nothing exceptional about that man having it. If Barabbas was called Jesus, it is easy to understand why scribes would omit it. Origen expressed it himself: the name of Jesus was not suitable for a criminal like Barabbas. This view prevailed in the church.

176

WHAT DID THE ANGELS SING?

'Glory to God in the
    highest,
And on earth peace,
    goodwill toward men'

The angels' song in Luke
2:14 is one of the most
familiar of all Christmas
texts. Twentieth-century
readers of Luke's Gospel
have wondered why
modern translations are
not the same as the
Authorized Version in
this verse. The Revised
Standard Version of 1946
has:

'Glory to God in the
    highest,
and on earth peace among
    men with whom he is
    well pleased.'

In the New English Bible
(1961) the verse reads:

'Glory to God in highest
    heaven,
And on earth his peace for
    men on whom his
    favour rests.'

The Good News Bible
(1976) and the New
International Version
(1973) are similar.

The scribe who copied Codex
Sinaiticus wrote 'peace to men
on whom his favour rests' in
the angels' song (Luke 2:14).
Later another scribe erased
the final 's' of the word for
'favour' to give the sense
'good will toward men'.

One letter in the Greek
makes the difference. The
word 'goodwill' stands
grammatically with 'peace'
in the traditional Greek text
as something wished for
mankind. A Christian
named Tatian who was
alive about
AD 170 knew this
interpretation. (He wove a
single 'gospel' out of the
four, leaving out duplicate
sections.) In the fourth
century the Christian
historian Eusebius also
knew it. On the other
hand, the fourth-century
Greek copies of Luke 2, the
oldest available, and the
Christian scholar Origen
who was active in the third
century, have the Greek
word for 'goodwill' with a
final 's', which gives it the
meaning 'of goodwill'.

How can anyone
decide which is right? A
final answer is impossible.
The early manuscripts
carry a lot of weight, but
the testimony of Tatian and
Eusebius partly count
against them. Here is a
case where scholars
maintain that the more
difficult form of the text is
to be preferred. Scribes
would make difficult words
and phrases simpler as
they copied, not make
them more awkward.
'Peace, goodwill toward
men' is the easier phrasing
in Greek. The expression
'men of goodwill' is now
known from the Dead Sea
Scrolls as one current
among some religious
Jews in the first century
(see The Scrolls and the
Teaching of Jesus).

DID THEY WASH BEDS?

'There are many other points on which they have a traditional rule to maintain, for example, washing of cups and jugs and copper bowls' (Mark 7:4, NEB). Mark's Gospel gives this list to explain the way religious Jews carried out the laws of purity. Archaeology has thrown light on the practical effect these laws had in daily life (see *Cleanliness is Next to Godliness?*).

To wash cups, jugs and metal bowls may not seem remarkable, merely an ordinary matter of hygiene. Rather odder is the fourth object which some copies of Mark add, 'and beds'. Among modern translations the Good News Bible has that; the Revised Standard Version and the New International Version have it in the margin. The translation 'tables', in the Authorized Version, is incorrect; the word is the one used for the bed of a sick girl later in the chapter (verse 30), and for the bed of the paralysed man whose story is told in Matthew 9:2,6 and Luke 5:18.

The oldest copy of Mark is a papyrus in the Chester Beatty Library, Dublin, made in the third century. It does not include 'and beds'. Neither does the Codex Sinaiticus nor the Codex Vaticanus. The Codex Alexandrinus, on the other hand, has 'and beds' at the end of the list, as do the Freer Codex in Washington and the Codex Bezae in Cambridge, both from the fifth century. The words continue into the traditional Greek text and so appeared in the older translations.

Did the Gospel writer put these words in his original text or not? At first sight the evidence of the oldest copies says he did not; the words were added later. Yet there is room for some doubt about that. The very fact that the idea of washing beds seems strange today may mean it seemed strange to ancient scribes, so they left the words out.

Certainly there are laws in the Old Testament that any beds which risked soiling from a bodily discharge should be washed (Leviticus 15:4, 20,26). When the rabbis applied Old Testament laws to every part of life in the first century, they observed the laws of purity or cleanliness strictly. Late in the second century, the Mishnah, a book of their interpretations, was made. In a long section devoted to rules of cleanliness applying to utensils it discusses the question of which parts of a bed should be washed.

Washing beds might, therefore, be an example which the Gospel writer would give to show the extent of the Jewish concern for such matters. This would be especially appropriate if he composed his book for Roman readers, as tradition claims. On the other hand, a reader of Mark who knew about those customs could have thought in the same way, and so added 'and beds' to the list.

In this case the question can be left open. Whether 'beds' was in the original Mark, or not, the copies that have the word represent the practice of the first century.

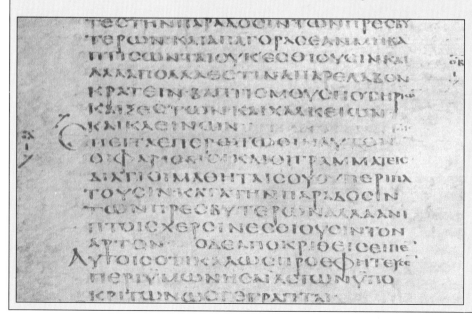

Codex Alexandrinus is the oldest copy of Mark 7:4 to say the Jews washed beds. This page covers Mark 6:54—7:23. (The words 'and beds' occur in the half-line two-thirds of the way down the first column.)

ARE THEY ORIGINAL?

Two passages in the Gospels call for comment because they are absent from many early copies, and so modern translations leave them out.

In John's Gospel (7:53–8:11) stands the famous account of Jesus' meeting with the woman taken in adultery and her hypocritical accusers.

'Then each went to his own home. But Jesus went to the Mount of Olives. At dawn he appeared again in the temple courts, where all the people gathered around him, and he sat down to teach them. The teachers of the law and the Pharisees brought in a woman caught in adultery. They made her stand before the group and said to Jesus, "Teacher, this woman was caught in the act of adultery. In the Law Moses commanded us to stone such women. Now what do you say?" They were using this question as a trap, in order to have a basis for accusing him.

'But Jesus bent down and started to write on the ground with his finger. When they kept on questioning him, he straightened up and said to them, "If any one of you is without sin, let him be the first to throw a stone at her." Again he stooped down and wrote on the ground.

'At this those who heard began to go away, one at a time, the older ones first, until only Jesus was left, with the woman still standing there. Jesus straightened up and asked her, "Woman, where are they? Has no one condemned you?"

'"No one, sir," she said.

'"Then neither do I condemn you," Jesus declared. "Go now and leave your life of sin."'

Although most Greek manuscripts of John have these verses, there are some which do not. Among those without the verses are the oldest copies of John, two papyri from Egypt made early in the third century (Papyrus Bodmer II and Papyrus Bodmer XIV). The Codex Sinaiticus and the Codex Vaticanus are also without them. Codex Alexandrinus has lost some pages from John's Gospel, including chapters 7 and 8. Calculation of the number of lines missing shows that there would not have been enough space for the lost pages to have contained the passage about the woman taken in adultery.

As well as several other Greek manuscripts that do not have the passage, translations of the Gospel made in the second and third centuries into Latin, Syriac and the Coptic dialects of Egypt show no signs of it.

The early Church Fathers add their evidence: none of them quotes these verses or comments on them. Moreover, the verses have several Greek expressions John does not have anywhere else.

On the other hand, some Christians of the fourth century knew these verses. Jerome translated them into Latin when he made the Vulgate (AD 384). In one of his books he observed that the verses were found in many manuscripts in Greek and in previous translations into Latin. Augustine, who wrote a little later than Jerome, also knew the verses.

Today the oldest surviving Greek manuscript which contains these verses

Excavations through the rubbish of centuries have uncovered parts of a pool deep below the modern surface just north of the Temple area in Jerusalem. This was apparently the Pool of Bethesda (John 5). There were colonnades around the four sides of the two pools, and between them, making five 'porches'.

men. When they heard this, they left everything on the ground and followed him.' These extra words were taken from the similar passage in Mark 1:17,18.

A few of the Codex Bezae's peculiarities, like the passage concerning the adulterous woman, are more interesting. They may well preserve traditions handed down from the first century, from the friends of Jesus. Why the Gospel writers did not see fit to put them into their four books is not known.

In the present case, the evidence of Jerome, Augustine, some later manuscripts of John, with the Codex Bezae, is strong. Scholars accept the story as likely to be a genuine account from the first century, although not originally part of John's Gospel.

The other passage absent from modern translations, or printed as a footnote, is at the end of Mark's Gospel (16:9–20). These verses pose a quite different problem from the account of the woman taken in adultery.

Codex Alexandrinus and Codex Bezae have them, and so do most later copies. Irenaeus, the bishop of Lyons at the end of the second century, knew them, and Tatian included them in the harmony of the Gospels which he made at that time (the *Diatessaron*). A century later Jerome knew they existed in a few copies. Although he saw many which had the passage about the woman taken in adultery, the majority he had seen did not have the long ending of Mark's Gospel.

Two like the latter survive—Codex Sinaiticus and Codex Vaticanus. By the accidents of survival and discovery, these are the oldest manuscripts of Mark which have the last chapter. There is an older copy on papyrus, at the Chester Beatty Library in Dublin. It is part of a book originally containing the four Gospels and the Acts, made in the third century. Alas, only six of the pages of Mark remain, ending in chapter 12. How the Gospel ended in that papyrus cannot be

is the Codex Bezae, now in Cambridge. This copy of the Gospels was made in the fifth or sixth century, with a Latin translation (older than Jerome's) beside the Greek. The Greek text of Codex Bezae stands apart from the other early copies, because it has a lot of additions found nowhere else. The majority of these additions have little value. They explain or harmonize passages in the Gospels. For example, Luke 5:10,11 has extra words: '. . . James and John the sons of Zebedee. He said to them, Come, do not fish for fish, for I will make you fishers of discovered. The problem about the end of Mark is not simply whether verses 6–20 were part of it or not. Jerome reported a form with extra verses, and one early Greek copy, the Washington Gospels produced about AD 400, preserves them. A few copies of later date, one manuscript of a Latin translation earlier than Jerome's and some other early translations have a very short ending, to which verses 9–20 have been added. Each of these endings uses words which are not used in the rest of Mark.

What do these things mean?

They appear to be signs that the Gospel ended in an unexpected way. Scholars guess that the author's manuscript was damaged; the end of the scroll or the last page of the codex was lost before anyone could copy it. Another guess is that the author never completed his book—perhaps he died suddenly. Of the several attempts to give it a tidy conclusion, the ending in the traditional text was accepted as the most suitable by comparison with the other three Gospels.

NEW KNOWLEDGE—
NEW TRANSLATIONS

One major achievement of the Reformation was the translation of the Bible into the chief languages of Europe. In previous centuries there had occasionally been translations which were made from the Latin Vulgate. John Wyclif's English version was one of these.

With the new learning of the Renaissance more scholars knew Greek, so now translations could be made directly from the Greek New Testament. The one Luther used for his German Bible and Tyndale for his English one was prepared by the famous scholar Erasmus. His Greek New Testament was the first to be printed and published (in 1516).

He put the text together from a few manuscripts which he happened to have to hand. Only one of them had

The great Renaissance scholar Erasmus saw the need for a standard printed text of the Greek New Testament. His work was the basis for most translations until the nineteenth century.

the Book of Revelation in it, and the last page with the six final verses was missing, so Erasmus translated the Latin Vulgate back into Greek!

With some corrections and changes, Erasmus' Greek text was printed over and over again. In the seventeenth century a Dutch publisher referred to it as 'the received text' (*textus receptus*), and that name has stuck. When King James I of England set up a committee to produce an English version without the bias of earlier ones, an edition of Erasmus' Greek New Testament was their basic text.

Although Erasmus' edition became the standard one, scholars soon showed that there were all sorts of differences between it and the Greek manuscripts, notably the older ones. When Patriarch Cyril Lucar presented the Codex Alexandrinus to the king of England he made available a copy older than any other known in the seventeenth century (see *The Oldest Bibles*). Walton's Polyglot, the New Testament part of a Bible in several ancient languages published in London in 1657, noted its variations.

Throughout the eighteenth century the work of examining manuscript copies of the New Testament and listing their variant readings continued. Studying the differences led to better understanding of how scribes made mistakes (see *Simple Mistakes*), and the creation of guidelines to help decide between one reading and another.

With Tischendorf's recovery of the Codex Sinaiticus, his researches on other manuscripts, and the labours of several scholars beside him, the nineteenth century saw a major change of opinion.

The limits of Erasmus' traditional or 'received' text became clear. It did preserve the authors' words, but after they had suffered some changes and harmonization. In order to read or translate accurately what the New Testament writers wrote, that text needed some revision to agree with older manuscripts.

In England the Revised Version of 1881 was the first translation to break away from the traditional text in certain places. Most translations made since then have done the same. For some Christians this is still puzzling. Why should there be these changes in

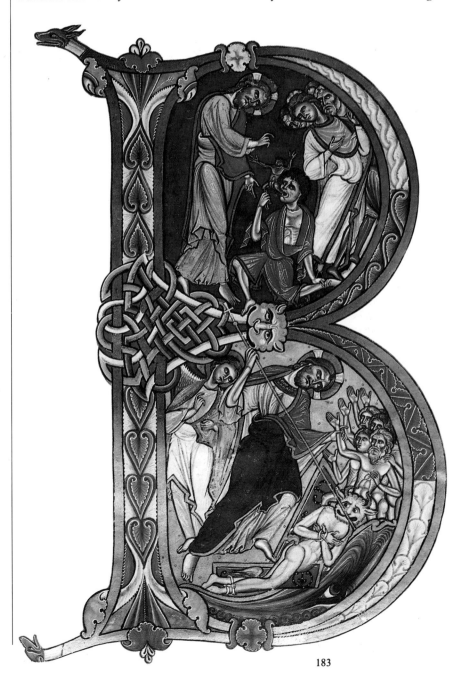

Preachers aim to 'bring the Bible to life'. To help the illiterate people of the Middle Ages, scribes added pictures to the text of the Bible. The biblical figures were shown as if they lived in the Middle Ages. In the twelfth-century 'Winchester Bible' Christ is shown 'harrowing' hell.

the Bible? How could the church have existed for so long with faulty copies of its foundation document? Are the very old manuscripts really superior to the traditional text?

These questions were asked a hundred years ago, and because they are still asked, they deserve attention. The last one is the key one: with most of the 5,000 or so Greek manuscripts of the New Testament, or parts of it, presenting texts very like Erasmus', why should anyone think a small number which disagree are better?

Age alone cannot put this small minority in first place. Older copies are not necessarily better copies (see *Finding the True Text*). Some people have argued that manuscripts such as the Codex Sinaiticus have survived because they were bad copies. Little used, they were not read to pieces like the good ones which have, therefore, disappeared.

Three lines of argument offer answers to these points. First, if only two or three fourth-century copies existed, like the Sinai or Vatican codices, their survival as faulty copies relegated to store-cupboards might be an acceptable explanation. As it is, their witness is joined by all the other copies of equal or greater age. Where there are differences from the traditional text, they often share them; rarely do any of them support the traditional form in these places. Their number and the circumstances of their discovery make it statistically unlikely that they were all rejects and that every 'good' copy has perished entirely.

Second, there is no democracy in textual studies; the voice of the majority does not dominate. Knowing the habits of scribes and the history of copying makes this plain (see *Finding the True Text*). Almost all New Testament manuscripts were made after the fourth century. Any coming from an earlier time will demand special scrutiny. They will disclose the forms of the New Testament books current in the first centuries of the church's life. If the normal means of

studying ancient texts shows that those have the characteristics of earlier texts, by comparison with the traditional text, then obviously they will be preferred.

Third, there is a separate body of very telling evidence. Passages from the New Testament occur often in the books of early Christian teachers and scholars (the Fathers). These men quoted from memory for short passages; longer passages may have been copied from manuscripts— although their memories were probably better than many people today imagine. What is noteworthy is the way these quotations tend to agree with the earlier texts rather than the traditional one, where there are points of difference. If the traditional text had been in use in their day, surely these Christian leaders would have quoted it!

These points are all valid. The traditional text has to be judged by the standards applied to all ancient texts and manuscripts. To claim that the New Testament text falls into a category of its own because it is Scripture is absurd. All of the manuscripts of the New Testament, whatever text they offer, suffer from the failings of their human copyists. Cases of expansion and harmonization are typical of a later text, and easily seen in the traditional text of the Greek New Testament. The Gospels are obvious candidates for harmonization.

One straightforward case is in Luke 23:38, 'And a superscription also was written over him in letters of Greek, and Latin, and Hebrew' (Authorized/King James Version). Modern translations leave out the list of 'letters'. These words occur in various copies in different orders, and are absent from the early third-century Bodmer papyrus and from Codex Vaticanus. This situation is best explained if the words were not part of the original text of Luke but were inserted into it from the account in John. If the words belonged to Luke from the start, there is no way to explain their omission or confusion.

Changes of fashion in piety also had an effect on the copyists. Where the traditional text has, 'Joseph and his mother marvelled at those things which were spoken of him' (Luke 2:23), the older copies have 'His father and mother' (compare RSV, GNB, NIV). As the position of Mary grew in the church, copyists felt a need to remove anything which might cast doubt on the doctrine of the virgin birth of Jesus.

The steps which the nineteenth-century scholars made in unravelling the history of the Greek New Testament text were part of a larger process. Copies of famous Greek and Latin classics found among the papyri from Egypt had similar effects on their study (see *Books from New Testament Times*). As a result, scribal mistakes can be corrected, lines left out can be restored, and phrases wrongly added can be removed, giving texts which are closer to the words the authors wrote.

To separate the New Testament text from this process would be quite wrong. Rather, all who value it should be glad that it can be treated on a level with texts of equal age. In this way its study is made more accurate. On one account it stands above the rest. In many of the classics scholars need to suggest changes to words in order to make sense of lines and sentences. The New Testament text has been preserved so well that not one passage demands such treatment. The New Testament text and all translations made by competent scholars can be trusted.

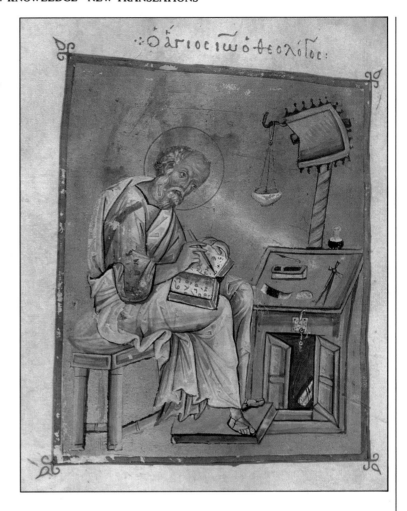

For 1400 years Christian scribes copied their holy books by hand, as St John is doing in this eleventh-century Greek Gospel book. The invention of printing enabled Erasmus and the Reformers to make the Bible available much more easily and cheaply.

EPILOGUE

King Herod, Pontius Pilate and some of the other figures of the Gospel story also appear in the books of Philo and Josephus. They would interest few outside the Jewish people had not Jesus of Nazareth lived at the same time. Coins are independent proof of Herod's existence, the Caesarea Stone of Pilate's. There is no sign of Jesus.

The discoveries described here reveal the context of his life story, bringing clearer understanding of incidents in it showing how reliably it has been recorded and transmitted. Yet they yield no trace of him.

Why?

The human desire to see, to touch, to own physical relics of a great man is understandable. But history shows how misleading it can be, and how easily misused.

The Gospel message, rooted in history, demands faith. Seeing a hero's bones or sitting in his chair may give a temporary thrill. Faith changes and inspires the whole of life. The Christian gospel calls for faith, simple but not blind; faith well-founded, not fantasy; faith in Jesus, God become man, who lived and died in Palestine and rose alive from the tomb.

For Further Reading

DAILY LIFE
N. AVIGAD, *Discovering Jerusalem*, Nelson, 1983; Blackwell, 1984.
M. AVI-YONAH, E. STERN, eds. *Encyclopaedia of Archaeological Excavations in the Holy Land*, 4 vols, Oxford University Press, 1976–79, gives information about individual sites.
J. MURPHY-O'CONNOR, *The Holy Land, An Archaeological Guide from Earliest Times to 1700*. Oxford University Press, 2nd edition, 1986.
J. STAMBAUGH, D. BALCH, *The Social World of the First Christians*, Westminster Press/SPCK, 1986.
J. WILKINSON, *Jerusalem as Jesus knew it: Archaeology as Evidence*, Thames and Hudson, 1982.

RULERS
M. AVI-YONAH, ed., *The World History of the Jewish People*, I.7, *The Herodian Period*, W. H. Allen, 1975.
A. H. M. JONES, *The Herods of Judaea*, Oxford University Press, 2nd edition, 1967.
Y. MESHORER, *Ancient Jewish Coinage*, 2 vols, Amphora Books, 1982.
E. SCHURER, *The History of the Jewish People in the Age of Jesus Christ (175BC–AD135)*, 4 vols, revised and edited by G. Vermes and F. Millar, T. and T. Clark/Fortress Press, 1973–87, gives a valuable survey of all written sources and reconstructs the history of the period.
E. M. SMALLWOOD, *The Jews under Roman Rule*, E. J. Brill, 1976.

RELIGION
M. BEN-DOV, *In the Shadow of the Temple, The Discovery of Ancient Jerusalem*, Harper and Row, 1985.
B. MAZAR, *The Mountain of the Lord. Excavations in Jerusalem*. Doubleday, 1975.
M. BLACK, *The Scrolls and Christian Origins*, Nelson, 1961; Scholars Press, 1988.
F. F. BRUCE, *Second Thoughts on the Dead Sea Scrolls*, Paternoster Press, 2nd edition, 1961.
J. C. TREVER, *The Dead Sea Scrolls, a Personal Account*, Eerdmans, revised edition, 1977.
G. VERMES, *The Dead Sea Scrolls: Qumran in Perspective*, SCM Press; Fortress Press, 2nd edition, 1982.

G. VERMES, *The Dead Sea Scrolls in English*, Penguin Books/Viking Penguin, 3rd edition, 1987.

WRITERS
JOSEPHUS, *The Jewish War*, translated by G. A. Williamson, revised and edited by E. M. Smallwood, Penguin Books, 1981.
JOSEPHUS, *Jewish Antiquities*, in Greek, with English translation by H. St. J. Thackeray, R. Marcus, L. Feldman, Loeb Classical Library, Harvard University Press/Heinemann, 1926–65.
PHILO, *Legatio ad Gaium* ('Embassy to Gaius'), in Greek, with English translation by E. M. Smallwood, E. J. Brill, 1961.
The Mishnah, translated by H. Danby, Oxford University Press, 1933.

GOSPEL RECORDS
K. ALAND and B. ALAND, *The Text of the New Testament*, E. J. Brill, Eerdmans, 1987.
J. N. BIRDSALL, 'The New Testament Text' in *The Cambridge History of the Bible* I, edited by P. R. Ackroyd and C. F. Evans, Cambridge University Press, 1970, pp. 308–77.
J. H. GREENLEE, *Introduction to New Testament Textual Criticism*, Eerdmans, 1964; Bagster, 1976.
J. H. GREENLEE, *Scribes, Scrolls and Scripture, A Layperson's Guide to Textual Criticism*, Eerdmans, 1985.
B. M. METZGER, *The Text of the New Testament*, Clarendon Press, 2nd edition, 1968.
T. S. PATTIE, *Manuscripts of the Bible*, The British Library, 1979.
C. H. ROBERTS, 'Books in the Graeco-Roman World and in the New Testament' in *The Cambridge History of the Bible* I, pp. 48–66.
C. H. ROBERTS and T. C. SKEAT, *The Birth of the Codex*, Oxford University Press, 1983.

Archaeological discoveries are often reported and discussed in *The Biblical Archaeologist*, published quarterly for the American Schools of Oriental Research by Johns Hopkins University Press, Baltimore, and in *The Biblical Archaeology Review* published bi-monthly by the Biblical Archaeology Society, Washington, DC, also available from Paternoster Press, Exeter.

Index

Acknowledgements

Illustrations
Dick Barnard 15, 84 (perspective drawings).
All others Lion Publishing.
Plans on pages 12, 15 based on the original drawing in N. Avigad,
Discovering Jerusalem, Shikmona Publishing Co. Ltd, Jerusalem,
in co-operation with Israel Exploration Society, 1980; Thomas Nelson,
Nashville, Tennessee; Blackwell, Oxford.
The drawings of Herod's Temple on pages 84–85 are based on those in
M. Ben-Dor, *In the Shadow of the Temple*, Harper and Row, New York, 1985
and B. Mazar, *The Mountain of the Lord*, Doubleday, New York, 1975.

Photographs
Ashmolean Museum Oxford: 61 (both), 91 (shekel), 98, 167
Professor N. Avigad: 14, 15, 24
Biblioteca Apostolica Vaticana: 158, 176
British Library: 154 MS Roy I D VIII f.41v, 155 Add MS 43725, 161 (above)
Papyrus 114 col 14–16, 171 Add MS 43725 f.260, 175 Add MS 43725 f.256,
177 Add MS 43725 f.229v, 178 MS Roy I D VIII f.10v.
British Museum: 16, 34, 62 (centre), 73 (all), 77, 142, 160 (below), 161 (below)
Cairo Museum: 143
Discoveries in the Judean Desert of Jordan III, les Petites Grottes de
Qumran, OUP 1962, plate XXX: 115
Dr Gideon Foerster, Department of Antiquities of Israel: 62
Sonia Halliday Photographs: Sonia Halliday; 25 (above), 46–47, 48 (above),
59, 68, 97, 110–111 and cover, 128, 129, 183; Jane Taylor: 57, 150, 163, 166;
Bibliothèque Nationale, Paris: 134

Robert Harding Picture Library: 160 (above)
Michael Holford: 50 (above), 76 (left)
Israel Museum Jerusalem: 17, 19 (below), 20 (above and below left), 21
(both), 33, 67, 83 (below, and cover), 96, 99, 104, 108
Dr John Kane: 53, 135
Kunsthistoriches Museum Vienna: 51
Landesmuseum Trier: H. Thornig; 74–75, 153, 168–169
Lion Publishing: David Alexander; 11, 38, 83 (above), 147 (below), 180;
David Townsend; endpapers, 12 (both), 19 (above), 22, 25 (below), 28, 35, 37,
42, 48 (below), 60 (both), 63 (centre and below), 66, 76 (right), 79, 86, 88, 89,
93, 100, 117, 120, 121, 123, 124, 125, 156
Liverpool Museum: 91 (half-shekel)
Mansell Collection: 147 (above), 168, 182
Magdalen College, Oxford: 162
Alan Millard: 23, 26, 31, 49, 50 (below), 56, 62 (below), 63 (above), 64, 71,
74, 75, 91 (all), 94, 98, 103, 106–7
Romisch-Germanische Museum Köln: 39
John Rylands Library: 165, 185
Scala: 149
Barrie Schwortz: 137
C. Vibert-Guigne: 152
Werner Forman Archive: 141
Ian Wilson: 138
Estate of Yigael Yadin: 20 (above right), 36 (all)
ZEFA: 5, 80–81, 119, 122, 144